Excel

Get the Results You Want!

Year 9 NAPLAN*-style Literacy Tests

Bianca Hewes

* This is not an officially endorsed publication of the NAPLAN program and is produced by Pascal Press independently of Australian governments.

Reprinted 2011
New NAPLAN Test question formats added 2012
Reprinted 2014, 2015
Conventions of Language questions updated 2017
Reprinted 2017

Revised in 2020 for the NAPLAN Online tests

Reprinted 2021, 2022, 2023

ISBN 978 1 74125 372 6

Pascal Press Pty Ltd
PO Box 250
Glebe NSW 2037
(02) 9198 1748
www.pascalpress.com.au

Publisher: Vivienne Joannou
Project editor: Mark Dixon
Edited by Christine Eslick and Rosemary Peers
Proofread by Barbara Bessant
Answers checked by Peter Little, Dale Little and Kim Elith
Cover design by DiZign Pty Ltd
Typeset by Julianne Billington and Leanne Richters (Grizzly Graphics)
Printed by Vivar Printing/Green Giant Press

All efforts have been made to gain permission for the copyright material reproduced in this book. In the event of any oversight, the publisher welcomes any information that will enable rectification of any reference or credit in subsequent editions.

Contents

NAPLAN AND NAPLAN ONLINE

WHAT IS NAPLAN?

- NAPLAN stands for National Assessment Program—Literacy and Numeracy.
- It is conducted every year in March and the tests are sat by students in Years 3, 5, 7 and 9.
- The tests cover Literacy—Reading, Writing, Conventions of Language (spelling, grammar and punctuation)—and Numeracy.

WHAT IS NAPLAN ONLINE?

Introduction

- In the past all NAPLAN tests were paper tests.
- From 2022 all students have taken the NAPLAN tests online.
- This means students complete the NAPLAN tests on a computer or tablet.

Tailored test design

- With NAPLAN paper tests, all students in each year level took exactly the same tests.
- In the NAPLAN Online tests this isn't the case; instead, every student takes a tailor-made test based on their ability.
- Please visit the official ACARA site for a detailed explanation of the tailored test process used in NAPLAN Online and also for general information about the tests: https://nap.edu.au/online-assessment.
- These tailor-made tests mean broadly, therefore, that a student who is at a standard level of achievement takes a test mostly comprised of questions of a standard level; a student who is at an intermediate level of achievement takes a test mostly comprised of questions of an intermediate level; and a student who is at an advanced level of achievement takes a test mostly comprised of questions of an advanced level.

Different question types

- Because of the digital format, NAPLAN Online contains more question types than in the paper tests. In the paper tests there are only multiple-choice and short-answer question types. In NAPLAN Online, however, there are also other question types. For example, students might be asked to drag text across a screen or listen to an audio recording of a sentence and then spell a word they hear.
- Please refer to the next page to see some examples of these additional question types that are found in NAPLAN Online and how they compare to questions in this book. As you will see, the content tested is exactly the same but the questions are presented differently.

NAPLAN ONLINE QUESTION TYPES

<table>
<tr><th>Additional NAPLAN Online question types</th><th>Equivalent questions in this book</th></tr>
<tr><td>

Sequencing

Order the seven stages of man into the order identified by Shakespeare. Use the tab to read the text. Put the first stage at the top.

1 ☐
2 ☐
3 ☐
4 ☐
5 ☐
6 ☐
7 ☐

soldier
wise man of justice
second childhood without teeth, hair or taste
crying baby
lover
old man
complaining school-boy

</td><td>

According to the text there are seven stages of man. Place the stages of man identified by Shakespeare in order.

☐ soldier
☐ wise man of justice
☐ second childhood without teeth, hair or taste
☐ crying baby
☐ lover
☐ old man
☐ complaining school-boy

</td></tr>
<tr><td>

Click

Which sentence has the correct punctuation?

☐ “Get back here!” , screamed Dai.
☐ Get back here! Screamed Dai.
☐ “Get back here!” Screamed Dai.
☐ “Get back here!” screamed Dai.

</td><td>

Which sentence has the correct punctuation?

A “Get back here!” , screamed Dai.
B Get back here! Screamed Dai.
C “Get back here!” Screamed Dai.
D “Get back here!” screamed Dai.

</td></tr>
<tr><td>

Drag and drop

Choose the words to correctly complete the sentence.

Ben knew he ____________________ somewhere before.

had seen her | has seen her
had saw her | will seen her

</td><td>

Write the correct words from the boxes to complete the sentence.

had seen her | has seen her
had saw her | will seen her

Ben knew he ☐ somewhere before.

</td></tr>
<tr><td>

Text entry

The cause of ______________ has only just been identified.

Click on the play button to listen to the missing word.

0.08 / 0.09

Type the correct spelling of the word in the box.

☐

</td><td>

Ask your teacher or parent to read the spelling words for you. The words are listed on page 175. Write the spelling word on the line below.

Word	Example
lightning	The cause of lightning has only just been identified.

____

</td></tr>
</table>

MAXIMISE YOUR RESULTS IN NAPLAN ONLINE

STEP 1: USE THIS BOOK

How *Excel* can help you prepare for NAPLAN Online

Tailored test design

- We can't replicate the digital experience in book form and offer you tailored tests, but with this series we do provide Standard, Intermediate and Advanced NAPLAN Online–style Literacy tests.
- This means that a student using these tests will be able to prepare with confidence for tests at different ability levels.
- This makes it excellent preparation for the tailored NAPLAN Online Literacy tests.

Remember the advantages of revising in book form

There are many benefits to a child using books to prepare for the online test:

- One of the most important benefits is that writing on paper will help your child retain information. It can be a very effective way to memorise. High-quality educational research has shown that writing by hand is more effective than using a keyboard for remembering what you write and assisting in learning.
- Students will be able to prepare thoroughly for topic revision using books and then practise computer skills easily. They will only succeed with sound knowledge of topics; this requires study and focus. Students will not succeed in tests simply because they know how to answer questions digitally.
- Some students find it easier to concentrate when reading a page in a book than when reading on a screen.
- It can be more convenient to use a book, especially when a child doesn't have ready access to a digital device.
- You can be confident that ***Excel*** books will help students acquire the topic knowledge they need, as we have over 30 years experience in helping students prepare for tests. All our writers are experienced educators.

STEP 2: PRACTISE ON *Excel Test Zone*

How *Excel Test Zone* can help you practise online

We recommend you go to www.exceltestzone.com.au and register for practice in NAPLAN Online–style tests once you have completed this book. The reasons include:

- for optimal performance in the NAPLAN Online tests we recommend students gain practice at completing online tests as well as completing revision in book form
- students should practise answering questions on a digital device to become confident with this process
- students will be able to practise tailored tests like those in NAPLAN Online, as well as other types of tests
- students will also be able to gain valuable practice in onscreen skills such as dragging and dropping answers.

Remember that ***Excel Test Zone*** has been helping students prepare for NAPLAN since 2009; in fact we had NAPLAN online questions even before NAPLAN tests went online!

We also have updated our website along with our book range to ensure your preparation for NAPLAN Online is 100% up to date.

ABOUT THE LITERACY TESTS AND THIS BOOK

THE YEAR 9 NAPLAN ONLINE LITERACY TESTS

About the tests

In Literacy there are three NAPLAN tests:

- **Reading** (comprehension)—there are 48 to 50 questions in this test
- **Conventions of Language** (spelling, grammar and punctuation)—there are 50 questions in this test
- **Writing** (written expression)—there is one piece of writing in this test.

About the report

- When your child completes the NAPLAN tests, you and your child's school will receive a report indicating their standard of proficiency in literacy and numeracy. There are four levels of achievement:
  - **Exceeding** (advanced proficiency)
  - **Strong** (average to high-average proficiency)
  - **Developing** (not yet proficient)
  - **Needs additional support** (help is needed).

The report will also show the national average.

ABOUT THIS BOOK

The Mini Reading and Conventions of Language Tests

In the first part of the book you will find ten tests for each subject. These tests are divided into three levels of difficulty:

- Standard level
- Intermediate level
- Advanced level.

- You will be able to see what level your child is at by finding the point where they start having consistent difficulty with questions. For example, if your child answers most questions correctly up to the intermediate level and then gets most questions wrong from then onwards, it is likely your child's ability is at an intermediate level.
- You will be able to see your child's strengths and weaknesses in different topics by completing the **Strengths and weaknesses chart** (see page viii).
- You will also be able to give your child intensive practice in short tests which have time limits based on the actual Reading and Conventions of Language test times.
- There are quick answers for every question so you can easily mark your child's work.
- For the **Reading tests**, line references and explanations are provided. The line references will help you find exactly where the answer to the question is found in the text. Questions in the reading answer section have been divided into three types: fact-finding, inferring and judgement. Explanations are provided within these answer scaffolds to help you teach your child how to answer the different types of reading questions. If you turn to the inside back cover you will see all these types of explanations explained fully.
- For the **Conventions of Language tests**, tips and explanations are provided. Your child can then learn to apply these general tips to similar questions and the explanations will help you explain the answers to your child.

The Mini Writing Tests

- There are three **Writing tests**.
- There are tips specific to the type of text of each question. These tips will provide guidelines for your child's writing.
- Each Writing test has writing samples at standard, intermediate and advanced levels. From this you will be able to see which level your child is writing at. For example, if your child's writing closely resembles the intermediate writing sample then their writing is at the intermediate level.
- Marking checklists are also provided so you can go through your child's writing and check that they have covered all of the necessary points.

The Sample Online-style Literacy Tests

- In the second part of the book we provide you with two sample tests which are modelled on actual NAPLAN Online Literacy tests.
- For the Conventions of Language and Reading tests there are answers, tips and explanations.
- For the Writing tests there are marking checklists and writing samples, one each at standard, intermediate and advanced levels. From this you will be able to see what level your child is writing at by comparing their writing to the writing samples.

STRENGTHS AND WEAKNESSES CHART

- As your child completes each test, mark it using the answer section at the back and then fill in this chart to record their progress.
- You will be able to see at a glance your child's strengths and weaknesses in different topics and different strands of Literacy.
- If you find your child needs more practice on specific topics, use the checklist of ***Excel*** books on the back cover to find the book to help them.

Area of Learning	Level	Mini test	Mark
Spelling	Standard	1	/25
Spelling	Standard	2	/25
Spelling	Intermediate	3	/25
Spelling	Intermediate	4	/25
Spelling	Intermediate	5	/25
Spelling	Intermediate	6	/25
Spelling	Advanced	7	/25
Spelling	Advanced	8	/25
Spelling	Advanced	9	/25
Spelling	Advanced	10	/25
Grammar	Standard	1	/25
Grammar	Intermediate	2	/25
Grammar	Intermediate	3	/25
Grammar	Advanced	4	/25
Grammar	Advanced	5	/25
Punctuation	Standard	1	/25
Punctuation	Intermediate	2	/25
Punctuation	Intermediate	3	/25
Punctuation	Advanced	4	/25
Punctuation	Advanced	5	/25
Reading	Standard	1	/8
Reading	Standard	2	/8
Reading	Intermediate	3	/8
Reading	Intermediate	4	/8
Reading	Intermediate	5	/8
Reading	Intermediate	6	/8
Reading	Advanced	7	/8
Reading	Advanced	8	/8
Reading	Advanced	9	/8
Reading	Advanced	10	/8

SPELLING

Standard level questions

Mini Test 1

Please ask your parent or teacher to read to you the spelling words on page 175.
Write the correct spelling of each word in the box.

1. The cause of ______ has only just been identified.
2. The child was involved in a ______ competition.
3. The fridge made a ______ humming sound.
4. The cables were left in a messy ______.
5. A town is larger than a ______, but smaller than a city.
6. The ______ was concerned about the impact of the urban sprawl.
7. Jasper couldn't believe what had happened. It was a ______!
8. He knew that his ______ would one day be repaid.
9. Even though his ankle was swollen and ______, he had managed to score the winning goal.
10. Moles create complex ______ of tunnels underground.
11. Fireworks never ______ to amaze me.
12. Swimmers of all ages can become a member of a swimming ______.
13. It doesn't matter what stage of your ______ you are at.
14. Joining a squad allows you to share your ______ for the water.
15. Samantha was shocked by the ______ of her mother's hair.

Answers and explanations on page 120

The spelling mistakes in these sentences have been highlighted. Write the correct spelling for each highlighted word in the box.

16 The team's stay in Melbourne was breef as a result of the bad weather.

17 Melanoma is the forthe most common cancer in the world.

18 Melanoma is detected by most people when they notise a mole changing colour or shape.

19 The risk of melanoma incresses with exposure to UV radiation.

20 On receipt of the trofy , Jemima wept openly.

Each sentence has one word that is incorrect. Write the correct spelling of the word in the box.

21 Scientists have conclluded that smallpox is an airborne virus.

22 The final verdict was that four people were responssabel for the damage from the fire.

23 The beuwty of the girl took Asha's breath away.

24 Asha knew that if he was to woo her, he would have to clime the hedge and speak with her.

25 Little did he know, she was eagarlly awaiting his words.

Answers and explanations on page 120

SPELLING

Standard level questions

Mini Test 2

Please ask your parent or teacher to read to you the spelling words on page 175. Write the correct spelling of each word in the box.

1. A thumbprint was all that was needed for the ______ to catch the thief.
2. The ______ 30-year-old woman in the United Kingdom owns twenty-one handbags.
3. Having waited what seemed like a lifetime, Harry finally had his ______ removed.
4. ______, the cost of living in Sydney is relatively cheap compared to that in Tokyo.
5. It was a ______ undertaking, yet Sami knew someone had to be responsible for it.
6. The protesters feared a violent backlash from their ______.
7. The wind ______ through the trees.
8. Upon the grass tiny slivers of moonlight shone to create ______.
9. However, this beauteous sight was ______ by none.
10. Following the politician's election, the gang chose to ______ him.
11. Would you like to highlight the key ______ in the passage?
12. In hindsight the experiment could have been better ______.
13. Clutching the glass ______, Andy struggled to remain calm.
14. Beneath his agitated feet the redwood floorboards were ______ to scuff.
15. If only Jasper had left that ______ alone, none of this would have happened!

Answers and explanations on page 121

The spelling mistakes in these sentences have been highlighted. Write the correct spelling for each highlighted word in each box.

16 It has been claimed that humankind desends from apes.

17 Tea leaves are soaked in boiling water to infusse the water with flavour.

18 It is somewhat unusual, but this plant must be cold before it will fllower.

19 Did you know that a strawbrry has over 200 seeds and the fruit are all hand-picked?

20 The best way to eat these sweet treats is with a teaspoon of wipped cream.

Each sentence has one word that is incorrect. Write the correct spelling of the word in the box.

21 Seeing Halley's Comet is for some people a once in a liftime event.

22 In its 29-year history, no prison inmmate ever escaped Alcatraz.

23 Throuhout the 16th century in England most people made their living from farming.

24 Men wore stockings called 'hose' and women didn't wear undawear!

25 For the poor in this time, the workeday was very long and hard.

Answers and explanations on page 121

SPELLING

Intermediate level questions

Mini Test 3

Please ask your parent or teacher to read to you the spelling words on page 176.
Write the correct spelling of each word in the box.

1. It was less than ten minutes since the ______ had arrived.
2. She was an ______ young woman and knew what the invitation meant.
3. She must ______ her fine manners and her willingness to marry Sir Albert.
4. Mother and Father celebrated their 50th wedding ______.
5. I study ______ this year. Do you?
6. The sports ______ fell off his chair when the team scored.
7. It is a ______ requirement of learning to surf that you know how to swim.
8. I could not hear the ______ on the other end of the phone.
9. Elms have a ______ for being ornamental.
10. Elms originated in Asia but they have ______ themselves as far as North America.
11. As a ______ of the development of Dutch elm disease the number of elms being sold is falling.
12. James did not grant me ______ to enter the building.
13. Ayden attempted to ______ me that he was a rock star.
14. When you are attending an interview for a job, it is important you ensure that your appearance is ______.
15. Be polite to all people you meet at the interview, as these people may be your ______ in the future.

Answers and explanations on pages 122–123

Mini Test 3 (continued)

The spelling mistakes in these sentences have been highlighted. Write the correct spelling for each highlighted word in each box.

16 You should ensure that the position you are being interviewed for is a stepping stone to your desired occupashon.

17 There is a shortadge of eligible young women in country towns.

18 Orthopaedic surgeons speshalise in the muscular-skeletal system.

19 There was an overwelming demand for tickets to the Helmet concert.

20 The Sydney Football Club was established in 2004 and is one of the most promanent soccer teams in Australia.

Each sentence has one word that is incorrect. Write the correct spelling of the word in the box.

21 The team recroots its younger players from the NSW State League and even from foreign teams.

22 The current senior sqwad includes Adam Casey and the captain, John Aloisi.

23 Belinda was glad to receive prayse for her hard work.

24 I took a stunning portrayte of Blake; his eyes looked amazing.

25 The stattistics for fatalities involving young people and cars are disturbing.

Answers and explanations on pages 122–123

SPELLING

Intermediate level questions

Mini Test 4

Please ask your parent or teacher to read to you the spelling words on page 176. Write the correct spelling of each word in the box.

1. It is ______ that young children drink full-cream milk.
2. Mothers should be ______ when giving their young children skim milk as it does not provide enough calcium.
3. If young children ______ to drink full-cream milk their bones and teeth can become brittle.
4. Despite having fallen over 20 metres to the ground, the man was still ______.
5. The flotation ______ was not buoyant enough to save all of the stranded men.
6. The teacher informed us that we needed to write up our spelling words in a ______.
7. The World Masters Games is a competition for ______ athletes.
8. Vegetarians must ensure that they include alternative ______ sources in their meat-free diets.
9. "Stop! Guards, ______ that man!" shouted the angry Roman emperor.
10. From a distance the ______ looked like a tiny blinking star moving slowly across the sky.
11. "It's not my ______ the car is broken!" exclaimed Judy to her frustrated husband.
12. The main colours for the Manly Warringah Sea Eagles are white and ______.
13. The prisoner found it difficult to ______ back into society.
14. He frequently had to attend parole meetings at the police ______.
15. The clock's ______ had a fault in it.

Answers and explanations on pages 123–124

The spelling mistakes in these sentences have been highlighted. Write the correct spelling for each highlighted word in each box.

16 Deep in the night the musishan could be heard practising for the show.

17 He believed this preparashon was essential to a successful performance.

18 Having prepared so well, he was surprised that the performance ended up as a nightmmare rather than a dream.

19 The husband thought to himself, "If I procrastanate any longer, the wife's going to go berserk."

20 As a workplace, the company's new office block was modern and scienetific looking.

Each sentence has one word that is incorrect. Write the correct spelling of the word in the box.

21 However, the nature of the work there had terrible physchological effects on the workers.

22 This made most of the employees relluctant to work there.

23 Having planned for five years, Alan was pleased when the day of his retirment arrived.

24 "Come on, be reasoneable. It's only $300," complained James to his mother.

25 Che Guevara is considered by some to be a terrorist, but by many to be a revolushonary.

Answers and explanations on pages 123–124

SPELLING

Intermediate level questions

Mini Test 5

Please ask your parent or teacher to read to you the spelling words on page 177. Write the correct spelling of each word in the box.

1. 'Don't ______ those who are different' was the motto of our school.
2. The great elm tree is ______ to a number of new diseases.
3. A ______ number of wizards had gathered for the first of four important tournaments.
4. The impact of the December 2004 tsunami was ______.
5. I could not believe that Gemma had such a flat ______ even though she had eaten three cheeseburgers.
6. When baking cookies it is essential that you have a ______ amount of chocolate chips.
7. Often little boys play ______ with their friends in order to understand the boundaries of acceptable behaviour.
8. On day seven the ______ set in. People began looking at one another suspiciously.
9. Food ______ always brings out the worst in people. This group was no exception.
10. The only ______ that existed in abundance on the island was bananas.
11. Jeff was trying to ______ his green P-plates, but the test seemed too difficult.
12. Police ______ with criminals on a daily basis and therefore require excellent patience and communication skills.
13. "The ______ that I hit the woman is entirely false," the defendant stated to the court.
14. Rubbing his hands continuously, the young man revealed to the interviewer that he was ______.
15. The ______ planned for Craig's birthday was even bigger than the one for Bianca's birthday.

☞ Answers and explanations on page 124

Mini Test 5 (continued)

The spelling mistakes in these sentences have been highlighted. Write the correct spelling for each highlighted word in each box.

16 The news station's coveradge of the election was biased; the opposition party was not impressed.

17 Sea Shepherd is an international not-for-profit whale conservashon organisation.

18 They are a group of couradgeous men and women who protect the wildlife in the world's oceans from illegal whaling activities.

19 Some people believe that this group is essenttially a group of pirates using violence to protect whales.

20 A fertile imagineation is the foundation for an exciting and rewarding life.

Each sentence has one word that is incorrect. Write the correct spelling of the word in the box.

21 For some people immigrateion is seen as a problem; however, many people view it as a natural part of a global community.

22 It was inittially believed by philosophers, merchants and explorers that the Earth was flat.

23 "Are you seriousely thinking about becoming a nun?" questioned Sophia.

24 Benny told me that, unfortunatly, there were no more pies left.

25 It is believed that within the next twenty years virttualy all schooling will occur online.

Answers and explanations on page 124

SPELLING

Intermediate level questions

Mini Test 6

Please ask your parent or teacher to read to you the spelling words on page 177. Write the correct spelling of each word in the box.

1 Everyone ______ Calvin was admitted to the show; Calvin didn't have enough money.

2 Children are often ______ to learn that the moon is not made out of cheese.

3 After 12 hours of shopping with my mother's credit card, a budget ______ halted my further spending.

4 "Did you see the ______ in the supermarket when the chocolate went on sale?" asked Samantha.

5 The footballer was arrested on suspicion of ______.

6 The boy's ______ revealed that he had contracted tuberculosis.

7 His lips were cracking ______ of constant exposure to wind.

8 Jack's tired eyes were ______ to be like those of a dead fish.

9 The children's hands were open and ______ for something.

10 In the Vietnam War the American soldiers often fell victim to the ______ warfare tactics of the Viet Cong.

11 The young boy had been wearing a maroon jumper on the night of his ______.

12 The police are on the lookout for a group of youths who consistently ______ outside the local mall.

13 The grandest piece of ______ in my house is my antique grandfather clock.

14 The cyclone left a trail of ______ all along the coast.

15 The army ______ was deployed to Fiji in October.

Answers and explanations on pages 124–125

Mini Test 6 (continued)

The spelling mistakes in these sentences have been highlighted. Write the correct spelling for each highlighted word in each box.

16 They were sent to help stabilise the island nation following the recent cou.

17 It is now being reported that there is dout as to whether the country's president will ever be reinstated.

18 It is essential to keep a record of all receitts, according to the Australian Taxation Office.

19 Silently the throng of mourners walked away from the grave; it was a solem occasion.

20 Deep, rustic reds, browns and oranges are the colours in fashion this autum.

Each sentence has one word that is incorrect. Write the correct spelling of the word in the box.

21 It has been recorded that between 10% and 15% of children and between 10% and 12% of adults have assma.

22 Detailed knowlage of the scene of the murder indicated that the man was involved in the crime.

23 "I have never been so offended! How dare you refer to me as a foregner!" screamed Heather at the interviewer.

24 The desine of the Sydney Opera House is iconic.

25 Due to an administration bungle, Karl was forced to resine from his job.

Answers and explanations on pages 124–125

SPELLING

Advanced level questions

Mini Test 7

Please ask your parent or teacher to read to you the spelling words on page 178. Write the correct spelling of each word in the box.

1. Janet told me that as a ________ of my wearing a hat I would have bad hair.
2. "The seating arrangement is ________! "yelled the frustrated teacher.
3. In the dead of night, Georgie sat hugging her legs in bed. The ________ was tense.
4. The fear of an ________ being had kept her awake for over two hours.
5. "Mother's idea of comfortable ________ is certainly unconventional," she thought to herself.
6. It is essential that we take an international ________ on the issue.
7. In the ________, mix two-thirds of a cup of yoghurt with 250 mL of low-fat milk.
8. The ________ of the contents of the entire storage container was a tiresome job.
9. "Where's your ________ mark?" enquired Ms Adams of little Jacob.
10. In English class Mr James explained that our narratives must be written in ________.
11. He also told us that a wide ________ was essential to express our ideas creatively.
12. Finally, Mr James said that really effective stories use poetic devices such as ________.
13. Crocodiles have been known to eat large stones to help their ________.
14. The ________ had started to build up on the windows, prompting Harry to turn on the car's engine.
15. The most advanced organism on Earth is the ________.

Answers and explanations on pages 125–126

The spelling mistakes in these sentences have been highlighted. Write the correct spelling for each highlighted word in each box.

16 The spinal cord, dorsal fin or notochords protect important nerves and allow for effective blood circulashon .

17 The advanced nervous systems of vertebrates have been studied closely in labratries around the world.

18 In class we learnt what longatude is.

19 The little boys were forced to sign a lengthy constatution before they were granted entry into Jake's tree-house.

20 An isoscalis triangle consists of two equal sides and one side that is different in length.

Each sentence has one word that is incorrect. Write the correct spelling of the word in the box.

21 "Look after that scientific aparattus, Adam! It's expensive," warned Mr Peters.

22 Through an impressive display of deducttion, the men uncovered the truth—the model had jumped to her death.

23 The scientific method, developed during the Enlightenment period, aims for the clarifacation of knowledge about the material world.

24 This method requires establishing a hypothasis, testing it, analysing the results and then drawing a conclusion from the results.

25 It is only through the employment of the scientific method that knowledge is considered emppirical—this means 'deduced from observation or experiment'.

 Answers and explanations on pages 125–126

SPELLING

Advanced level questions

Mini Test 8

Please ask your parent or teacher to read to you the spelling words on page 178.
Write the correct spelling of each word in the box.

1 Grand ______ sounds rumbled from the belly of the school hall.

2 Charlie was told to leave the group; his ______ was affecting their chances of winning the competition.

3 The ______ of the drums during the song's coda was unexpected.

4 Jo is the more ______ of the twins; Sam is happier reading a book alone.

5 I will never forget the ______ of my host mother, reflected Komei.

6 The length of the ______ is dependent on the quality of the players participating.

7 Leg extension exercises are designed to specifically target the ______ .

8 The term ______ refers to art that has been created using a variety of different forms.

9 The combination of magazine and newspaper clippings with paint and fabric often creates a piece with ______ qualities.

10 Of course, some people have a ______ for traditional art made simply from paint and canvas.

11 A broad ______ of musicians performed at the charity gig.

12 The young labourers were forced to ______ the scaffolding at the end of the workday.

13 Many children no longer look to an ______ when they want the answer to a question.

14 The attitudes of the group were particularly ______, and as a result Ji felt frustrated and resentful.

15 It is ______ the job of all mothers to clean the rooms of their children.

Answers and explanations on pages 126–127

The spelling mistakes in these sentences have been highlighted. Write the correct spelling for each highlighted word in each box.

16 The prime minister wished to introduce **legisllation** that would ban young people from congregating in public.

17 My meal was the **equivallent** of three large burger meals.

18 "You will find that **elswwhere** in the world, people do not enjoy the same liberties that we do in Australia," instructed Mr Anderson.

19 Despite the best efforts of the **ambbasador** to resolve the dispute between the nations, war was declared.

20 Those in government had to **conseed** that it was not possible to reach a peaceful agreement between the two nations.

Each sentence has one word that is incorrect. Write the correct spelling of the word in the box.

21 One analist suggested that the need for oil was so great by both countries that war was bound to happen.

22 I believe Jacob's leaving Jessica was inevatable; the two of them are complete opposites.

23 Hitler's Nazi regeeme is known for its cruelty and lack of humanity.

24 Through the microscope we watched a tiny bactereum squirm.

25 It is surprising to find that there are three weather bureus in Australia.

Answers and explanations on pages 126–127

SPELLING

Advanced level questions

Mini Test 9

Please ask your parent or teacher to read to you the spelling words on page 179.
Write the correct spelling of each word in the box.

1. The word ______ originates from the Greek word *per-aa* meaning 'great house'.
2. The word was originally used to describe the ______ and grand royal court of the Egyptian king.
3. It was not until the late 18th dynasty that the word was used to describe the ______ king himself.
4. The students looked very ______ lying around on the beanbags.
5. "Have you got ______ rope to hold the boat steady?" enquired Lee.
6. The ______ to a good life is a satisfying, enjoyable and fulfilling career.
7. The largest of the known ______ is *Tyrannosaurus rex*.
8. Anji was disappointed that the ______ bureaus had got the forecast incorrect for the second day in a row.
9. William Shakespeare is renowned for his impeccable use of ______ in his sonnets.
10. The boys were told to stop playing tag. They were being too ______.
11. The science teacher had a ______ hanging next to the whiteboard.
12. Even his ______ at work had begun to complain.
13. The presenter was ______ with his message; surprisingly, Harry managed to understand what was being said.
14. Ashley is frequently concerned that his children may not be getting the correct ______ from their unhealthy diet.
15. The finale of *Hamlet* was a ______ of the dead characters arranged artistically around the stage.

Answers and explanations on pages 127–128

Mini Test 9 (continued)

The spelling mistakes in these sentences have been highlighted. Write the correct spelling for each highlighted word in each box.

16 It is believed that liquorice has been consummed for thousands of years.

17 The ancient Egyptians enjoyed it as a sweet liquid, like a saurce.

18 The liquorice we know and love today is still prodduced from extracts from the root of the liquorice plant.

19 "Commercialism is coruppting the minds of the young," admonished the poet.

20 During this experiment the students will learn how and why water disolves salt crystals.

Each sentence has one word that is incorrect. Write the correct spelling of the word in the box.

21 The young men at Gallipoli made the ultimate saccrifise for the freedom of future generations of Australian men and women.

22 The position of apprentise in a busy kitchen is difficult and trying; most apprentices don't last more than six months.

23 Simi had always loved to dance, and when she attended her first synkronised swimming lesson, she was hooked!

24 She had formaly been committed to ballet and jazz.

25 However, she felt this new activity to be an apropreate alternative during the summer months.

Answers and explanations on pages 127–128

SPELLING

Advanced level questions

Mini Test 10

Please ask your parent or teacher to read to you the spelling words on page 179.
Write the correct spelling of each word in the box.

1 The boy was ______ sorry to have missed his grandfather's funeral.

2 I had to admit to the parents that, ______, their daughter was missing.

3 The line for the tickets had ______ 500 people in it.

4 Exhausted and emotionally drained, Jill spread herself ______ on the couch.

5 The families were delighted by the prospect of a ______ funded day-care system.

6 The women were dressed ______ in the traditional Palestinian attire.

7 Alana was impressed by the ______ numbered labels that adorned all of the filing cabinets.

8 Tania confessed to being ______ illiterate.

9 Amanda ______ made the decision to cease eating meat.

10 We ______ drove the long way home in order to avoid the afternoon traffic.

11 Gough Whitlam was ______ dismissed by the governor-general in 1975.

12 My mother is ______ opposed to the teaching of Intelligent Design at school.

13 The man in the dark coat leered ______ into the window of a parked car.

14 I was impressed with my younger brother's resistance to the ______ of his silly friends.

15 The costume worn by Lady Gaga at her most recent concert was ______!

Answers and explanations on pages 128–129

The spelling mistakes in these sentences have been highlighted. Write the correct spelling for each highlighted word in each box.

16 The knowledge that he had stolen the cookie weighed heavily on Herb's conschence.

17 The Mexican axolotl is an amfibian that lives under water and eats meat.

18 The products of resparation are carbon dioxide and water.

19 Seed dispersil is the process whereby insects and birds help plants spread their seed.

20 Scientists believe that it is inevatable that Earth will become too hot to sustain human life.

Each sentence has one word that is incorrect. Write the correct spelling of the word in the box.

21 The columns holding up the beautiful dome of Hagia Sophia in Istanbul are not symetrical.

22 My teacher informed us that one of the great dangers of a strong Western economy is cultural imperiallism.

23 When writing a resume, it is important to list your experience in chronologgical order.

24 Mr Henry was certainly the most popular parishoner; all of the members wanted to be well acquainted with him.

25 The country was suffering badly as a result of the harsh economic sanctons it had endured.

Answers and explanations on pages 128–129

GRAMMAR Standard level questions

Mini Test 1

Highlight the pronouns in the sentences below.

1 He was stunned by the beauty of the pyramids.

2 The doctor diagnosed him as suffering from night tremors.

3 The teacher stressed that she saw Mathematics as the most valuable of all subjects.

4 Which sentence is correct?

A Samantha shouldn't have touched those cats.
B Samantha shouldn't have touched that cats.
C Samantha shouldn't have touched them cats.
D Samantha shouldn't have touched this cats.

5 Which sentence is correct?

A He cut himself on the barbed wire fence.
B He cut themself on the barbed wire fence.
C He cut herself on the barbed wire fence.
D He cut yourself on the barbed wire fence.

6 Which words correctly complete this sentence?

Despite assurances by ______ private sector, it is no longer considered ______ good idea for ______ individual to invest in the stock market.

A the an a **B** the a an **C** an the an **D** a an the

Read *Tennis* and answer questions 7 and 8.

Tennis

Playing tennis looks easy, but you require a great deal of skill to play this sport successfully. Once the basic skills are mastered, playing tennis is both fun and good for your health.

The first thing that you must master is the serve. A serve involves throwing the ball in the air and timing your hit perfectly to ensure that the ball gets across the net and lands in your opponent's side of the court. Professional tennis players spend many years perfecting their own style of serving.

7 This text is written in the

A present tense. **B** past tense. **C** future tense.

8 This text is written in the

A first person. **B** third person. **C** second person.

 Answers and explanations on pages 129–130

9 *The Catcher in the Rye* is a very popular novel with teenage boys.

In the sentence above, the words *The Catcher in the Rye* are in italics because

A this is difficult to understand.
B this is a title.
C this is an unfamiliar phrase.

10 The word *democracy* has its origins in the Greek word *dēmokratía*, which means 'rule of the people'.

In the sentence above, the word *dēmokratía* is in italics because it is

A a title. **B** a technical word.
C difficult to pronounce. **D** a word from another language.

11 Which of the following is correct?

A He didn't know that he will look under the table.
B He didn't know that he should look under the table.
C He didn't know that he shall look under the table.
D He didn't know that he were look under the table.

Write the correct words from the boxes to complete the sentence.

12 had seen her | has seen her | had saw her | will seen her

Ben knew he ______ somewhere before.

13 will lost her | has lost her | had lost her | losing her

Isabel noticed she ______ final baby tooth.

14 would find an | will find an | you finds an | you had find an

Travel anywhere in the world and you ______ Australian.

15 Which of the following correctly completes the sentence?

Harry ______ gone to the zoo if his friends hadn't gone.

A did not have **B** would not have
C should not have **D** would not

Highlight the verbs in the sentences below

16 Unauthorised people are not allowed in the intensive care unit.

17 Specially trained dogs helped the rescuers find the trapped man.

18 The magician conjured a rabbit out of his slender hat.

Answers and explanations on pages 129–130

Read the text *Sunshine* and answer questions 19 to 21.

Sunshine

Cool air filtered across the young boy's feet and he slowly dug further into the sand. He sat alone on the bare dune waiting for the sharp rays of sunlight to warm him. The night had been long and far colder than he had expected.

19 In the first sentence, the word *slowly* is used as

A a verb. **B** a noun. **C** an adjective. **D** an adverb.

20 This text is written in the

A present tense.
B past tense.
C future tense.

21 This text is written in the

A first person.
B third person.
C second person.

22 Which words in this sentence are adjectives?

The fat dog panted as he trudged up the steep hill.

A dog, panted
B fat, trudged
C steep, fat
D panted, he

23 Which words in this sentence are common nouns?

The first film that I watched as a child was *E.T.*

A I, as **B** child, E.T. **C** watched, first **D** film, child

24 Which word correctly completes the sentence?

The great white shark ________ one of the most deadly killers in the world.

A is **B** was **C** are **D** were

25 Which word correctly completes the sentence?

In January every year I ________ my birthday.

A celebrating **B** celebrated **C** celebrate **D** celebration

Answers and explanations on pages 129–130

GRAMMAR

Intermediate level questions

Mini Test 2

Write the correct word or words in the box to complete each sentence.

1. will have | would have | won't have | won't

   It [ ] been a good idea for Lee to hang out the wet clothes.

2. have had | hasn't have | has not had | have not had

   Ruby [ ] a cold for over two years.

3. have not | had | haven't not | has not

   Even though it is sunny, Jack still [ ] washed the car.

4. their | I am | There | They're

   [ ] the largest species of dinosaur ever to roam the Earth.

5. we've | we were | we has | we had

   Even though the other school is selective, [ ] got smarter teachers.

6. Which word is not needed in this sentence?

   The shop was giving out free gifts to every customer.

   A giving **B** free **C** every **D** shop

7. Which of the following correctly completes the sentence below?

   Many Australians ____ more money on fast food meals than on homemade meals.

   A spend **B** spends **C** spent **D** spending

8. Which of the following correctly completes the sentence below?

   Today's busy lifestyles are thought ____ of this shift in expenditure.

   A to be caused **B** to causing **C** to be cause **D** to be the cause

9. Which of the following correctly completes the sentence below?

   Unfortunately many fast foods ____ low in fibre and high in sugar and saturated fats.

   A are **B** is **C** were **D** am

10. Which of the following correctly completes the sentence below?

    As a result, more and more Australians ____ to be suffering heart disease and diabetes.

    A had been show **B** was shown **C** were showed **D** have been shown

Answers and explanations on pages 130–131

11 Highlight the preposition in the sentence below.

The mountain appears smaller since the hotel complex was built.

12 Highlight the prepositions in the sentence below.

Down fell the rain and up went the umbrellas, mused Emma.

13 Highlight the preposition in the sentence below.

Hermit crabs are often difficult to spot as they like hiding inside their shells.

14 Highlight the preposition in the sentence below.

Darkness fell upon the sleepy town as the band of bushrangers lurked.

15 Highlight the preposition in the sentence below.

Wikis are essentially collaborative tools that are designed to allow multiple users to edit and add information on a website.

16 Highlight the preposition in the sentence below.

Wikis provide a number of valuable, and also enjoyable, learning opportunities for students as they learn to communicate and collaborate on a new medium.

17 Highlight the preposition in the sentence below.

The mother wrapped the fish in two sheets of newspaper.

18 Which word correctly completes the sentence?

Spiders can be seen by day or night ________ just about any habitat.

A under B off C at D in

19 Which words correctly complete the sentence?

These sites ________ and public, such as Wikipedia—the world's best-known wiki—an online collaborative encyclopedia.

A is usually open B was usually open C won't usually open D are usually open

20 Which words correctly complete the sentence?

However, wikis can be tailored to suit a particular class, school or region of schools where only those who have registered ________ permission to edit or add information to the wiki site.

A will be granted B were granted C is granted D will grant

Answers and explanations on pages 130–131

21 Which words correctly complete the sentence?

The most common is the creation for a small group of a wiki that ______ the basis for their collaboration on class assignments or activities.

A will then become **B** was becoming **C** will not become **D** then became

22 James was uncomfortable when he visited the hospital at the quarantine station.

The sentence above is written in the

A past tense.
B present tense.
C future tense.

23 Green tree frogs are an endangered species according to the World Wildlife Fund.

The sentence above is written in the

A past tense.
B present tense.
C future tense.

Read *Blue-ringed octopus* and answer questions 24 and 25.

Blue-ringed octopus

Did you know that the name *octopus* comes from the Latin word *octopoda*, which means 'eight-footed'? All octopuses have eight arms. An octopus is a mollusc, just like squids and cuttlefish. Molluscs are invertebrates—this means they don't have backbones. Blue-ringed octopuses live in Australia and are highly poisonous. These very small octopuses, distinguished by the vibrant blue rings that pattern their skin, can be lethal to humans.

24 This text is written in the

A past tense.
B present tense.
C future tense.

25 In the second sentence the word *have* is a

A verb. **B** noun. **C** adverb. **D** adjective.

Answers and explanations on pages 130–131

Mini Test 3

1 Which sentence is correct?

A Danny shouldn't have made an appointment with the doctor: the waiting time was three hours.
B Danny should have made an appointment with the doctor: the waiting time was three hours.
C Danny should had made an appointment with the doctor: the waiting time was three hours.
D Danny should has made an appointment with the doctor: the waiting time was three hours.

2 Which sentence is correct?

A "Everyone will wanted to be in my group," boasted Jamie.
B "Everyone will wants to be in my group," boasted Jamie.
C "Everyone will wanting to be in my group," boasted Jamie.
D "Everyone will want to be in my group," boasted Jamie.

3 Which sentence is correct?

A Scientists believe there couldn't have been a number of factors contributing to the tsunami.
B Scientists believe there could had been a number of factors contributing to the tsunami.
C Scientists believe there could have been a number of factors contributing to the tsunami.
D Scientists believe there could of been a number of factors contributing to the tsunami.

4 Which set of words completes this sentence correctly?

Balin changed ________ mind about going to the movies; ________ going to go to ________ friend's birthday party instead.

A	he's	he	his
B	his	he's	his
C	his	he's	he's
D	he's	his	he's

5 Which sentence is correct?

A The photograph had brung back fond memories for Claudine.
B The photograph had brought back fond memories for Claudine.
C The photograph has bringed back fond memories for Claudine.
D The photograph had bring back fond memories for Claudine.

6 Which words correctly complete the sentence?

In the distance, far from the farmhouse, Haty ________ make out a dark figure.

A can just **B** is just **C** was just **D** could just

Answers and explanations on pages 131–132

7 Which words correctly complete the sentence?

It [ ] quiet all night and Haty longed to see her father return from his journey.

A has been **B** has being **C** had being **D** had been

8 Which word correctly completes the sentence?

Her father [ ] a missionary and travelled to foreign lands frequently.

A were **B** is **C** are **D** was

9 Which word or words correctly complete the sentence?

Tonight Haty [ ] greeted by new smells, exotic sweets and stories of adventure.

A expected **B** expect to be **C** expects to be **D** expected to be

10 Which words correctly complete the sentence?

As the figure grew larger, Haty knew that she [ ] delighted with the unknown.

A would soon be **B** will soon be **C** could be **D** would soon have

Highlight the verb that correctly matches the noun in the sentences below.

11 *Jabberwocky* by Lewis Carroll [is/has/was/will be] thought by many to be the greatest nonsense poem ever written in English.

12 A number of the nonsense words that Carroll created for the poem are so well known that they [has/having/will have/have] entered the Oxford English Dictionary

13 The poem appears in the book *Through the Looking Glass* and the main character, Alice, [putting/will put/is putting/puts] her finger on the reason the poem is so special.

14 "It seems to fill my head with ideas—only I don't know exactly what they [are/is/were/am]."

15 While the strange words appear to [has no precise/have no precise/having no precise/haven't precise] meaning, they seem to create a certain mood appropriate to the poem's subject matter.

16 It seems that there is no other activity that [capture/captures/capturing/captured] the human imagination more than the possibility of time travel.

17 You could go back and meet yourself at an earlier age, or even better, go forward and see how you [look/looked/will look/is looking] in the future!

18 Select the correct word or words from the boxes to complete the sentence.

is was are is being

Ashley [ ] embarrassed after he yawned loudly during the lecture.

Answers and explanations on pages 131–132

19 Select the correct word from the boxes to complete the sentence.

were | is | was | are

Jupiter [ ] the fifth planet from the sun.

20 Write the correct words from the boxes to complete the sentence.

that have made | that will make | that is making | that have make

It is these fantasies about the future and the past [ ] time travel the focus of thousands of the last century's science fiction novels and films.

21 Write the correct words from the boxes to complete the sentence.

that were there | who were there | who are there | who was there

A fully functioning time machine could allow you to witness major events in history and even talk to the people [ ].

22 Which sentence is correct?

A Eat a balanced diet is essential for a long and healthy life.
B Eats a balanced diet is essential for a long and healthy life.
C Eating a balanced diet is essential for a long and healthy life.
D Eaten a balanced diet is essential for a long and healthy life.

23 Although the situation wasn't too dramatic, the teacher made a drama out of it.

In this sentence, *dramatic* and *drama* are:

	dramatic	drama
A	noun	verb
B	adjective	noun
C	verb	adjective
D	verb	noun

24 It will be interesting to hear what the prime minister has to say about funding for youth projects.

The sentence above is written in the

A past tense. B present tense. C future tense.

25 Which sentence is correct?

A Students who don't focus in class were find it hard to excel in examinations.
B Students who don't focus in class finds it hard to excel in examinations.
C Students who don't focus in class will finds it hard to excel in examinations.
D Students who don't focus in class will find it hard to excel in examinations.

Answers and explanations on pages 131–132

GRAMMAR

Advanced level questions

Mini Test 4

Highlight the adverbs in the sentences below.

1 The young child fell violently ill and was swiftly rushed to hospital.

2 The injured bird lifted itself effortlessly off the ground, amazing the onlookers.

3 Jemima walked across the stage nervously because it was the first time she had won an award.

Highlight the adjectives in the sentences below.

4 James laughed heartily at the boy's silly joke.

5 Inside the tiny corridor were squeezed the refugee families.

6 Last Christmas we had a phenomenal light display.

7 As the trees danced in the light breeze, the word 'forever' danced on Hannah's lips.

Write the correct words from the boxes to complete the sentence.

8 real quick | real quickly | really quick | really quickly

He threw the burning stick into the fire [ ].

9 Mary skipped past the tackle, [ ] the ball over the ashy-white tryline.

hasty thrusted | hastily thrusting | hasty thrust | hastingly thrusting

10 The wobbly mirrors fascinated the young boy: [ ] to be reality.

the illusion appeared | an illusion this good is | a illusion imagined | illusions seem can

11 My [ ] intimidates my friend Becky.

Which words correctly complete the sentence above?

A new teacher, who is French,
B new teacher, French,
C new speaking French teacher
D posh French teacher scares

Answers and explanations on pages 132–133

12 Every night ________ on the sleepy village below.

Which words correctly complete the sentence above?

A a brightly shining stars
B brightly shined the stars
C the stars shine brightly
D the bright stars shine

13 It had been three hours since those lips had delicately touched the lips of another.

In this sentence, the word *delicately* is used as

A a verb.
B a noun.
C an adjective.
D an adverb.

14 He had dark green eyes and sandy hair.

In this sentence, the word *sandy* is used as

A a verb.
B a noun.
C an adjective.
D an adverb.

15 Which sentence is correct?

A Compared with Holly's, my typing skills are quite good.
B In regards to Holly, my typing skills are quite good.
C Regarding Holly, my typing skills are quite good.
D In comparison with Holly, my typing skills are quite good.

16 Which words correctly complete the sentence below?

An ________ has six steel strings of varying thickness.

A guitar is ordinary
B ordinary electric guitar
C ordinary guitar will
D the guitar and

Read *Easter Hat Parade.* The text has some gaps. Choose the correct option to fill each gap.

Easter Hat Parade

17 working all day on their Easter hats. The very next day was the Easter Hat Parade and both boys wanted 18 . Last year their mother 19 filled with tiny chicks and colourful eggs. 20 their new baby sister and it was up to the boys to make their own hats and make her proud.

17 A Those boys has been
B The two boys had been
C Them there boys is
D Yet it was raining and they were

18 A to have the biggest and best hat
B their hat to be big and best
C thought the bigger the hat the better
D their hat to be the most biggest

19 A has crafted extravagantly bonnets
B had crafted extravagant bonnets
C will craft extravagant bonnets
D is crafting extravagant bonnets

20 A Their mother is the busiest with
B This year she was busy with
C There were others with their
D Next year their mother will be

Answers and explanations on pages 132–133

Read the text *Black holes*. The text has some gaps. Choose the correct option to fill each gap.

Black holes

Black holes develop where 21 intensified to such a point that it engulfs all other forces in the universe. 22 powerful that, once trapped inside, nothing can escape—not even light. Contemporary astronomy can tell us how black holes develop, where in the universe they occur and why they exist in different sizes. The 23 revealed one of the strangest objects in the universe, and there's still much that is not known about this phenomenon.

21
A gravity has lost
B ordinary gravity has
C gravity ordinary is
D it seems gravity is not ordinary

22
A This hole is almost
B Black holes don't have
C A black hole is so
D The powerful black hole is

23
A discoveries of astronomers have
B telescopes are strong enough to
C astronomers have discovered
D the discovering astronomers did

24 Which sentence is correct?
A Being the betterest shot-putter earned Jan a medal.
B I am the bestest bike rider in the neighbourhood.
C Do you think you're the most best at tennis?
D Jan was the best shot-putter in her school.

25 Which words are all adverbs?
A longer, longest, long, length
B swiftly, quickly, fast, hastily
C shock, dismay, awe, surprise
D throw, heave, chuck, hurl

Answers and explanations on pages 132–133

GRAMMAR

Advanced level questions

Mini Test 5

1 Write the correct word from the boxes to complete the sentence.

what who that why

Dean is [ ] you would call an eccentric character!

2 Write the correct words from the boxes to complete the sentence.

[ ] my mother would call the spirit of a great land.

Germans invaded the land and delivered that

Visiting Germany prior to the Great War,

In Germany I came into contact with what

I love the German nation for those which

3 Write the correct word from the boxes to complete the sentence.

Yelling at a group of students in public will make [ ] resent the teacher.

it them those that

4 Which part of this sentence is an adjectival clause?

The Kombi that was 34 years old jolted to a halt and the driver let out a yell of frustration.

A The Kombi
B that was 34 years old
C jolted to a halt
D and the driver let out a yell of frustration

5 Which sentence uses conjunctions correctly?

A Mary not only enjoyed fishing since kayaking but also rowing.
B Emily didn't desire Charles because she married him anyway.
C The fish is translucent as a means of camouflage.
D It was unfortunate that the animals were given time to graze however they were caught in the rain.

6 Which words correctly complete the sentence below?

He loved being in the snow [ ].

A but this year his leg was broken
B because he had been suffering from a broken leg
C since he was afraid of breaking his leg
D and always broke his leg

7 Which of the following sentences is correct?

A I cannot abide by this rules any longer; this school will not do.
B This is the coldest day on record but I feel this children aren't feeling the cold.
C Is June playing Scrabble with those new girl?
D Have you seen that new boy in Mr Moran's class?

Answers and explanations on pages 133–134

8 Which of the following correctly completes this sentence?

_______________ are responsible for crop circles.

A Those girls who said aliens
B Little Joe thinks aliens that which
C Some people believe aliens
D The Jones family who

9 Which sentence tells the reader who performed the action?

A John opened the can of baked beans.
B The beans were heated on the hot plate.
C The electric hot plate was designed to stop working if it became too hot.
D The bread was quickly toasted.

10 Which sentence is correct?

A Today's carnival are cancelling due to bad weather and limited public transport options.
B Training all evenings, she starting to feel frustrated by plays professional soccer.
C It's not uncommon to see a well-groomed dogs being walking along the beach at Bondi.
D Patrick felt that he had spent enough time at work, and so he decided that he should leave.

11 Which sentence is correct?

A Territory locals believed that the young boy would not have been killed had the government maintained the crocodile culling.
B Dancing each night have taken its toll on Gigi that is now feeling exhausted.
C Dark blue would been a favourite colour of the kindergarten children today.
D It were unacceptable for the builders to create such a mess in the school yard.

12 Which sentence uses pronouns correctly?

A I felt delightfully joyous playing with the eldest of they in the class.
B Each morning on my way to school I was confronted by children who thought they were very important.
C Psychologists are only interested in studying that who suffer from unusual thoughts or behaviours.
D Are you aware of the implications of the experiments who you are conducting?

13 Which sentence uses conjunctions correctly?

A After much deliberation, Bianca and Belinda flew down to Melbourne because they needed a break.
B Telecommunication stations own vast stretches of land in Australia since this contributes to a significant amount of money for regional communities.
C 'Ignorance is bliss' was tattooed on his right and left wrists while he lived life investigating the meaning of life.
D Within a rather short space of time Dylan had reached out for the lollies and he felt tired.

14 Highlight the pronoun in the sentence below.

The sport of canyoning is becoming popular as it allows people to have fun with nature.

Answers and explanations on pages 133–134

15 Highlight the adjectives in the sentence below.

Jumping into rock pools can be dangerous, so it is important to try and hit the water feet first and keep as straight as possible.

16 Highlight the adjectives in the sentence below.

Following these simple rules will ensure a smooth landing.

17 Highlight the conjunction in the sentence below.

German researchers have indicated that chocolate may contribute to controlling blood pressure but also protect the heart.

18 Highlight the adjective in the sentence below.

Chocolate is being studied for its potential benefits to the heart.

19 Highlight the past-tense verbs in the sentence below.

Recently the research team found that chocolate reduces the risk of strokes associated with high blood pressure.

Read the text *Breathe* and answer questions 20 to 23.

Breathe

"It only takes one breath," instructed the midwife.

Just one breath, thought Belinda, as her eyes zoomed around the room and fell on the face of her husband. Just one breath.

It may have been just one small breath, but after thirteen hours of labour Belinda felt as exhausted as a marathon runner. She couldn't breathe.

From somewhere in the room, she couldn't work out exactly where, a slow counting started and each number reminded her to breathe. One. Breathe. Two. Breathe. Yes—she could breathe.

20 This extract is written in the

A past tense. **B** present tense. **C** future tense.

21 This extract is written in the

A first person. **B** second person. **C** third person.

22 Which of the following is an example of a metaphor?

A *after thirteen hours of labour Belinda felt as exhausted as a marathon runner*

B *her eyes zoomed around the room and fell on the face of her husband*

C *One. Breathe. Two. Breathe. Yes—she could breathe.*

23 The clause *after thirteen hours of labour Belinda felt as exhausted as a marathon runner* is an example of

A metaphor. **B** personification. **C** simile.

Answers and explanations on pages 133–134

24 Which sentence below uses personification?

A Her heart felt as if it could crash into a thousand minute pieces.

B The deep, dark woods swished in the evening breeze.

C The trees danced in the breeze and waved to the people passing by.

D Annie rode to work dog-tired and ready to claw at the throats of her opponents.

25 Which of the sentences below is an example of second-person narrative? You may choose more than one.

A It's not like I don't like boys—I think they're worth a stare and occasionally they provide comic relief—but what I'm saying is that I have more to do with my time than to follow one around like a lost puppy.

B Walking swiftly across the room, you look furtively behind you to ensure you are completely alone.

C You sidle up to the nearest barman and throw a killer smile in his direction. You mean business, and anyone around can see it

D Just because I'm not wearing two-inch heels and a push-up bra doesn't mean I'm disinterested. It just means I've got some self-respect, right?

Answers and explanations on pages 133–134

PUNCTUATION Standard level questions

Mini Test 1

1 Which of the following has the correct punctuation?
- **A** Jo asked, “Where are you going, Jasmine?”
- **B** Jo asked. “Where are you going, Jasmine?”
- **C** Jo asked “Where are you going, Jasmine?”
- **D** Jo asked “Where are you going, Jasmine.”

2 Which of the following has the correct punctuation?
- **A** My favourite novel is *My Love Lies Bleeding* by alyxandra harvey.
- **B** My favourite novel is *my Love Lies Bleeding* by Alyxandra Harvey.
- **C** my favourite novel is *My Love Lies Bleeding* by Alyxandra Harvey.
- **D** My favourite novel is *My Love Lies Bleeding* by Alyxandra Harvey.

3 Which sentence has the correct punctuation?
- **A** Did you know that an octopus has three hearts!
- **B** Did you know that an octopus has three hearts?
- **C** Did you know that an octopus has three hearts.
- **D** Did you know that an octopus has three hearts,

4 How could this sentence be rewritten correctly with the same meaning?

“Can I get another ice-cream?” asked Joni.
- **A** Joni asked for another ice-cream.
- **B** Joni asked if “he could have another ice-cream.”
- **C** Joni asked for “another ice-cream”.
- **D** Joni wanted to know if you asked for another ice-cream.

5 Which sentence has the correct punctuation?
- **A** “Get back here!”, screamed Dai.
- **B** Get back here! Screamed Dai.
- **C** “Get back here!” Screamed Dai.
- **D** “Get back here!” screamed Dai.

6 Which sentence has the correct punctuation?
- **A** Last november was the warmest ever recorded.
- **B** last November was the warmest ever recorded.
- **C** Last November was the warmest ever recorded?
- **D** Last November was the warmest ever recorded.

7 Which of the following has the correct punctuation?
- **A** After eating breakfast, I went to the beach pool for a swim.
- **B** After eating breakfast I went to the beach pool for a swim.
- **C** After eating breakfast, I went to the beach pool for a swim!
- **D** After eating breakfast I went to the beach pool for a swim?

Answers and explanations on pages 134–135

8 Which **two** sentences have the correct punctuation?

A Ali said he was sorry that he couldn't make it to the play.

B Ali said "He was sorry that he couldn't make it to the play."

C Ali said, "He was sorry that he couldn't make it to the play."

D Ali, the boy with the red hair, said he was sorry.

9 Which **two** sentences use speech marks (" and ") correctly?

A I appreciate your "honesty in this difficult matter," said George.

B "I appreciate your honesty" in this difficult matter, said George.

C George said, "I appreciate your honesty in this difficult matter."

D "I appreciate your honesty in this difficult matter," said George.

10 Circle the letter to show where the missing apostrophe (') should go.

A B C

Your brother↓s are crazy. They think it↓s↓ funny to dance in their underwear.

11 Circle **one** letter to show where the missing apostrophe (') should go.

A B C D

Octopuse↓s are highly intelligent creature↓s; it↓s amazing the complex behaviour↓s they can learn.

12 Circle **one** letter to show where the missing apostrophe (') should go.

A B

Global warming↓s impact is becoming more apparent as sea levels rise. It↓s impact will affect many countries.

13 Circle **one** letter to show where the missing apostrophe (') should go.

A B

It↓s hard to believe that there are over 200 million motorcycle↓s in use worldwide.

14 Which apostrophe is used correctly in this sentence?

A B C D

Don't you dare touch that computer—it belong's to Ari and he like's that it sit's just there.

15 Circle **two** letters to show where the missing speech marks (" and ") should go.

A B C

"It's absolutely unbelievable! ↓exclaimed↓ Tarma.↓ Where did you find it?"

Answers and explanations on pages 134–135

16 Circle a letter to show where the missing apostrophe (') should go.

A ... B

Jamie↓s shoulders were red and blistered. The sun was high and it↓s heat had burnt her skin.

17 Which sentence has the correct punctuation?

A Ben said that "working in the orphanage was the best experience he had ever had."
B Ben said that working in the orphanage was the best experience he had ever had.
C Ben said "that working in the orphanage" was the best experience he had ever had.
D Ben said that working in the orphanage was the best experience he had ever had?

18 Which sentence has the correct punctuation?

A "Don't worry about the concert tomorrow," her teacher said, "because it is cancelled."
B "Don't worry about the concert tomorrow", her teacher said, "Because it is cancelled."
C Don't worry about the concert tomorrow, her teacher said, "because it is cancelled."
D "Don't worry about the concert tomorrow." her Teacher said, "because it is cancelled."

19 Which sentence has the correct punctuation?

A I certainly wouldn't trust a teacher who didn't have a degree?
B I certainly wouldn't trust a teacher who didnt have a degree.
C I certainly wouldn't trust a teacher who didn't have a degree.
D I certainly wouldnt trust a teacher who didnt have a degree.

20 How could this sentence be rewritten correctly with the same meaning?

"Why is Sammy walking through the house wearing muddy shoes?" asked Dad.

A Dad asked why "Sammy is walking through the house with muddy shoes?"
B Dad asked why Sammy was walking through the house with muddy shoes.
C Why is Sammy walking through the house "wearing muddy shoes" asked Dad.
D Dad asked if Sammy should "be wearing muddy shoes in the house."

21 How could this sentence be rewritten correctly with the same meaning?

"It's too late for the children to be up watching movies," explained Mum.

A Mum explained that "it was too late for the children to be up watching movies."
B Mum explained that it was too late for the children to be up watching movies.
C Mum explained that you shouldn't be watching movies.
D "Mum explained that it was too late for the children to be up watching movies."

22 How could this sentence be rewritten correctly with the same meaning?

"I just saw the biggest cake in the whole world!" exclaimed Arji.

A Arji exclaimed that he had just seen the biggest cake in the whole world.
B Arji asked if he had just seen the biggest cake in the whole world.
C Arji was looking at the biggest cake he has ever seen.
D Arji exclaimed, I just saw "the biggest cake in the whole world."

Answers and explanations on pages 134–135

Write the correct punctuation mark from the boxes to complete each sentence.

23 colon (:) semicolon (;) comma (,) full-stop (.)

To service a car you will require the following items [ ] oil, rags, coolant and oil filters.

24 colon (:) semicolon (;) comma (,) full-stop (.)

I must pack my own lunch box today, so I included items I like [ ] chips, lollies, and chocolate.

25 colon (:) semicolon (;) comma (,) full-stop (.)

December was the best month for fruit. We harvested such a variety [ ] mangoes, peaches, strawberries and cherries.

Answers and explanations on pages 134–135

Mini Test 2

1 Which sentence has the correct punctuation?

A Keenan said, "I love playing the drums."
B Keenan said: "I love playing the drums."
C Keenan said. "I love playing the drums."
D Keenan said—"I love playing the drums"

2 Which sentence has the correct punctuation?

A Balin cried: "I didn't hit Hunter!"
B Balin cried, "I didn't hit Hunter!"
C Balin cried. "I didn't hit Hunter!"
D Balin cried! "I didn't hit Hunter!"

3 Which sentence has the correct punctuation?

A "It's unbelievable the number of people who prefer dark chocolate over milk" gasped Tabitha.
B "It's unbelievable the number of people who prefer dark chocolate over milk." gasped Tabitha.
C "It's unbelievable the number of people who prefer dark chocolate over milk," gasped Tabitha.
D "It's unbelievable the number of people who prefer dark chocolate over milk", gasped Tabitha.

4 Which sentence has the correct punctuation?

A "Every man, woman and child should feel confident that a doctor will see them promptly at the nearest hospital" proclaimed the politician.
B "Every man, woman and child should feel confident that a doctor will see them promptly at the nearest hospital", proclaimed the politician.
C "Every man, woman and child should feel confident that a doctor will see them promptly at the nearest hospital," proclaimed the politician.
D "Every man, woman and child should feel confident that a doctor will see them promptly at the nearest hospital." proclaimed the politician.

5 Which sentence has the correct punctuation?

A Ashley asked, "Have you ever seen a lunar eclipse?"
B Ashley "asked, Have you ever seen a lunar eclipse?"
C Ashley asked ", Have you ever seen a lunar eclipse?"
D Ashley asked, "Have you ever seen a lunar eclipse."

6 Which sentence has the correct punctuation?

A Josh said to look out for dragons, so we held our swords high.
B Josh said to "look out for dragons, so we held our swords high."
C Josh said "to look out for dragons, so we held our swords high."
D Josh said to "Look out for dragons, so we held our swords high."

Answers and explanations on pages 135–136

7 Which sentence has the correct punctuation?

A The leader told us that we must keep a close eye out for brown snakes.

B The leader told us that we must “keep a close eye out for brown snakes.”

C The leader told us “that we must keep a close eye out for brown snakes.”

D “The leader told us that we must keep a close eye out for brown snakes.”

8 Which sentence has the correct punctuation?

A I informed the station that “I would not comment on the incident.”

B I informed the station “that I would not comment on” the incident.

C “I informed the station that” I would not comment on the incident.

D I informed the station that I would not comment on the incident.

9 Which sentence has the correct punctuation?

A It was John F kennedy who famously asked for people to consider not what the country could do for them—but what they could do for their country.

B It was John F Kennedy who famously asked for people to consider not what the country could do for them, but what they could do for their country.

C It was John F Kennedy who famously asked for people to consider not what the country could do for them. but what they could do for their country.

D It was John F Kennedy who famously asked for people to consider not what the country could do for them, But what they could do for their country.

10 Which sentence has the correct punctuation?

A The teacher promised the students that they would spend a term doing group work.

B The teacher promised the students that “they would spend a term doing group work.”

C The teacher promised the students that they would “spend a term doing group work.”

D “The teacher promised the students that they would spend a term doing group work.”

11 Which sentence uses speech marks (“ and ”) correctly?

A With emotion in his voice, “he cried, We will unite against racism in this country.”

B With emotion in his voice, he cried, We will unite “against racism in this country.”

C With emotion in his voice, he cried “, We will unite against racism in this country.”

D With emotion in his voice, he cried, “We will unite against racism in this country.”

12 Which sentence uses speech marks (“ and ”) correctly?

A Softly she whispered, I don’t think I can do this anymore.”

B Softly she whispered “I don’t think I can do this anymore”.

C “Softly she whispered, I don’t think I can do this anymore.”

D Softly she whispered, “I don’t think I can do this anymore.”

Answers and explanations on pages 135–136

13 Which sentence uses speech marks (" and ") correctly?

A "It is against human morality to allow animal cruelty to continue as it has for the last 50 years, declared the student" passionately.

B "It is against human morality to allow animal cruelty to continue as it has for the last 50 years," declared the student passionately.

C "It is against human morality to allow animal cruelty to continue as it has for the last 50 years, declared the student passionately.

D "It is against human morality to allow animal cruelty to continue as it has for the last 50 years", declared the student passionately.

14 Which sentence uses speech marks (" and ") correctly?

A "I'm sorry about breaking your pencil case", apologised Ellie.

B "I'm sorry about breaking your pencil case," apologised Ellie.

C "I'm sorry about breaking your pencil case, apologised" Ellie.

D "I'm sorry about breaking your pencil case, apologised Ellie.

15 Which sentence uses speech marks (" and ") correctly?

A "Quickly she admitted, I was the one who ate the last chocolate biscuit."

B Quickly she admitted ",I was the one who ate the last chocolate biscuit."

C Quickly she admitted, "I was the one who ate the last chocolate biscuit."

D Quickly she admitted, I was the one "who ate the last chocolate biscuit."

16 Which sentence has the correct punctuation?

A "It isn't my fault, she pleaded, the glass slipped from my fingers."

B "It isn't my fault" she pleaded "the glass slipped from my fingers."

C "It isn't my fault," she pleaded. "The glass slipped from my fingers."

D "It isn't my fault," she pleaded, "The glass slipped from my fingers."

17 Which sentence has the correct punctuation?

A "Let me have a chance," he begged. "I won't disappoint you."

B "Let me have a chance," he begged, I won't disappoint you."

C "Let me have a chance, he begged, I won't disappoint you."

D "Let me have a chance", he begged, "I won't disappoint you."

18 Which sentence has the correct punctuation?

A "Everyone hates me, cried Annie, "because they think I'm annoying."

B "Everyone hates me" cried Annie, "because they think I'm annoying."

C "Everyone hates me," cried Annie, "because they think I'm annoying."

D "Everyone hates me," cried Annie, "Because they think I'm annoying."

Answers and explanations on pages 135–136

19 Which contraction is used correctly in this sentence?

The children we're (A) in trouble with they're (B) teacher; they'd (C) eaten three lollies out of they're (D) class lolly jar.

20 Circle the letters to show where the missing commas (,) go.

The Kombi van (A) which had (B) been sitting in the rain for three days (C) was beginning to leak (D) and smell damp inside.

21 Circle the letters to show where the missing commas (,) go.

Eddie (Koiki) Mabo (A) an intelligent (B) and determined Indigenous Australian (C) won his fight in the High Court (D) against the claim of *terra nullius*.

22 Highlight where the missing commas (,) should go.

Our dentist Dr Johnston believed that my adult teeth are brittle.

23 Circle the word that should be in italics.

Surfache, a novel written by Gerry Bobsien, is my favourite novel.

Which **two** sentences have the correct punctuation?

24 **A** My father, John, is the man with the kindest heart in the world.
B My father John, is the man with the kindest heart in the world.
C My father is John, the man with the kindest heart in the world.
D My father is John, the man with the kindest heart, in the world.

25 **A** Mr Anderson the one with bushy eyebrows. was my fourth-grade teacher.
B Mr Anderson, the one with bushy eyebrows—was my fourth-grade teacher.
C My fourth grade teacher, Mr Anderson, is the one with the bushy eyebrows.
D Mr Anderson, the teacher with bushy eyebrows, taught me in fourth grade.

Answers and explanations on pages 135–136

Mini Test 3

1 Which sentence has the correct punctuation?

A "It may seem surprising to you," said Mrs McLeod, "but I think it's important to love reading."
B "It may seem surprising to you," said Mrs McLeod, "But I think it's important to love reading."
C "It may seem surprising to you." said Mrs McLeod, "But I think it's important to love reading."
D "It may seem surprising to you" said mrs McLeod, "but I think it's important to love reading."

2 Which sentence has the correct punctuation?

A "I do not like turquoise," asserted Bandy, "Although I am fond of aubergine."
B "I do not like turquoise," asserted Bandy, "although I am fond of aubergine."
C "I do not like turquoise," asserted Bandy "Although I am fond of aubergine."
D "I do not like turquoise," asserted bandy, "although I am fond of aubergine."

3 Which sentence has the correct punctuation?

A "You've already eaten a tub of ice-cream." said Dad, "So I don't think a can of soft drink is a good idea."
B "You've already eaten a tub of ice-cream," said dad, "so I don't think a can of soft drink is a good idea."
C "You've already eaten a tub of ice-cream," said Dad, "so I don't think a can of soft drink is a good idea."
D "you've already eaten a tub of ice-cream," said dad, "so I don't think a can of soft drink is a good idea."

4 Which sentence has the correct punctuation?

A "Indigenous health must be a priority for any government" stated the politician "Because these people do matter."
B "Indigenous health must be a priority for any government," stated the Politician, "because these people do matter."
C "Indigenous health must be a priority for any government" stated the politician, "because these people do matter"
D "Indigenous health must be a priority for any government," stated the politician, "because these people do matter."

5 Which sentence has the correct punctuation?

A "public safety campaigns continue to target drink driving," Explained the activist, "yet people are still driving and dying under the influence of alcohol."
B "Public safety campaigns continue to target drink driving," explained the activist, "yet people are still driving and dying under the influence of alcohol."
C "Public safety campaigns continue to target drink driving," explained the activist, "Yet people are still driving and dying under the influence of alcohol."
D "Public safety campaigns continue to target drink driving" explained the activist, yet people are still driving and dying under the influence of alcohol."

Answers and explanations on pages 136–138

6 Which sentence has the correct punctuation?
A "The accident occurred," reported the newsreader "at Precisely 12.35 am."
B "The accident occurred," Reported the newsreader, "at precisely 12.35 am."
C "The accident occurred," reported the newsreader, "at precisely 12.35 am."
D "The accident occurred" reported the newsreader "at precisely 12.35 am."

7 Which sentence has the correct punctuation?
A "Without even thinking of the consequences," admitted sara, "I left the baby alone for three hours."
B "without even thinking of the consequences," admitted Sara, "I left the baby alone for three hours."
C "Without even thinking of the consequences," admitted Sara, "I left the baby alone for three hours."
D "Without even thinking of the consequences" admitted Sara "I left the baby alone for three hours."

8 Which sentence has the correct punctuation?
A Sunglasses should be worn when driving during the day: in fact, they are useful for all outdoor activities.
B Sunglasses should be worn when driving during the day. in fact, they are useful for all outdoor activities.
C Sunglasses should be worn when driving during the day; in fact, they are useful for all outdoor activities.
D Sunglasses should be worn when driving during the day, in fact, they are useful for all outdoor activities.

9 Which sentence has the correct punctuation?
A Crop circles continue to bewilder farmers in the US, no explanation has come from elsewhere either.
B Crop circles continue to bewilder farmers in the US: no explanation has come from elsewhere either.
C Crop circles continue to bewilder farmers in the US. no explanation has come from elsewhere either.
D Crop circles continue to bewilder farmers in the US; no explanation has come from elsewhere either.

10 Which sentence has the correct punctuation?
A I remember John when he was just a student; now he's the manager of Sony.
B I remember John when he was just a student, now he's the manager of Sony.
C I remember John when he was just a student! now he's the manager of Sony.
D I remember John when he was just a student now he's the manager of Sony.

Answers and explanations on pages 136–138

11 Which sentence correctly uses a colon (:)?

A I would like to order a large meal: three burgers, two fries and a coke.
B I would like to order a large meal three burgers: two fries and a coke.
C I would like: to order a large meal three burgers, two fries and a coke.
D I would like to order a large meal three burgers, two fries: and a coke.

12 Which sentence correctly uses a colon (:)?

A This article will focus on the following cities Toronto, London: and Sydney.
B This article will focus on the following cities: Toronto, London and Sydney.
C This article will focus on: the following cities Toronto, London and Sydney.
D This article will focus on the following: cities Toronto, London and Sydney.

13 Which sentence has the correct punctuation?

A "I don't think you're hopeless" explained Claudia, "but you do seem to be taking a long time to fix that bike."
B "I don't think you're hopeless," explained Claudia, "But you do seem to be taking a long time to fix that bike."
C "I don't think you're hopeless," explained claudia, "but you do seem to be taking a long time to fix that bike."
D "I don't think you're hopeless," explained Claudia, "but you do seem to be taking a long time to fix that bike."

Write the correct punctuation mark from the boxes to complete each sentence.

14 colon (:) semicolon (;) comma (,) full-stop (.)

The traffic was really heavy today [ ] I'm not sure why.

15 colon (:) semicolon (;) comma (,) full-stop (.)

I witnessed a three car pile-up [ ] six people were injured.

16 colon (:) semicolon (;) comma (,) full-stop (.)

My son loves dinosaurs [ ] he collects all the dinosaur models he can.

17 Which sentence has the correct punctuation?

A Yesterday I ate seven cheeseburgers, tomorrow I'll try for eight!
B Yesterday I ate seven cheeseburgers: tomorrow I'll try for eight!
C Yesterday I ate seven cheeseburgers. tomorrow I'll try for eight!
D Yesterday I ate seven cheeseburgers; tomorrow I'll try for eight!

Answers and explanations on pages 136–138

18 Circle **two** letters to show where the missing speech marks (" and ") should go.

"It's absolutely unbelievable! **A**↓ exclaimed **B**↓ Tarma. **C**↓ Where did you find it?"

19 Circle **two** letters to show where the missing speech marks (" and ") should go.

A↓ I'm ashamed to admit it," confessed Jan **B**↓, **C**↓ but I'm a chocoholic."

20 Highlight where the missing semicolon (;) should go.

Easter is celebrated with chocolate for many the origins of the holiday are being forgotten.

21 Highlight where the missing semicolon (;) should go.

Jessie was unforgettable her sister Ann was equally memorable.

22 Highlight where the missing semicolon (;) should go.

Every night I have trouble getting to sleep every morning I am tired.

23 Highlight where the missing semicolon (;) should go.

Last night I watched four episodes I've got two more to go.

24 Which **two** sentences correctly use a colon (:)?

A I have one rule in my house: you must remove your shoes before walking on the carpet.
B My favourite flavours of soda are: raspberry, lemon, ginger and cola.
C It isn't every day that you decide you want to become a rock star: it was for me today.
D Too many people waste water when they are showering: you should only shower for five minutes at a time.

25 Which **two** sentences have the correct punctuation?

A "Those oranges," pointed out Dad, "are nearly ready to be harvested."
B Dad pointed out that "those oranges are nearly ready to be harvested"
C Dad pointed out that the oranges were nearly ready to be harvested.
d "Those oranges", pointed out Dad "Are nearly ready to be harvested."

Answers and explanations on pages 136–138

PUNCTUATION Advanced level questions

Mini Test 4

1 Which of the following has the correct punctuation?

A "Sergeant Anthony will show you to the cell," the detective informed shocked Amanda.
B "Sergeant Anthony will show you to the cell" the detective informed shocked Amanda.
C "Sergeant Anthony will show you to the cell", the detective informed shocked Amanda.
D "Sergeant anthony will show you to the cell," The detective informed shocked Amanda.

2 Which of the following has the correct punctuation?

A "I can't see any reason why we shouldn't go to the game. It's only $10 each," whined Jessie.
B "I can't see any reason why we shouldn't go to the game. It's only $10 each," whined jessie.
C "I can't see any reason why we shouldn't go to the game. It's only $10 each." whined Jessie.
D "I can't see any reason why we shouldn't go to the game. It's only $10 each, whined Jessie.

3 Which of the following has the correct punctuation?

A In an authoritative tone, Professor hewes informed the students, "This essay is worth 50% of your final mark for psychology 1001."
B In an authoritative tone, Professor Hewes informed the students, "This essay is worth 50% of your final mark for psychology 1001."
C In an authoritative tone, Professor Hewes informed the students, "This essay is worth 50% of your final mark for Psychology 1001."
D In an authoritative tone, Professor Hewes informed the students, This essay is worth 50% of Your final mark for Psychology 1001."

4 Which of the following has the correct punctuation?

A "Did you know that Bear grylls is the youngest ever Chief Scout?" asked Joseph in surprise.
B "Did you know that Bear Grylls is the youngest ever Chief Scout?" asked Joseph in surprise.
C "Did you know that bear Grylls is the youngest ever Chief Scout?" asked Joseph in surprise.
D "Did you know that Bear Grylls is the youngest ever Chief Scout!" asked joseph in surprise.

5 Which of the following has the correct punctuation?

A Upon arriving at the capital city of London, detective Jones was summoned to Washington DC.
B Upon arriving at the capital city of london, Detective Jones was summoned to Washington DC.
C Upon arriving at the capital city of London, Detective Jones was summoned to Washington DC.
D Upon arriving at the capital city of London, Detective Jones was summoned to washington DC.

6 Which of the following has the correct punctuation?

A Lisa, Joe and Anthony spent over four hours shopping at Warringah Mall.
B Lisa, joe and Anthony spent over four hours shopping at Warringah Mall.
C Lisa, Joe and Anthony spent over four hours shopping at warringah Mall.
D Lisa, Joe and anthony spent over four hours shopping at Warringah Mall.

Answers and explanations on pages 138–139

7 Which sentence has the correct punctuation?
A The little boy, wearing only his pyjamas! raced after the ice-cream truck.
B The little boy—wearing only his pyjamas, raced after the ice-cream truck.
C The little boy. wearing only his pyjamas, raced after the ice-cream truck.
D The little boy, wearing only his pyjamas, raced after the ice-cream truck.

8 Which sentence has the correct punctuation?
A The class was unruly, even the clever kids and, the teacher could not cope.
B The class was unruly, even the clever kids and the teacher, could not cope.
C The class was unruly, even the clever kids, and the teacher could not cope.
D The class was unruly even the clever kids, and the teacher could not cope.

9 Which sentence has the correct punctuation?
A Cycling as fast as his legs would move Harry, sped down the hill.
B Cycling as fast as his legs, would move Harry sped down the hill.
C Cycling as fast as his legs would move, Harry sped down the hill.
D Cycling as fast, as his legs would move Harry sped down the hill.

10 Which sentence has the correct punctuation?
A Thinking only of himself—Peter began eating the chocolates in the box.
B Thinking only of himself Peter began eating the chocolates in the box.
C Thinking only of himself, Peter began eating the chocolates in the box!
D Thinking only of himself, Peter began eating the chocolates in the box.

11 Which sentence has the correct punctuation?
A I certainly wouldn't trust a surgeon who wasn't registered as a professional.
B I certainly wouldn't trust a surgeon, who wasn't registered as a professional.
C I certainly would'nt trust a surgeon who wasn't registered as a professional.
D I certainly wouldn't trust a surgeon who was'nt registered as a professional.

12 Which sentence has the correct punctuation?
A "Don't worry about coming in to work tomorrow, her boss said, "As the office is flooded."
B "Don't worry about coming in to work tomorrow," her boss said, "as the office is flooded."
C "Don't worry about coming in to work tomorrow" her boss said, "as the office is flooded."
D "Don't worry about coming in to work tomorrow", her boss said, "as the office is flooded."

13 Which sentence has the correct punctuation?
A There are obvious dangers in rock-climbing … climbers must be aware of the risks they are taking.
B There are obvious dangers in rock-climbing. climbers must be aware of the risks they are taking.
C There are obvious dangers in rock-climbing; climbers must be aware of the risks they are taking.
D There are obvious dangers in rock-climbing, climbers must be aware of the risks they are taking.

Answers and explanations on pages 138–139

14 Which sentence has the correct punctuation?
- A “Thank goodness it’s finished!” exclaimed Ms Peters. “I thought it would never end.”
- B “Thank goodness it’s finished! exclaimed Ms Peters, “I thought it would never end.”
- C “Thank goodness it’s finished” exclaimed Ms Peters, I thought it would never end.”
- D “Thank goodness it’s finished” exclaimed Ms Peters. “I thought it would never end.”

15 Which sentence has the correct punctuation?
- A My father once commented “that the difficulty of life lies in forging your own identity.”
- B My father once commented that the difficulty of life lies in forging your own identity.
- C My father once commented that “the difficulty of life lies in forging your own identity.”
- D My father “once commented that the difficulty of life lies in forging your own identity.”

Write the correct words or punctuation marks from the boxes to complete each sentence.

16 should of | should’ve | shouldv’e | should’ave

My family [ ] listened to me when I warned them about the storm.

17 could of | could’ave | could’ve | couldv’e

Dad reckons the army [ ] won the war if they had thought more strategically.

18 Isnit | I’snt | Isn’t | Isnot

[ ] it impossible for a human being to live on Mars?

19 Jasper and Jasmine [ ] preferred to be going to the park rather than staying at home.

would’ve | would of | wouldve | would’ave

20 dashes (–) | full stops (.) | semicolons (;) | exclamation marks (!)

This is the longest [ ] and worst [ ] novel that I have been forced to read!

21 Were | We’re | Where | We’are

[ ] unaware of the impact that consuming animal products is having on our bodies and our planet.

22 I’ve | Iv’e | I’ave | I of

Did you notice that [ ] cut my hair recently?

 Answers and explanations on pages 138–139

23 Which sentence correctly combines the information in this table?

Child	Favourite food
Marty	pizza, hot chips and fried rice
June	curry, chocolate and pizza

A Marty and June like curry while they also like to eat pizza, hot chips, fried rice and chocolate.
B Both Marty and June like to eat food; they eat curry, pizza, hot chips, fried rice and chocolate.
C The favourite food of both Marty and June is pizza; Marty also likes eating hot chips and fried rice while June also likes eating curry and chocolate.
D Marty and June eat pizza together; June likes to eat chocolate and curry, and Marty likes hot chips and fried rice.

24 Which **two** sentences have the correct punctuation?
A Lord Darcy felt sick and was forced to leave the ceremony early.
B Feeling sick, Lord Darcy left the ceremony early.
C Lord darcy felt sick and was forced to leave the ceremony early.
D Feeling sick, Lord darcy left the ceremony early.

25 Which **two** sentences have the correct punctuation?
A Clearly the young children, two of whom were no older than ten years old, were not prepared for their trip to Italy.
B Clearly the young children two of whom were no older than ten years old were not prepared for their trip to Italy.
C Clearly, the young children two of whom were no older than ten years old were not prepared for their trip to italy.
D Clearly the young children were not prepared for their trip to Italy.

Answers and explanations on pages 138–139

PUNCTUATION Advanced level questions

Mini Test 5

1. Circle the letter where the missing apostrophe (’) should go.

   The accident, which resulted in three death[A]s, was caused by the car[B]s faulty accelerator.

2. Circle the letter where the missing apostrophe (’) should go.

   Japan[A]s force[B]s entered World War II in December 1941 and swiftly achieved a serie[C]s of victorie[D]s.

3. Circle the letter where the missing apostrophe (’) should go.

   The laboratory[A]s equipment made investigating the germination of rare seed[B]s much easier.

4. Circle the letter where the missing apostrophe (’) should go.

   His parent[A]s were unimpressed with James[B]s poor behaviour at the movie[C]s.

5. Circle the letter where the missing apostrophe (’) should go.

   CSIRO[A]s partnership with the wool industry has allowed for numerou[B]s advance[C]s in wool technologie[D]s.

6. Circle the letter where the missing apostrophe (’) should go.

   Craig[A]s ideas about shopping centre[B]s seem strange to me.

7. Circle the letter where the missing apostrophe (’) should go.

   Deliverie[A]s made overnight made it easier for the continuation of the school[B]s agriculture project.

8. Circle the letter where the missing apostrophe (’) should go.

   Doctor[A]s believe that an individual[B]s decision[C]s made about drinking early in life can drastically affect his/her health in the future.

Answers and explanations on pages 139–140

Write the correct word from the boxes to complete each sentence.

9 performers | performer's | performers' | performers's

The teacher told the children that backstage was for [ ] only.

10 spectators' | spectators | spectator's | spectators's

Soccer has become almost as popular in Australia for [ ] as AFL.

11 Jones' | Jones's | Jones | Joneses

My family has never been interested in keeping up with the [ ].

12 where | wear | we're | were

I have no clue [ ] the team got their new jackets from; I want one.

13 who's | whose | whose' | whos

The boy [ ] the best in the class is Charlie.

14 they're | their | there | the'yre

You know that [ ] not the only people ready to sacrifice themselves, don't you?

15 could'nt | couldn't | couldnt | could'not

It had been believed that the *Titanic* [ ] be sunk.

16 Which option correctly completes this sentence?

I decided to leave university [ ] yesterday.

A last Thursday; reality hit
B last Thursday: reality hit
C last Thursday, reality hit
D last Thursday … reality hit

17 Which option correctly completes this sentence?

The building is infested with [ ] destroyed.

A vermin, it is to be
B vermin; it is to be
C vermin! it is to be
D vermin … it is to be

Answers and explanations on pages 139–140

18 Which option correctly completes this sentence?

After much discussion the decision was made to leave ________ stranded for seventeen days.

A the island; they had been
B the island, they had been
C the island … they had been
D the island—they had been

19 Which punctuation mark should be used in both spaces in this sentence?

Belinda's three children ____ Ayden, Blake and Claudine ____ are the most delightful children I have met.

A — (dash)
B : (colon)
C ... (ellipsis)
D ; (semicolon)

20 Which punctuation mark should be used in both spaces in this sentence?

"I haven't been sleeping well since ____ you know ____ it's really hard losing such a close friend," cried Angie.

A — (dash)
B : (colon)
C ... (ellipsis)
D ; (semicolon)

21 Which punctuation mark should be used in the space in this sentence?

I have only ever wanted what's best for you ____ I don't know why you fight me.

A , (comma)
B : (colon)
C ... (ellipsis)
D ; (semicolon)

22 Which sentence has the correct punctuation?

A With his heart beating fast. Ryo pulled open the door.
B With his heart beating fast, Ryo pulled open the door.
C With his heart beating fast—Ryo pulled open the door.
D With his heart beating fast! Ryo pulled open the door.

23 Which sentence has the correct punctuation?

A Dancing with glee, the tiny girl accepted her certificate.
B Dancing with glee! the tiny girl accepted her certificate.
C Dancing with glee. the tiny girl accepted her certificate.
D Dancing with glee—the tiny girl accepted her certificate.

24 Which sentence has the correct punctuation?

A Every summer, even the very hot one last year! I visit the Lake District.
B Every summer, even the very hot one last year. I visit the Lake District.
C Every summer, even the very hot one last year, I visit the Lake District.
D Every summer, even the very hot one last year—I visit the Lake District.

25 Which sentence has the correct punctuation?

A Swiftly and softly, Smaug the dragon flew over the mountain.
B Swiftly and softly: Smaug the dragon flew over the mountain.
C Swiftly and softly. Smaug the dragon flew over the mountain.
D Swiftly and softly—Smaug the dragon flew over the mountain.

☞ Answers and explanations on pages 139–140

READING Standard level questions

Mini Test 1: Narrative

A narrative:

- is a fiction text that is also known as a story
- has entertainment, amusement or information as its main purpose
- traditionally has a structure consisting of an orientation (the introduction of the setting and characters), a series of events including a complication (a problem faced by the character that must be overcome), a climax (a scene of increased tension where the character is faced with some kind of danger), a resolution (the problem is overcome) and a coda (a lesson is learned and life returns to normal)
- uses language features such as descriptive language, figurative language, adjectives, action verbs and sometimes dialogue.

Read the narrative *Night worker* and answer the questions.

Night worker

The night was cold and dark. Yet this was not the first time that JT had felt the unnatural chill of the wind as it howled through the empty hallways. He knew this place and the way it made his heart beat a little faster. He expected his breath to catch in his throat at the smallest sound.

At 12.30 am, it was early for JT. Despite his seeming isolation, there was still the possibility of a nurse walking down to his ward, doing the final checks before leaving for a warm meal and comfortable bed. It wouldn't be for an hour or two that the night would really settle in and he would be on his own.

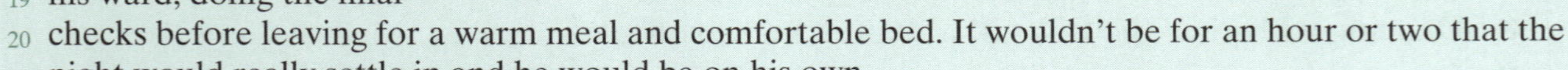

A nursing home at night is a strange place, full of seemingly unearthly sounds. The slightly too wide corridors, illuminated by outdated fluoro lights and covered in dull linoleum, begin to fill with low moans of half-asleep residents. Muffled notes of pain join together with the whispers of words unsaid and cries of loneliness to create a sombre soundtrack to his nightly shift.

Sitting at his small desk and studying the roster for the coming week, JT was startled by a new sound. Shuffling. Putting down his handful of papers, he turned his attention to the hallway behind him. The glow of the hall light seeped into the office in which he sat, throwing strange colours and patterns onto the thick carpet. The hall was empty of any presence but for the shuffling sound. This sound appeared to grow louder with each breath JT inhaled. Feeling sure he was imagining things, JT rose from his seat and edged his way to the door. Nothing.

He had been working here for six months. During this time he had become accustomed to the eeriness of his environment and the fact that one must always expect the unexpected. He sat back at the desk and distracted himself with the roster.

Note: the numbers in the margin are line references to help you use the answer section more effectively.

1 The nursing home was a strange place because
A JT was afraid.
B there was a shuffling noise.
C it was full of unearthly sounds.
D it was full of strange people.

2 JT would be on his own because
A he worked late at night.
B the residents of the nursing home had left.
C the nurse had gone home.
D the nursing staff would finish their shift and he worked the late night shift alone.

3 JT worked in
A a hospital full of ghosts.
B a hallway lit by fluoro lights.
C a nursing home.
D an office with a desk and chair.

4 *He knew this place and the way it made his heart beat a little faster.* Why did JT know this place?
A He had worked there for six months.
B He lived in the nursing home.
C He spent every night there.
D He was a nurse in the nursing home.

5 Why did JT stop reading the roster?
A He was bored.
B He felt afraid.
C He was frustrated with his job.
D He heard an unusual sound.

6 This text would be appropriate for what type of audience? There are **two** correct answers.
A anyone who likes being scared by stories
B adults thinking about putting their parents in a nursing home
C the elderly who live in nursing homes
D anyone who enjoys reading a story full of suspense
E young children about to go to bed

7 How did JT feel about the nursing home?
A comfortable because it was his workplace
B scared because there were strange noises
C familiar with it, yet wary of the unknown
D wary because he knew strange things could happen there

8 JT went back to reading the roster because
A he couldn't find a cause for the strange shuffling noise.
B he was afraid and wanted to distract himself.
C the roster needed to be checked.
D he had become accustomed to strange things happening in the nursing home.

 Answers and explanations on page 141

Standard level questions

Mini Test 2: Procedure

A procedure:
- is a non-fiction text (sometimes referred to as instructions) that is intended to instruct someone how to do something
- features a goal to be achieved, a series of steps (often numbered) to be followed and sometimes a list of materials and equipment to be used
- often includes diagrams or images to support the instructions given
- uses language features such as verbs in the imperative mood, phrases that indicate location and time, and sometimes jargon (technical language specific to the subject area).

Read these instructions and answer the questions.

1. Take an A4 sheet of paper and fold it in half.

2. Fold the short edge of one side down to the first fold. This will produce a 45 degree angle. Do this for the other side too.

3. Fold down the new fold you have created to the original fold you did in (1). Repeat for the other side.

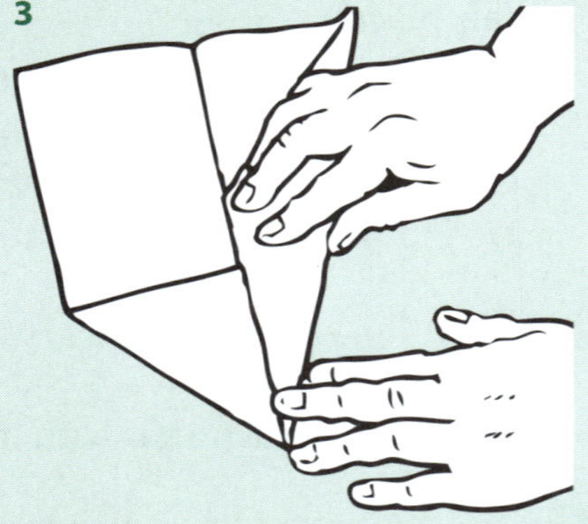

4. Do (3) again for both sides.

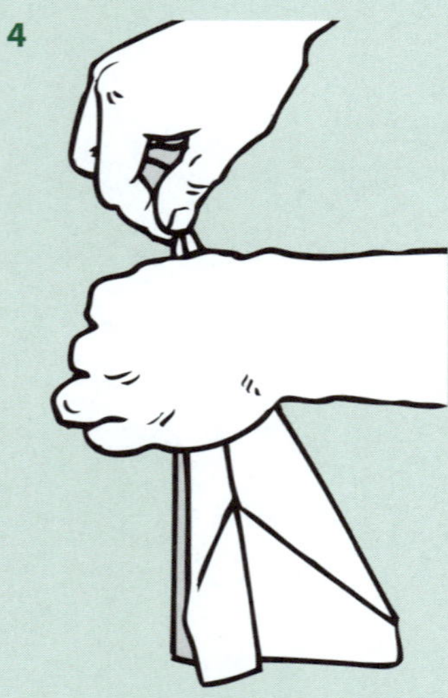

5. Hold the centre and fold the wings out.

6. Now throw!

Source: <http://www.paperairplanes.co.uk/peteplan.php>

1 What is the main purpose of this text?
A to teach how to fold paper
B to instruct how to create a paper plane
C to state how many folds are needed to create a paper plane
D to demonstrate how to create a paper boat

2 What sized sheet of paper is needed to create this plane?
A A4 **B** A3 **C** B3 **D** A6

3 What angle is produced when you fold the short edge of one side down to the first fold?
A a 47 degree angle **B** a 90 degree angle
C a 45 degree angle **D** a 180 degree angle

4 Who is the intended audience of this text? There are **two** correct answers.
A young children
B young adults
C people who want to create paper planes
D people who don't know how to make paper planes but want to learn
E experts in paper plane design

5 How does step 4 connect with step 3?
A Step 4 requires an understanding of step 3.
B Step 4 is harder than step 3.
C Step 4 is a repeat of step 3.
D Step 3 is essential for step 4.

6 What is the purpose of the second diagram?
A to show the second step in making the paper plane
B to show when to fold the paper
C to produce a 45 degree angle
D to show how to fold the short edge

7 How many times do you fold the piece of paper to make the plane?
A 9 **B** 7 **C** 5 **D** 4

8 What does the last step mean?
A The plane must be thrown now.
B A ball must be thrown at the plane.
C The only purpose of a plane is to throw it.
D The plane is now ready to use.

Answers and explanations on page 141

READING

Intermediate level questions

Mini Test 3: Procedure

Read these instructions and answer the questions.

Go to page 58 to read about **Procedures**.

1. Safety first

Flat tyres always seem to happen in inconvenient places, so make sure you pull over in a safe area, clear of passing traffic, and on a surface that is hard and flat to change it. Ensure the car is in 'park' and apply the handbrake.

2. Use the right equipment

You will need a jack and a wheel brace to replace your flat tyre, both of which should be in the car's boot. Once you have located them, get down on your knees and look for small notches or grooves on the underside of your car (see diagram)—this is where you need to place the jack. Once the jack is in place, slowly turn the handle until you remove some of the car's weight from the flat tyre.

3. Loosen the wheel nuts

Place the wheel brace on one of the wheel nuts (see diagram) and, with a straight arm and a straight back, 'crack' each of the wheel nuts in turn in an anti-clockwise direction (looking at the wheel). Keep the wheel brace horizontal to the ground and you'll find that your body weight alone is adequate to loosen the wheel nuts. Now, use the jack to lift the car up so that it is some way off the ground to accommodate the fully inflated tyre.

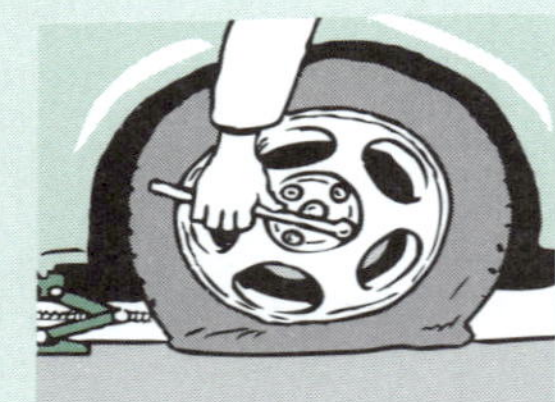

4. Remove the wheel

You should now be able to remove the wheel nuts one by one and gently lift the wheel from the car (see diagram). If the wheel will not come free, it could be that corrosion has caused the wheel to stick. If this happens, put one nut back on the wheel and give the wheel a kick in order to free it.

5. Replace the wheel

Remove your spare wheel from the boot and place it against the car's wheel assembly. By lining up the wheels' holes first, it will make it easier to lift the wheel straight onto the car. Then tighten all the wheel nuts by hand. If you tighten the bottom nut first, it will hold the wheel in place. Using the wheel brace, give all the wheel nuts a small 'nip' to tighten them. The idea is not to tighten the nuts completely at this point because the car is not completely stable while it is still on the jack.

6. Remove the jack

Unwind the jack slowly until the new wheel takes the weight of the car and then remove it (see diagram). Remember to keep a straight arm and back, and with the wheel brace horizontal to the ground, use the weight of your body to tighten all of the wheel nuts.

Source: <http://www.openroad.com.au/How_to_Change_a_Tyre_mar07.htm>. Reprinted courtesy of NRMA Motoring & Services.

1 What might cause the wheel to *not come free* once the wheel nuts are removed?

A The tyre is old.
B Corrosion has caused the tyre to stick.
C Someone has been kicking the tyre.
D The wheel nuts are too tight.

2 Why should you pull over in a safe area to change a flat tyre?

A to avoid being involved in a car accident
B because it is difficult changing a tyre with cars driving past
C because a flat surface is needed
D so that you are clear of passing traffic

3 Choose the **two** correct answers. Step 4 suggests that

A people often have difficulty removing wheels from cars.
B you must kick a tyre to remove it.
C people may need to be determined and improvise when removing a tyre.
D wheel nuts are hard to remove.
E wheels can be difficult to remove for a range of reasons.

4 Step 6 suggests that

A people must be careful changing tyres.
B a jack must be unwound carefully.
C a specific technique is needed to remove the jack.
D moving a jack is difficult.

5 Which procedure is illustrated in the third image?

A removing wheel nuts
B loosening wheel nuts
C using a wheel brace
D changing a tyre

6 The specific directions regarding the *small notches or grooves on the underside of your car* in step 2 indicate that

A people often place the jack in the wrong spot.
B these notches or grooves are hard to find.
C placing a jack in the right spot is easy.
D the notches or grooves are small.

7 Images are included in these instructions to

A show the reader what each part of the car looks like.
B add interest to the instructions.
C help people who can't read.
D support the written instructions.

8 What is likely to affect an individual's success when changing a tyre?

A traffic on the road
B placing the jack in the wrong spot
C tightening the wheel nuts as the very last step
D all of the above

 Answers and explanations on pages 141–142

READING

Intermediate level questions

Mini Test 4: Response

A response:

- is a non-fiction text that responds to a work of art or other stimulus and presents a person's judgement on it (e.g. film and book reviews)
- usually features a brief description of the stimulus material, the writer's judgement on it and examples to support this judgement
- uses language features such as descriptive language, emotive words and persuasive language.

Read about the Guringai people and answer the questions.

I would like to acknowledge the Guringai people who are the Traditional Custodians of this Land.

How many times have you heard that welcome at assembly? But just what does 'the Traditional Custodians of this Land' mean and who were the Guringai people?

Mum told me that I should throw some jokes into my speech because everyone loves to have a laugh and the funny kids always win this competition. But then I started thinking about the fate of our Indigenous people, especially the Guringai people, and—well, it's not really funny, is it? But I'm not here today to focus on the bad stuff. I want to share with you some of the beautiful stories of the traditional custodians of the land on which I now stand, the Guringai people.

By the time the settlers arrived in 1788, the Indigenous culture of the shire we live in today was at least 15 000 years old. That even makes my grandad seem young! But do you know what's even older still? The stars! You probably don't know this, but the Aboriginal people were among the first ever astronomers! They knew a lot about the sun, stars, planets and the moon and they shared this through their Dreaming stories for over 40 000 years.

The Guringai people were the traditional inhabitants of the northern Sydney region. They knew a lot about marine life and how to hunt effectively on land and in the water. They celebrated the giants of the sea—whales and sharks—and you can see this today in rock carvings just down the road! Even North Head in Manly is a sacred place for the Guringai people. It was there that the senior law men, or *karadji*, came together for healing ceremonies.

You've probably all heard the names Captain Cook and Governor Phillip, but have you ever heard of a man called Bungaree? Bungaree was the chief of the Guringai Broken Bay tribes and he was born close to Brisbane Waters. He was described as witty and intelligent. Some people said that he was 'smart enough to keep his foot in both black and white camps'. In 1801 he sailed with Matthew Flinders around the entire coast of Australia, mapping the coastline. How cool is that?

Unfortunately not all of the Guringai people were this lucky. The Guringai people struggled to survive but lost. Most of them were killed by the vicious smallpox disease that the settlers brought with them from England. Those who didn't die from smallpox fled out West to live with other Aboriginal tribes.

So, how can you help to celebrate the traditional custodians of our land? Ask Mum and Dad to take you to look at the Aboriginal rock carvings and other sacred sites at Ku-ring-gai Chase and attend next year's Guringai Festival. We are the future of our nation and we must work together to remember and celebrate those who came before us.

Thank you.

1 In the third paragraph the speaker refers to *the bad stuff*. What does this suggest?

A The speech could be sad.
B Indigenous people had bad experiences.
C The speaker wants the speech to be funny.
D There are no happy things to talk about.

2 One opinion expressed by the speaker is that

A smallpox killed all of the Guringai people.
B the Guringai people were kind people.
C the settlers killed the Guringai people.
D Guringai history must be remembered.

3 According to the speaker, Bungaree is cool because

A he sailed around the Australian coastline with Matthew Flinders.
B he could keep one foot in the white camp and one in the black camp.
C he was witty and intelligent.
D he was born near Brisbane Waters.

4 Why does the speaker open the last paragraph with a question?

A to question the audience about the Guringai people
B to prompt the audience to take action and protect the memory of the Guringai people
C because he does not like the audience
D because he wants the audience to think about the future of the Guringai people's memory

5 What does the line *I want to share with you some of the beautiful stories of the traditional custodians of the land on which I now stand, the Guringai people* suggest about the speaker's attitude towards the Guringai people?

A He is interested in their stories.
B He respects and values their culture.
C He is critical of their stories.
D He thinks the Guringai people were clever.

6 Which of the following contains an example of figurative language?

A *They celebrated the giants of the sea—whales and sharks—and you can see this today in rock carvings just down the road!*
B *Even North Head in Manly is a sacred place for the Guringai people.*
C *You probably don't know this, but the Aboriginal people were among the first ever astronomers!*
D *They knew a lot about marine life and how to hunt effectively on land and in the water.*

7 The question *How cool is that?* suggests that

A Bungaree was a cool person.
B the speaker finds Bungaree dull.
C the speaker is impressed by Bungaree.
D the weather was cold when Bungaree was sailing around Australia.

8 Why does the speaker believe that *We are the future of our nation*? There are **two** correct answers.

A He thinks young people are powerful and they will shape their nation in the future.
B Young people will be responsible for remembering and celebrating the history of the Guringai people.
C The Guringai people are important.
D The Guringai people attend festivals.
E He has an over-inflated sense of self-importance.

Answers and explanations on pages 142–143

READING Intermediate level questions

Mini Test 5: Poem

Poetry:
- is an intense expression of emotion, experience or ideas in a compact form, often intended to change the reader's experience of the world in some way
- is usually tightly structured and features lines instead of sentences and stanzas instead of paragraphs—popular forms are ballads, haiku, lyric poems and sonnets
- can feature a regular rhyme scheme and a regular rhythm
- uses language features such as figurative language (metaphor, simile and personification) and sound devices such as assonance, alliteration and onomatopoeia.

Read *Ozymandias* by Percy Bysshe Shelley and answer the questions.

Ozymandias

I met a traveller from an antique land
Who said: "Two vast and trunkless legs of stone
Stand in the desert. Near them on the sand,
Half sunk, a shattered visage lies, whose frown
And wrinkled lip and sneer of cold command
Tell that its sculptor well those passions read
Which yet survive, stamped on these lifeless things,
The hand that mocked them and the heart that fed.
And on the pedestal these words appear:
'My name is Ozymandias, King of Kings:
Look on my works, ye mighty, and despair!'
Nothing beside remains. Round the decay
Of that colossal wreck, boundless and bare,
The lone and level sands stretch far away".

1 *'My name is Ozymandias, King of Kings:*
Look on my works, ye mighty, and despair!'
Nothing beside remains.

These lines suggest that

A individuals who desire power are destined to fail.
B the work of the artist will outlive the memory of a king.
C Ozymandias was a cruel king.
D the statue is now broken.

2 *Tell that its sculptor well those passions read* is best interpreted as

A the sculptor is friends with the king.
B the sculptor was told that the king was angry and temperamental.
C the sculptor was familiar with the temper of the king.
D the sculptor enjoys reading books about kings.

3 When the poet uses the word *lifeless* he

A reveals his belief that the king is powerless in death.
B shows that people in power should not abuse it.
C shows that the statue reflects the loss of power all individuals must eventually experience.
D captures the pain of the king's death.

4 *a shattered visage lies* is best interpreted as

A the statue is shattered.
B a face lies broken.
C there is a mirage of broken glass.
D the king's face can't be seen clearly.

5 The description of the statue in this poem creates feelings of

A respect and admiration.
B happiness and satisfaction.
C frustration and despair.
D contemplation and awe.

6 Which statement best describes the underlying assumptions in the poem?

A Individuals don't survive but art does.
B There is no power over death.
C A man is vulnerable to the passage of time despite his claims to power.
D Memories of great individuals can last through the ages.

7 Highlight **one** example of figurative language in the text. ______________________

8 Which of the following is an example of figurative language?

A *I met a traveller from an antique land*
B *Two vast and trunkless legs of stone*
C *My name is Ozymandias, King of Kings*
D *The hand that mocked them and the heart that fed*

Answers and explanations on page 143

READING Intermediate level questions

Mini Test 6: Narrative

Read the narrative below and answer the questions.

Go to page 56 to read about Narratives.

9.29 am and I'm pleased to still be in bed. The thick doona has kept me warm and secure for the last 12 hours—well, really for the last 12 years. I often wonder why Mum doesn't chuck it. There's enough reason to. There's that yellow stain at the bottom where Gemma at age 6 decided to chat in bed with a cup of OJ. Boy was Mum aggro when she saw that! You know, my whole room's a bit of an exhibition of me, a homage to myself if you will. Mum would say it's an archaeological dig!

There isn't much light in my room at the moment even though the sun is well above the horizon and the birds are tiring of their morning songs. In here it's dark and stuffy, just the way any 16 year old likes his room. Glancing around my haven I see that over the years I've accumulated some pretty cool stuff. Stuff that reeks of me and reminds me of how fortunate I am that the fever broke during the night.

Picture this: a slender yet healthy 16-year boy, top of Science and PE, but bottom of French. He crouches eagerly at the starting line of the 100-metre sprint, breathing calmly and visualising the first place position he always gets. Then, without warning, the boy's knees buckle and his blemish-free face hits the red rubber. His eyes stare blankly up at the nothingness in front of them. Darkness.

That was me just over 24 hours ago. Since the darkness dropped I've been in and out of the light—the shades of grey I'll call them. I remember one moment when everything just seemed one massive contraction of aching and throbbing muscles. My head was the worst. It seemed far larger than normal, and even though they assure me they had me lying in bed, I swear it seemed as though I were balancing the head of an elephant on the neck of a stork. Delirium came soon after. I remember Mum singing an obscure jazz tune somewhere in the distance and Gemma seemed to radiate from the walls. Her voice was just a tinkling that echoed around my room, bouncing at odd angles from bed-head to Nirvana poster and coming to roost on that faint yellow stain.

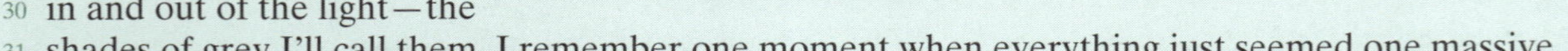

Then, precisely halfway through this dalliance with delirium, came my knight in grey three-piece suit and faux hair—Mr Harrison, the family doctor. The magic he worked is beyond the comprehension of mere mortals such as me—but it worked!

I am comfortable and I am conscious. These are two things that have brought me to this moment of rumination upon a light yellow stain on my doona. As the light of the sun attempts to squeeze through my defiant curtains, I realise that life is a light I don't want to let go of for a long, long time.

1 The words *Boy was Mum aggro when she saw that!* (line 4) give the impression that
A the boy is scared of his mother.
B the narrator is a young boy.
C the boy feels bad about spilling the juice.
D the boy appreciates how valuable the doona is to his mother.

2 What made the narrator's head hurt?
A He was suffering from a fever.
B His head was like that of an elephant.
C He had a headache because of his delirium.
D He hit his head on the ground when he fainted.

3 *I often wonder why Mum doesn't chuck it* (line 2) implies that the narrator
A believes his mother likes to keep old things.
B thinks his mother is untidy.
C wishes his mother would buy new blankets.
D doesn't see the value in keeping the doona.

4 In this short story, the narrator feels
A shocked by how quickly he became sick.
B thankful that the doctor cured him.
C frustrated at being stuck in his bedroom.
D appreciative of his life having come so close to death.

5 The mood of this story is
A calm. **B** energetic. **C** negative. **D** reflective.

6 The detailed description of the boy's bedroom helps to build an atmosphere of
A comfort. **B** fear.
C disorder. **D** security and familiarity.

7 Highlight **one** example of figurative language in the text.

---

8 Which statement best describes this short story?
A Life is precious and we must treasure every moment.
B An individual's health is important and must be looked after.
C Sometimes unexpected events change our view of the world.
D Teenagers don't respect their parents or value their own lives.

Answers and explanations on pages 143–144

READING

Advanced level questions

Mini Test 7: Poem

Read *All the world's a stage* by William Shakespeare (from the play *As you like it*, Act 2, Scene 7) and answer the questions.

Go to page 64 to read about **Poetry**.

All the world's a stage,
And all the men and women merely players:
They have their exits and their entrances;
And one man in his time plays many parts,
His acts being seven ages. At first the infant,
Mewling and puking in the nurse's arms.
And then the whining school-boy, with his satchel
And shining morning face, creeping like snail
Unwillingly to school. And then the lover,
Sighing like furnace, with a woeful ballad
Made to his mistress' eyebrow. Then a soldier,
Full of strange oaths and bearded like the pard,
Jealous in honour, sudden and quick in quarrel,
Seeking the bubble reputation
Even in the cannon's mouth. And then the justice,
In fair round belly with good capon lined,
With eyes severe and beard of formal cut,
Full of wise saws and modern instances;
And so he plays his part. The sixth age shifts
Into the lean and slipper'd pantaloon,
With spectacles on nose and pouch on side,
His youthful hose, well saved, a world too wide
For his shrunk shank; and his big manly voice,
Turning again toward childish treble, pipes
And whistles in his sound. Last scene of all,
That ends this strange eventful history,
Is second childishness and mere oblivion,
Sans teeth, sans eyes, sans taste, sans everything.

1 Why is the lover *Sighing like furnace*?

A He is in love but cannot express his thoughts.
B He believes this behaviour will attract the attention of his lover.
C He thinks this is what a person in love should sound like.
D He is expressing his emotions to the person he loves.

2 *Sans teeth, sans eyes, sans taste, sans everything.* Commas are used in this line to

A make the reader pause in certain places.
B separate items in a list.
C create tension.
D add emphasis to the repetition of the word *sans* and to create a cumulating effect.

3 The attitude towards the life of man suggested in this extract is one of

A dismay. B understanding. C alarm. D acceptance.

4 The words *bubble reputation* (line 14) suggest that

A reputation is temporary and should not be desired.
B reputations are false.
C an individual's reputation can be seen through by others.
D people can get stuck with their own reputation in society.

5 According to the text there are seven stages of man. Place the stages of man identified by Shakespeare in order.

☐ soldier
☐ wise man of justice
☐ second childhood without teeth, hair or taste
☐ crying baby
☐ lover
☐ old man
☐ complaining school-boy

6 What does Shakespeare find fascinating about humanity?

A Life is nothing but a series of performances with individuals playing predefined roles.
B Life is over suddenly.
C People occupy themselves with meaningless tasks, only to die anyway.
D Men and women pretend to be something or someone different at each stage of their life.

7 The tone of this extract is best described as

A sarcastic. B frustrated. C humorous. D philosophical.

8 Shakespeare would likely be intrigued by human behaviour because

A life is like a cycle.
B people change their behaviour at different times of their lives.
C people follow familiar patterns throughout their lives.
D people do unusual things as they age.

Answers and explanations on page 144

READING

Advanced level questions

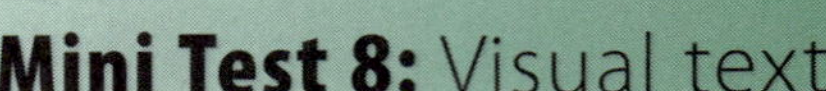

Mini Test 8: Visual text

A visual text:
- can be fiction or non-fiction—forms include comics, films, posters and advertisements
- uses pictures, diagrams and images to express ideas, persuade, inform or educate
- is unlike written text as it can be read in many ways, including from bottom to top or from right to left
- uses features such as familiar symbols (e.g. stop signs, love hearts, crosses), colour, and the size and placement of objects within a frame to convey information.

Read the cartoon and answer the questions.

Source: <http://farm1.static.flickr.com/194/512991135_2408284c48.jpg>

1 For the first boy, the iPhone is

A a common ground between the boys.

B a reason to be friends with the other boy again.

C a surprise.

D an exciting possession to own.

2 What would be the best way to describe the second boy in this comic?

3 How does the first boy feel towards the second boy by the end of the text?

A He feels excited that the second boy is getting an iPhone.

B He believes that the two can still be friends.

C He is happy that they both have an iPhone.

D He doesn't want to show him the iPhone.

4 What does the word *OUCH* imply about the second boy?

A He likes the first boy and wants to remain friends.

B He is hurt that the first boy thinks they have nothing in common.

C The first boy hurt his feelings.

D He doesn't like the other boy's words.

5 Choose the **two** correct answers. The mood of this comic is

humorous.	critical.	sad.	joyful.	cynical.
A	B	C	D	E

6 The second and third frames are similar in order to

A show the confusion of both boys.

B capture the difficulty of sustaining friendship between young people.

C make a comment on the materialistic attitudes of young people.

D create tension between the two boys as they confront problems with their relationship.

7 When the cartoonist draws the first boy smiling in the final frame he

A implies that young people bond over material possessions.

B captures the relief of the first boy, who feels he now has a reason to keep his friend.

C shows the excitement young people feel regarding new technology.

D suggests the boy is shallow.

8 This cartoon uses stereotypes to convey its message. Write down **one** stereotype from this cartoon.

Answers and explanations on pages 144–145

READING Advanced level questions

Mini Test 9: Poem

Read *I wandered lonely as a cloud* by William Wordsworth and answer the questions.
Go to page 64 to read about **Poetry**.

I wandered lonely as a cloud

I wandered lonely as a cloud
That floats on high o'er vales and hills,
When all at once I saw a crowd,
A host, of golden daffodils;
Beside the lake, beneath the trees,
Fluttering and dancing in the breeze.

Continuous as the stars that shine
And twinkle on the milky way,
They stretched in never-ending line
Along the margin of a bay:
Ten thousand saw I at a glance,
Tossing their heads in sprightly dance.

The waves beside them danced; but they
Out-did the sparkling waves in glee:
A poet could not but be gay,
In such a jocund company:
I gazed—and gazed—but little thought
What wealth the show to me had brought:

For oft, when on my couch I lie
In vacant or in pensive mood,
They flash upon that inward eye
Which is the bliss of solitude;
And then my heart with pleasure fills,
And dances with the daffodils.

1 William Wordsworth uses figurative language to convey his message in this poem. Write down one example of figurative language from this poem.

____

____

____

2 Nature helped the poet to

A overcome great sadness.
B appreciate the benefits of being alone.
C overcome boredom.
D feel connected to the universe.

3 For the poet, the daffodils are

A a reminder of the beauty of nature.
B difficult to describe in words.
C inspiration for his poetry.
D perfect company for a poet.

4 This four-stanza poem describes the poet's experience of seeing daffodils in the wild. Put the following one-sentence summaries of each stanza in the correct order.

- [ ] The poet describes how the memory of seeing the flowers continues to bring him joy and happiness when alone at home.
- [ ] The poet describes the vast number of daffodils.
- [ ] The poet is sad and alone but suddenly sees some daffodils.
- [ ] The poet begins to feel happier having seen the flowers.

5 The words *They flash upon that inward eye* are best interpreted as

A the poet imagining the flowers.
B the intrusion of the flowers on the imagination of the poet.
C the poet's eye being harmed by the colour of the flowers.
D the daffodils being bright and powerful.

6 The mood of the final stanza changes to

A critical.
B sad.
C reflective.
D philosophical.

7 How do the daffodils change the mood of the poet?

A They dance in the breeze and look happy, making the poet feel the same.
B There are so many of them that their colour attracts the poet's thoughts.
C The poet felt alone but the daffodils gave him company.
D The daffodils made the poet think about nature.

8 In the line *A poet could not but be gay*, the word *gay* refers to

A the happiness the poet feels.
B the poet's ideas about the daffodils.
C the beauty of the daffodils.
D the frustration of the poet.

Answers and explanations on pages 145–146

READING Advanced level questions

Mini Test 10: Narrative

Read the extract from *To build a fire* by Jack London (1876–1916) and answer the questions.
Go to page 56 to read about **Narratives**.

To build a fire

DAY had broken cold and gray, exceedingly cold and gray, when the man turned aside from the main Yukon trail and climbed the high earth-bank, where a dim and little traveled trail led eastward through the fat spruce timberland. It was a steep bank, and he paused for breath at the top, excusing the act to himself by looking at his watch. It was nine o'clock. There was no sun nor hint of sun, though there was not a cloud in the sky. It was a clear day, and yet there seemed an intangible pall over the face of things, a subtle gloom that made the day dark, and that was due to the absence of sun. This fact did not worry the man. He was used to the lack of sun. It had been days since he had seen the sun, and he knew that a few more days must pass before that cheerful orb, due south, would just peep above the sky-line and dip immediately from view.

The man flung a look back along the way he had come. The Yukon lay a mile wide and hidden under three feet of ice. On top of this ice were as many feet of snow. It was all pure white, rolling in gentle undulations where the ice jams of the freeze-up had formed. North and south, as far as his eye could see, it was unbroken white, save for a dark hairline that curved and twisted from around the spruce-covered island to the south, and that curved and twisted away into the north, where it disappeared behind another spruce-covered island. This dark hair-line was the trail—the main trail—that led south five hundred miles to the Chilcoot Pass, Dyea, and salt water; and that led north seventy miles to Dawson, and still on to the north a thousand miles to Nulato, and finally to St. Michael on Bering Sea, a thousand miles and half a thousand more.

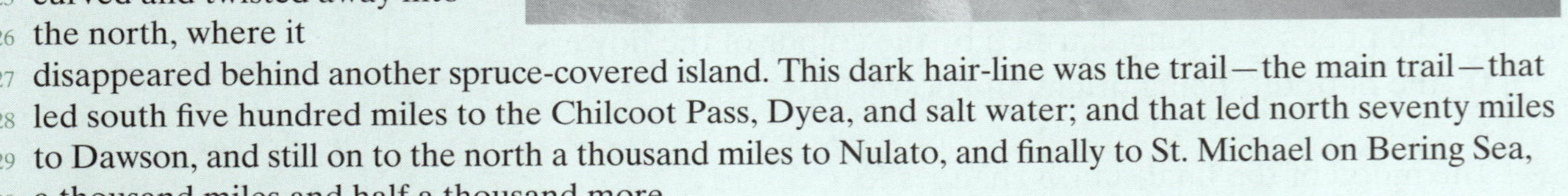

But all this—the mysterious, far-reaching hair-line trail, the absence of sun from the sky, the tremendous cold, and the strangeness and weirdness of it all—made no impression on the man. It was not because he was long used to it. He was a newcomer in the land, a chechaquo, and this was his first winter. The trouble with him was that he was without imagination. He was quick and alert in the things of life, but only in the things, and not in the significances. Fifty degrees below zero meant eighty-odd degrees of frost. Such fact impressed him as being cold and uncomfortable, and that was all. It did not lead him to meditate upon his frailty as a creature of temperature, and upon man's frailty in general, able only to live within certain narrow limits of heat and cold; and from there on it did not lead him to the conjectural field of immortality and man's place in the universe. Fifty degrees below zero stood for the bite of frost that hurt and that must be guarded against by the use of mittens, ear-flaps, warm moccasins, and thick socks. Fifty degrees below zero was to him just precisely fifty degrees below zero. That there should be anything more to it than that was a thought that never entered his head.

1 The attitude towards the man described in this extract is one of

A criticism. **B** admiration. **C** disbelief. **D** confusion.

2 *But all this—the mysterious, far-reaching hair-line trail, the absence of sun from the sky, the tremendous cold, and the strangeness and weirdness of it all—made no impression on the man.*

The list within the two dashes in this sentence shows

A the many difficult conditions the man is confronted with.
B different obstacles in this landscape.
C the ignorance of the man to the dangers of the environment.
D the writer's attitude to the man's ignorance.

3 The words *intangible pall* tell us that

A the weather is terrible.
B the man should be cautious on his travels.
C something bad will happen.
D the landscape will play an important role in the story.

4 The tone of this extract is best described as

anxious.	gloomy.	suspenseful.	mysterious.	reflective.
A	**B**	**C**	**D**	**E**

5 What intrigues the narrator about the man in the story?

A He is not concerned with the possibility of dying.
B He is walking alone in such a dangerous landscape.
C He has no fear of death or interest in philosophical problems such as the meaning of life.
D He looked back the way he had come.

6 The description of the landscape in the second paragraph suggests that the narrator

A feels a sense of awe towards nature. **B** is impressed by its size and beauty.
C has visited there himself. **D** understands the dangers of the landscape.

7 The metaphor *that cheerful orb* refers to

A the light of the day. **B** a fire in the distance.
C the moon. **D** the sun.

8 In the line *It was a steep bank, and he paused for breath at the top, excusing the act to himself by looking at his watch* the writer suggests that the man is

A a determined individual who does not like to admit that he needs to rest.
B unfit and must rest.
C not used to walking in harsh weather.
D determined to reach his destination.

Answers and explanations on page 146

TIPS FOR WRITING A PERSUASIVE TEXT

Check the Writing section (www.nap.edu.au/naplan/writing) of the official NAPLAN website for up-to-date and important information on the Writing Test. Sample Writing Tests and marking guidelines that outline the criteria markers use when assessing your writing are also provided. Please note that, to date in NAPLAN, the types of texts that students have been tested on have been narrative and persuasive writing.

The Australian Curriculum for English requires students to be taught three main types of texts:

- imaginative writing (including narratives and descriptions)
- informative writing (including procedures and reports)
- persuasive writing (expositions).

Informative writing has not yet been tested by NAPLAN. The best preparation for writing is for students to read a range of texts and to get lots of practice in writing different types of texts. We have included information on all types of texts in this book.

Persuasive texts

A **persuasive text** is sometimes known as an exposition or an argument. A persuasive text aims to argue a position and support it with evidence and reasons.

When writing persuasive texts it is best to keep the following points in mind. They will help you get the best possible mark.

Before you start writing

- Read the question carefully. You will probably be asked to write your reaction to a particular question or statement, such as *Excessive Internet usage is bad for teenagers*. Most of the topics that you will be asked to comment on are very general. This means you will probably be writing about something you know and can draw upon your experience.
- Give yourself a few minutes before you start writing to get your thoughts in order and jot down points.

Structure of persuasive texts

A persuasive text has a specific structure:

- The **introduction** is where you clearly state your ideas about the topic. You must ensure your position is clearly outlined. It is a good idea to list your main points in your introduction—three points is perfect.
- The **body** is a series of paragraphs where your opinions are developed. Evidence and/or reasons are given to support your opinions about the topic. Each paragraph usually opens with a sentence that previews what the paragraph will focus on.
- The **conclusion** is a paragraph where the main points of your argument are summarised and where you restate your opinion on the topic. Your conclusion should not include any new information.

Language features of persuasive texts

You can use some or all of the following features:

- **Emotive language**: Use words or phrases that express emotion, e.g. *I find it shocking, terrible crime, terrific, heartless, desirable*.
- **Third-person narrative**: Avoid using *I* in your argument. The third person is more formal and appropriate for a persuasive text.
- **Connectives**: These words link your points together, e.g. *firstly*, *secondly*, *finally*, *on the other hand*, *however*, *furthermore*, *moreover*, *in conclusion*.
- **Modality**: Use modals to express different levels of certainty. High modal verbs, including *should*, *must*, *will not* and *ensure*, are strongly persuasive.
- **Repetition**: Repeat key words or phrases to have a dramatic effect on the reader by emphasising a point or idea.
- **Rhetorical questions**: These questions are designed to make the reader think, e.g. *Have you ever lost a loved one?*
- **Statements of appeal**: These affect the emotions of your readers and encourage action, e.g. *The world owes it to the children of the future to act now on climate change*.

Don't forget to:

- plan your argument before you start
- write in correctly fomed sentences and take care with paragraphing
- choose your words carefully and pay attention to your spelling and punctuation
- write neatly but don't waste time
- make no more than three different points
- quickly check your argument once you have finished.

WRITING

Mini Test 1
Persuasive text

Before you start, make sure you read the Tips for Writing on page 76.

Today you are going to write a persuasive text, often called an exposition. The topic is:

White chocolate is better than milk chocolate.

What do you think about this idea?
Do you support or reject this proposal?

Write to convince a reader of your opinions.

Before you start writing, give some thought to:

- whether you strongly agree or disagree with this statement
- the way you will present your ideas—clearly list or order your points
- the reasons or evidence for your arguments
- your brief but definite conclusion. In your conclusion list some of your main points—you may add a personal opinion.

Don't forget to:

- plan your argument before you start (three points will make a strong argument)
- write in correctly formed sentences and take particular care with paragraphing
- choose your words carefully and pay attention to your spelling and punctuation
- write neatly but don't waste time
- quickly check your argument once you have finished. Your position must be clear to your reader.

Remember: The stance taken in a persuasive text is not wrong, as long as the writer has evidence to support his or her opinion. How the opinion is supported is as important as the opinion itself.

Start writing here or type your answer on a tablet or computer.

Once you have completed the Writing Test, turn to page 147 and use the Marking checklist to check your writing. Also go to pages 160–162 where sample pieces of writing (Standard, Intermediate and Advanced levels) can be used to see at what level you are writing. These writing samples have been analysed based on the marking criteria used by markers to assess the NAPLAN Writing Test.

TIPS FOR WRITING A NARRATIVE TEXT

Narrative texts

A **narrative** is a fiction text and is also known as a story. The purpose of a narrative is to entertain, amuse or inform.

Before you start writing

- Read the question and check the stimulus material carefully. *Stimulus material* means the topic, title, picture, words, phrases or extract of writing you are given to base your writing on.
- Decide if you are going to be writing in the first person (you become a character in your story) or in the third person (you are writing about other characters). When writing in the first person, be careful not to overuse the pronoun *I* (e.g. *I did this*, *I did that*).
- Take a few moments to plan the structure of your story. Remember: Stories have a beginning, middle and end. It sounds simple but many stories fail because one of these three parts is not well written.

Structure of narrative texts

A narrative has a specific structure, containing:

- **Orientation**—the introduction of the setting and characters
- **Complication**—a problem faced by the character(s) that must be overcome
- **Climax**—a scene of increased tension where the character is faced with some kind of danger
- **Resolution**—the problem is overcome
- **Coda**—a lesson is learned and life returns to normal.

Language features of narrative texts

You should give some thought to the language features of this text type:

- **Engage the senses** of your reader through description of what can be seen, heard, felt, tasted or smelled. To do this you should include figures of speech such as similes, metaphors and personification.
- **Use strong action verbs** to capture mood and create tension. Instead of *The girl took the food* you could say *The girl lunged for the food*.
- **Use emotive words** to help engage the emotions of your reader. It is important to consider what emotions you would like your reader to feel for a character in a specific situation. Once you have decided, use emotive words and phrases to evoke these emotions, e.g. *Lee sat alone feeling despair descend upon him* or *Rob's desire for the cookie caused her stomach to tangle*.
- **Use dialogue sparingly.** It should be used to develop a character or situation. Remember that dialogue tags should elaborate on the attitude of the speaker. Instead of writing *Jane said* you should be more specific, such as *Jane cried* or *Jane moaned, flicking her hair over her shoulder*.

Don't forget to:

- plan your narrative before you start
- write in correctly formed sentences and take care with paragraphing
- choose your words carefully and pay attention to your spelling and punctuation
- write neatly but don't waste time
- quickly check your narrative once you have finished.

WRITING Mini Test 2

Narrative text

42 MIN

Before you start, make sure you read the Tips for Writing on page 78.

Today you are going to write a narrative. The idea for your narrative is **An accident**.

Your narrative might be about a car accident, the accidental breaking of a window or a person accidentally opening a portal into another dimension. It could be the accidental discovery of how to fly, of a bag of money or of the first ever use of fire for cooking. Your narrative could be about the accidental breaking of a friend's car, a friend's heart or a promise.

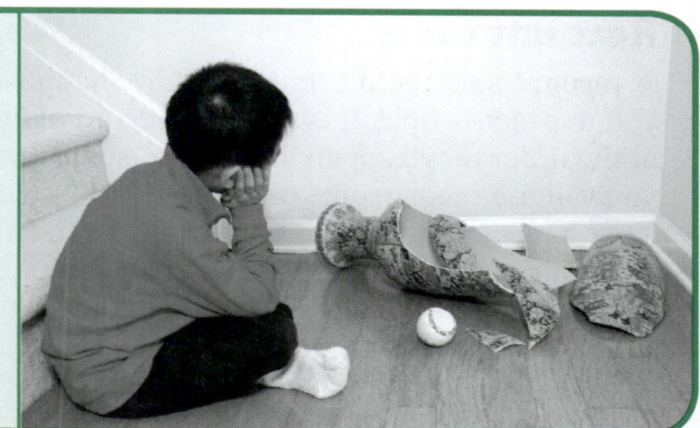

Before you start writing, give some thought to:

- where your narrative takes place (the setting)
- the character(s) and what they do in your narrative
- the events that take place in your narrative and the problems that have to be resolved
- how your narrative begins, what happens in your narrative, and how your narrative ends.

Don't forget to:

- plan your narrative before you begin writing
- write in correctly formed sentences and take care with paragraphing
- choose your words carefully and pay attention to your spelling and punctuation
- write neatly but don't waste time
- quickly check your narrative once you have finished.

Start writing here or type your answer on a tablet or computer.

Once you have completed the Writing Test, turn to page 147 and use the Marking checklist to check your writing. Also go to pages 163–165 where sample pieces of writing (Standard, Intermediate and Advanced levels) can be used to see at what level you are writing. These writing samples have been analysed based on the marking criteria used by markers to assess the NAPLAN Writing Test.

TIPS FOR WRITING A RECOUNT TEXT

Recount texts

A **recount** tells about events that have happened to you or other people. It is usually a record of events in the order they happen. If it is a personal recount, you will use the personal pronoun *I*. You could also write a recount of an event in the third person. A recount can conclude with a personal opinion of the event. Recounts are always written in the past tense.

Before you start writing

- Read the question and check the stimulus material carefully. *Stimulus material* means the topic, title, picture, words, phrases or extract of writing you are given to base your writing on.
- Give some thought to:
  - where your recount takes place
  - the characters and what they do in your recount
  - the events that take place in your recount and the problems that have to be resolved
  - how you and others reacted to the event. You may make brief personal comments on events as you write about them.
- Remember that a recount is told in the past tense because the events have already happened.
- When you have chosen your topic it might be helpful to jot a few ideas quickly on paper so you don't forget them. Decide if you will write a first-person recount (using *I* as the main character) or a third-person recount.

Structure of informative texts (recounts)

The introduction

- The first paragraph of a recount is important as it must provide the reader with a brief overview of the event being recounted. It must inform the reader about who, what, when and where.
- The introduction may feature proper nouns such as the names of places and people—this helps orient the reader.

The body

- Recounts recall events in the order in which they happened. The body of a recount is a series of chronological paragraphs detailing important aspects of the event being recounted.
- Use conjunctions and connectives to indicate when events occurred. Examples are *firstly, then, next, later, finally.*
- Correctly paragraph your writing. You need a new paragraph when there is a change in time or place or a new idea is introduced.
- Include personal comments, e.g. about your feelings, your opinions and your reactions, but only include comments that add to your recount.

The conclusion

- A conclusion is necessary as it informs the reader how the event ended. It is also a good idea to include a final comment on the events or experiences. This may be as simple as reflecting on the impact that the event had on the individuals involved.

Language features of informative texts (recounts)

You should give some thought to the language features of this type of text:

- **Engage the senses** of your reader through description of what can be seen, heard, felt, tasted or smelled. To do this you should include figures of speech such as similes, metaphors and personification.
- **Use strong action verbs** to capture mood and create tension. Instead of *The girl took the food* you could say *The girl lunged for the food*.
- **Use emotive words** to engage the emotions of your reader. It is important to consider what emotions you would like your reader to feel for a character in a specific situation. Once you have decided, use emotive words and phrases to evoke these emotions, e.g. *Lee felt anxious having lost his wallet*.

Don't forget to:

- plan your recount before you start
- write in correctly formed sentences and take care with paragraphing
- choose your words carefully and pay attention to your spelling and punctuation
- write neatly but don't waste time
- quickly check your recount once you have finished.

WRITING

Mini Test 3
Recount text

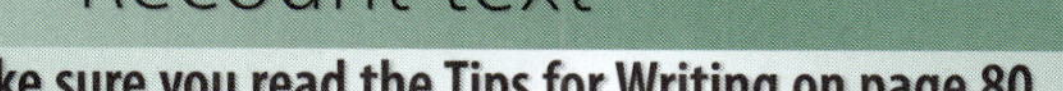

Before you start, make sure you read the Tips for Writing on page 80.

Today you are going to write a recount. The idea for your recount is **The hunt**.

Your recount might be about the hunt for a cure for cancer, the hunt for the perpetrator of a crime or the hunt for the perfect dress. It could be the hunt for water, food or treasure. Your story could be about the hunt for car keys in a messy house or the hunt for the best-tasting hamburger in your town.

Before you start writing, give some thought to:

- where your recount takes place (the setting)
- the characters and what they do in your recount
- the events that take place in your recount and the problems that have to be resolved
- how you and others reacted to the event. You may make brief personal comments on events as you write about them.

Don't forget to:

- plan your recount before you start writing
- write in correctly formed sentences and take care with paragraphing
- choose your words carefully and pay attention to your spelling and punctuation
- write neatly but don't waste time
- quickly check your story once you have finished.

Start writing here or type your answer on a tablet or computer.

☞ **Once you have completed the Writing Test, turn to page 148 and use the Marking checklist to check your writing. Also go to pages 166–168 where sample pieces of writing (Standard, Intermediate and Advanced levels) can be used to see at what level you are writing. These writing samples have been analysed based on the marking criteria used by markers to assess the NAPLAN Writing Test.**

DIFFERENT TEST LEVELS

- There are six tests for students to complete in this section. These sample tests have been classified as either intermediate or advanced according to the level of the majority of questions. This will broadly reflect the NAPLAN Online tailored testing experience where students are guided into answering questions that match their ability.
- The following tests are included in this section:
  - two Reading Tests at intermediate and advanced levels
  - two Conventions of Language Tests at intermediate and advanced levels
  - two Writing Tests.

CHECKS

- The NAPLAN Online Conventions of Language and Reading tests will be divided into different sections.
- Students will have one last opportunity to check their answers in each section when they have reached the end of that section.
- Once they have moved onto a new section, they will not be able to go back and check their work again.
- We have included reminders for students to check their work at specific points in the Sample Tests so they become familiar with this process before they take the NAPLAN Online tests.

Excel Test Zone

- After students have consolidated their topic knowledge by completing this book, we recommend they practise NAPLAN Online–style questions on our website at www.exceltestzone.com.au.
- Students will be able to gain valuable practice in online skills.
- Students will also become confident in using a computer or tablet to complete NAPLAN Online–style tests so they will be fully prepared for the actual NAPLAN Online tests.

Year 9 Conventions of Language Sample Online-style Test 1

Intermediate level

1 Which sentence is correct?

A "I did not damage that house!" exclaimed joey loudly.
B "Everyone will want to be in my group." stated Dilio angrily.
C Liam Cried, "Everyone hates me!"
D "Everyone will want to be in my group," boasted Jamie.

2 Which sentence is correct?

A The little pie-man from up the road had brought boxes of pastries and pies to our home.
B The little pie-man from up the road had bring boxes of pastries and pies to our home.
C The little pie-man from up the road wasn't brought boxes of pastries and pies to our home.
D The little pie-man from up the road was brought boxes of pastries and pies to our home.

3 Which sentence is correct?

A She let himself into the house; the door closed with a bang.
B She let themself into the house; the door closed with a bang.
C She let herself into the house; the door closed with a bang.
D She let ourself into the house; the door closed with a bang.

4 Which sentence uses speech marks (" and ") correctly?

A "I wonder if you're surprised by today's findings"? enquired the professor.
B "I wonder if you're surprised by today's findings? enquired the professor."
C I wonder if you're surprised by today's findings?" enquired the professor."
D "I wonder if you're surprised by today's findings?" enquired the professor.

5 Which sentence has the correct punctuation?

A Juni asked, "Have you ever even wondered what happened to Mr Gee from down the street?"
B "Don't you think Sarah has the strangest laugh? giggled jessie.
C Jessabelle threw down her Novel and pronounced. "I will be a great writer!"
D Feeling that the day was dragging on, Lolly sighed "isn't it time to go home now?"

6 Which words complete the sentence?

We began looking for a new place to live ______________.

A even though we had no money for the bond
B although we were looking hard
C even if it was good for a short time
D though the owner had kicked us out

7 Which of the following has the correct punctuation?
A Nancy begged, “Please let me have something to drink!”
B Nancy begged. “Please let me have something to drink!”
C Nancy begged “Please let me have something to drink!”
D Nancy begged, “Please let me have something to drink.”

8 Running from one store to another and carrying large bags of clothes and shoes. Does this sound like your idea of the perfect holiday? It isn’t desirable for some, but for my mum it’s the *only* way to relax.

In the last sentence italics are used
A to show that the word is foreign.
B to show that the word is important.
C to add emphasis to what is being said.
D because the word is misspelt.

Choose the correct option to complete each sentence.

9 The items being recycled must be as clean as possible as even small amounts of food residue ______ affect the paper, glass and steel recycling process.
A is B are C can D was

10 People must make an effort to clean out all solid food scraps from jars and cans ______ them in the recycling bin.
A and may putting B and then putted C and can puts D and then put

11 Concern over ______ left food residue behind can be alleviated with a quick rinse of jars, cans and bottles
A have B had C having D has

12 Which sentence correctly uses italics?
A On *1 January 1901*, the constitution of Australia came into force.
B The *Governor-General* visited local schools and hospitals.
C The Stolen Generations refers to the children of *Australian Aboriginal* and *Torres Strait Islander* descent who were taken from their families by the Australian Federal and State governments.
D The word *democracy* has its origins in the Greek word *dēmokratía*, which means ‘rule of the people’.

13 Which of the following sentences has the correct punctuation?
A Yesterday, I went to the promenade for a stroll.
B Yesterday I went, to the promenade for a stroll.
C Yesterday I went to the promenade for a stroll.
D Yesterday I went, to the promenade for a stroll?

 Answers and explanations on pages 149–150

Write the correct word or punctuation mark from the boxes to complete each sentence.

14 about for around from

A frequent question asked by people ______ recycling relates to the cleanliness of the items being recycled.

15 I love playing board games with my family ______ a rainy evening.

on in over around

16 – (dash) : (colon) ... (ellipsis) ; (semicolon)

"Candy was the greatest artist our school had produced. The fact that she has died so young is ______ um ______ an absolute tragedy."

17 Highlight the pronoun in the sentence below.

The weatherman indicated that this coming Thursday may result in rain. Jack didn't believe him.

18 Highlight where the missing commas go in the sentence below.

The fortnightly inspection which was designed to detect faulty wiring was a complete success.

19 Highlight the words that should be in italics in the sentence below.

No Country for Old Men was a very popular movie with film critics; it was not so popular with the general public.

20 Highlight the pronoun in the sentence below.

Alison is better friends with Jade because they spend each day together.

21 Highlight the adjective in the sentence below.

Bitter was the wind which blew under the door.

22 Circle where punctuation is used incorrectly in the sentence below.

Each december we pack up our car and head north?

23 Highlight the nouns in the sentence below.

Eating foods high in protein will help you lose weight.

24 Some sentences below contain a cause and an effect. Which sentences contain both a cause and an effect?

A Inevitably he dived into the sparkling and clear salt water.
B The rain was falling very hard on the roof of our car and it was giving me a headache.
C It therefore became impossible for me to continue living in the premises.
D Josh was afraid of being burnt, so he threw the burning stick into the fire really quickly.

25 Highlight the pronouns in the sentence below.

Kathy was afraid of monkeys because one had bitten her in Bali.

It would be a good idea to check your answers to questions 1 to 25 before moving on to the other questions.

Answers and explanations on pages 149–150

Year 9 Conventions of Language Sample Online-style Test 1

To the student

Ask your teacher or parent to read the spelling words for you. The words are listed on page 180. Write the spelling words on the lines below.

26 ______________ 27 ______________

28 ______________ 29 ______________

30 ______________ 31 ______________

32 ______________ 33 ______________

34 ______________ 35 ______________

36 ______________ 37 ______________

38 ______________ 39 ______________

40 ______________

The spelling mistakes in these sentences have been highlighted. Write the correct spelling of each highlighted word in each box.

41 Soon the children had built themselves a sturdy **causway** between the small sandbank.

42 Each evening the children rebel vocally against the **beddtime** prescribed for them.

43 For the teachers the swimming **carnavool** is a great opportunity to spend time with their students.

44 Arriving in the hands of the courier was a beautiful **parsal** for Deirdre.

45 Tiny Annie hated it when her big brother Andy pulled her **piggtails**.

Each sentence has one word that is incorrect. Write the correct spelling of the word in the box.

46 The current government is showing significant dissregard for the welfare of its citizens.

47 "I can't believe that the children's departtment was so busy!" exclaimed Aunt Peg.

48 His breath began to kach in his throat as he neared the 12-kilometre mark of the half marathon.

49 The actions of Ned Kelly are viewed as heroec by many scholars.

50 Bald John likes to encouradge the younger skaters to take risks on the ramps.

Answers and explanations on pages 149–150

Sample Online-style Test 2

Advanced level

1 Which words correctly complete the sentence below?

The phoenix is a mythical bird ______ around the world as a symbol of immortality.

A them is think B that is regarded C that was thought D who is regarded

2 Which words correctly complete the sentence below?

According to Greek legend, the phoenix ______ well in Arabia.

A living on the B lives over another C lives under a cool D lived near a cool

3 Which words correctly complete the sentence below?

The legend tells how this magnificent bird rose every morning to bathe in the water of the well ______ beautiful songs.

A and singing B and sang C and sung D and sing

4 Which word correctly completes the sentence below?

Close to the end of its life, it built a nest of sweet ______ wood.

A smelled B smelling C smell D smellier

5 Which word correctly completes the sentence below?

When the fire cooled a baby phoenix ______ from the ashes of the nest.

A arises B arising C arisen D arose

6 Which words correctly complete the sentence below?

John Donne is considered by many as the ______ revitalised the sonnet form.

A poet who B poet what C poet that D poet who'd

7 How does the suffix *er* change the word *listen* in this sentence?

Samuel didn't like to listen but he tried hard so he would get a gold star for being a good listener.

It changes

A an adverb into a noun. B a verb into a noun.

C a noun into an adverb. D an adjective into an adverb.

8 Umbrellas poke the sky; car doors open and close.

In this sentence, a semicolon (**;**) is used to

A introduce a list. B separate two complete ideas.

C separate items in a list. D introduce an idea

9 In which sentence is the word *back* used as a verb?

A He stood at the back of the stage.

B I entered the house via the back entrance.

C Who are you going to back in the football match?

D I was kept in after school for talking back to my teacher.

Answers and explanations on pages 151–152

10 Brackets ( ) are needed in this sentence. Which part of the sentence needs brackets?

My favourite time of the year in America is fall September to December because this is when the leaves change from dark green to rich red.

A of the year **B** leaves change **C** September to December **D** dark green

11 Where do the missing commas go?

The house, crumbling and, dilapidated, was being prepared for, demolition.

(A: after "house"; B: after "and"; C: after "dilapidated"; D: after "for")

12 Read these three sentences.

Ten years went by.
Then Les joined the air force.
Then Les was deployed to Afghanistan.

Which option accurately combines the information about Les into a single sentence?

A Ten years later, Les joined the air force and was deployed to Afghanistan.
B Les joined the air force three years after he was deployed to Afghanistan.
C Ten years after Les joined the air force, he was deployed to Afghanistan.
D Les joined the air force and ten years later was deployed to Afghanistan.

13 What does the prefix *un* in the word *unmade* mean?

A without **B** very **C** not **D** against

14 Highlight the pronouns in the sentence below.

Holden Caulfield is the most authentic character in literature as he is true to himself.

Write the correct word or words from the boxes to complete each sentence.

15 Their | I am | There | They're

[ ] the silliest dogs I have ever seen; they can't keep quiet or still.

16 its its | its it' | it's it's | it's its

The lizard flicked [ ] tongue out of [ ] mouth and scared the children.

17 Highlight the pronoun in the sentence below.

Despite finding her little sister annoying, Janie's parents did nothing to alleviate her annoyance.

18 Highlight where the missing apostrophe should go in the sentence below.

Our mums are angry. They think its wrong that we stayed out until 12.30 am.

19 Highlight the pronouns in the sentence below.

I just couldn't believe it when you spoke to me with such an aggressive tone. I do hope you know it is unacceptable!

20 Highlight the adjectives in the sentence below.

Black clouds gather on the horizon, angry and grim.

Answers and explanations on pages 151–152

21 Highlight the conjunction in the sentence below.

The group, having already hiked for several hours, realised that not only were they heading in the wrong direction but they were heading towards a steep waterfall.

22 Highlight the prepositions in the sentence below.

The winning team, of whom three were from Davidson High School, celebrated with a rousing chorus of *Waltzing Matilda*.

23 Which of the following sentences uses quotation marks (' and ') correctly to tell the reader not to take the words literally?

A Jay-Jay didn't go to school for two days because he was 'feeling sick'.
B My father described my little brother as having the 'gift of the gab'.
C Mark told his mum he didn't want to wear the school shoes she bought him as they were 'too cool'.
D My dad's favourite football player is Steve 'Beaver' Menzies.

24 Which **two** sentences say who is responsible for the broken vase?

A After breaking her vase, the boys begged their mother to forgive them.
B The mother will be angry because her vase was broken.
C After having her vase broken, the boys' mother was very angry.
D The boys broke a vase and their mother was very angry.

25 Highlight the proper nouns in the sentence below.

With all sincerity, I did not wish harm to befall Alfred, and yet, when he was struck ill, I wasn't upset in the least.

It would be a good idea to check your answers to questions 1 to 25 before moving on to the other questions.

To the student

Ask your teacher or parent to read the spelling words for you. The words are listed on page 180. Write the spelling words on the lines below.

26 ______________________ 27 ______________________

28 ______________________ 29 ______________________

30 ______________________ 31 ______________________

32 ______________________ 33 ______________________

34 ______________________ 35 ______________________

36 ______________________ 37 ______________________

38 ______________________ 39 ______________________

40 ______________________

 Answers and explanations on pages 151–152

Year 9 Conventions of Language Sample Online-style Test 2

The spelling mistakes in these sentences have been highlighted. Write the correct spelling of each highlighted word in each box.

41 You won't be disappointed with this story if you like adventure. Our relluctant hero must face off against dwarves, elves, goblins, eagles and wizards in this tale of courage.

42 Interestingly, the guppy is native to the Americas but has been introduced to many countries around the world in an attempt to control moscquitoe populations.

43 Each week I try to overcome my chocolate addicshon. Each week I fail.

44 The inishul days of high school can be daunting for Year 7 students.

45 My words fell away into insignifikants as Mathew turned his back and walked away.

Each sentence has one word that is incorrect. Write the correct spelling of the word in the box.

46 The new hair dye was very good at lightning my brown hair.

47 Dylan was glad to receive aclaym for his art.

48 Standing to one side of the expansive window was an imposing anteek clock.

49 "Gosh you give bad advise, Dolly," complained her sister Lou-Lou.

50 Many find it difficult to distinguish the important numbers from those that are arbitry.

Answers and explanations on pages 151–152

Year 9 Reading

Sample Online-style Test 1

Intermediate level

Read *The llama* and answer questions 1 to 6.

The llama

The llama is a really interesting and unusual animal. It originates from South America, and is a member of the camel family, known as lamoids. However, unlike camels, llamas do not have humps. Llamas can be identified by their long legs and necks, small heads, and pointed ears. They are a hardy, fertile breed of pack animal that feeds on grass and other plants. A female llama gives birth to one young following a gestation period of 11 months.

The llama is a very useful animal, and large herds are maintained by Indigenous peoples in Bolivia, Peru and Argentina. Many of these regions are known for their harshness, with llamas being bred way up on the bleak plateaus of the Andes. Llamas are used by the Indigenous peoples in a variety of ways. They can be killed and eaten as a source of food or their hides used for material. Llamas are also farmed for their wool, yet it is not as valuable as that of their fellow lamoid, the alpaca. However, one of the most important roles of llamas for Indigenous peoples is for carrying loads. A single llama can carry a load of up to 60 kilograms, and they can travel a long way each day—between 25 and 30 kilometres. This makes them a very valuable resource.

The llama is sometimes confused with the alpaca. The main difference between llamas and alpacas is their size, their faces and their ears. Llamas are much bigger than alpacas, have a longer face, and much longer ears. The llama and alpaca have similar dispositions, as they can be gentle but they also have a tendency to kick and spit if they are unhappy.

A llama at Macchu Pichu, photo Joseph L Hartman, https://commons.wikimedia.org/wiki/File:Llama_in_Machu_Picchu-1.jpg

Year 9 Reading Sample Online-style Test 1

1 For the llama, life can be
- **A** easy.
- **B** hard.
- **C** fun.
- **D** relaxing .

2 This information is mainly useful for
- **A** people interested in llamas.
- **B** young children.
- **C** the elderly.
- **D** llama farmers.

3 The text states that female llamas give birth to
- **A** seven young.
- **B** two young.
- **C** one young.
- **D** five young.

4 According to the text, how many kilometres can a llama travel each day?
- **A** 5 to 10 kilometres
- **B** 25 to 30 kilometres
- **C** 15 to 35 kilometres
- **D** 20 to 40 kilometres

5 Choose the **two** correct answers.
- **A** Llamas have small heads and no humps.
- **B** Llamas have pointed ears and a low thirst tolerance.
- **C** Llamas have large heads and small humps.
- **D** Llamas are usually black with long tails.

6 Tick the correct option. A llama would make a good pet for small children.

☐ True ☐ False

Answers and explanations on page 153

Year 9 Reading Sample Online-style Test 1

Read this extract from the short story *A little cloud* by James Joyce and answer questions 7 to 13.

A little cloud

Eight years before he had seen his friend off at the North Wall and wished him God-speed. Gallaher had got on. You could tell that at once by his travelled air, his well-cut tweed suit, and fearless accent. Few fellows had talents like his, and fewer still could remain unspoiled by such success. Gallaher's heart was in the right place and he had deserved to win. It was something to have a friend like that.

Little Chandler's thoughts ever since lunch-time had been of his meeting with Gallaher, of Gallaher's invitation, and of the great city London where Gallaher lived. He was called Little Chandler because, though he was but slightly under the average stature, he gave one the idea of being a little man. His hands were white and small, his frame was fragile, his voice was quiet and his manners were refined. He took the greatest care of his fair silken hair and moustache, and used perfume discreetly on his handkerchief. The half-moons of his nails were perfect, and when he smiled you caught a glimpse of a row of childish white teeth.

As he sat at his desk in the King's Inns he thought what changes those eight years had brought. The friend whom he had known under a shabby and necessitous guise had become a brilliant figure on the London Press. He turned often from his tiresome writing to gaze out of the office window. The glow of a late autumn sunset covered the grass plots and walks. It cast a shower of kindly golden dust on the untidy nurses and decrepit old men who drowsed on the benches; it flickered upon all the moving figures—on the children who ran screaming along the gravel paths and on everyone who passed through the gardens. He watched the scene and thought of life; and (as always happened when he thought of life) he became sad. A gentle melancholy took possession of him. He felt how useless it was to struggle against fortune, this being the burden of wisdom which the ages had bequeathed to him.

He remembered the books of poetry upon his shelves at home. He had bought them in his bachelor days and many an evening, as he sat in the little room off the hall, he had been tempted to take one down from the bookshelf and read out something to his wife. But shyness had always held him back; and so the books had remained on their shelves. At times he repeated lines to himself and this consoled him.

When his hour had struck he stood up and took leave of his desk and of his fellow-clerks punctiliously. He emerged from under the feudal arch of the King's Inns, a neat modest figure, and walked swiftly down Henrietta Street. The golden sunset was waning and the air had grown sharp. A horde of grimy children populated the street. They stood or ran in the roadway, or crawled up the steps before the gaping doors, or squatted like mice upon the thresholds. Little Chandler gave them no thought. He picked his way deftly through all that minute vermin-like life and under the shadow of the gaunt spectral mansions in which the old nobility of Dublin had roistered. No memory of the past touched him, for his mind was full of a present joy.

Source: http://www.world-english.org/stories.htm

7 For Little Chandler, Gallaher's invitation was
- **A** exciting and scary.
- **B** something to look forward to in an otherwise dull life.
- **C** keeping him happy despite his unhappiness with life.
- **D** occupying his mind.

8 Highlight the imagery in the second-last sentence of the text.

---

9 *A gentle melancholy took possession of him.* What literary device is this an example of?
- **A** metaphor
- **B** simile
- **C** personification
- **D** alliteration.

10 What would be the best way of describing Little Chandler's way of thinking about Gallaher?
- **A** admiring
- **B** envious
- **C** loving
- **D** nostalgic

11 Where does Little Chandler work?
- **A** King's Inns
- **B** London
- **C** Henrietta Street
- **D** North Wall

12 The detailed description of the city streets in the final paragraph helps to build an atmosphere of
- **A** melancholy.
- **B** despair and loneliness.
- **C** emptiness and isolation.
- **D** hopelessness.

13 Why doesn't Little Chandler give any thought to the grimy children on the street?
- **A** He is too busy thinking about his meeting with Gallaher.
- **B** He accepts their presence as part of life.
- **C** He is unfeeling and cruel.
- **D** He doesn't care about them.

Answers and explanations on page 153

Year 9 Reading Sample Online-style Test 1

Read *My Grandfather's Ice Pigeons* by Robert Adamson and answer questions 14 to 18.

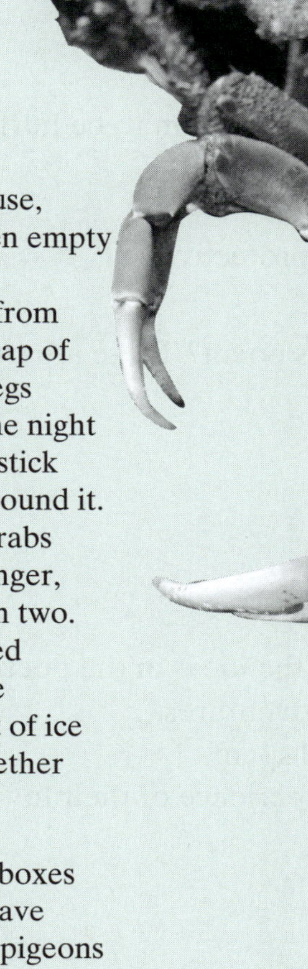

My Grandfather's Ice Pigeons

My grandfather would walk into the house,
on a summer evening after his work, then empty
his catch of mudcrabs into the bath-tub;
they'd flow out in a stream of ice-flurry from
his four gallon drums, then settle in a heap of
black and olive speckled claws, spikey legs
and back flappers waving frantically. One night
my mother caught me holding a broom-stick
with an angry muddie's claw clamped around it.
She ordered me to stay away from the crabs
reminding me why Uncle Eric lost his finger,
besides they could snap a clothes prop in two.
My mother went back to the city. I stayed
a week and my grandmother showed me
what to do, first throw one into a bucket of ice
to slow it down, then bind the claws together
with kingfisher-blue twine in a slip knot.
Old Dutch would come to take them
to the Co Op in his truck, packed in fishboxes
covered in ice. My grandfather would leave
again for his next catch, he'd take some pigeons
with him in a cage on his trawler. If he
had a good haul, he'd let one of the birds go,
when it came home it was my job to ride my bike
into town to order the ice. When I reached
the Co Op, Dutch would ask how many pigeons?
If more than one, it was a box of ice a bird.
He'd send the ice to my grandfather next morning
on the mail boat. They talk about the time
Fa Fa got drunk up the river at Spencer,
the river postman saw him through the mist
one morning, balancing on net-boards at the stern
of his boat, singing aloud, throwing pigeons at the sky.

Source: <http://www.redroomcompany.org/poet/robert-adamson>. Copyright the Red Room Company. Commissioned for the Red Room Company's 'Pigeon Poetry' 2008.

14 *She ordered me to stay away from the crabs*
reminding me why Uncle Eric lost his finger,
besides they could snap a clothes prop in two.

These lines suggest that

A the speaker's mother doesn't want him to be hurt.
B the crabs are dangerous.
C Uncle Eric wasn't careful.
D the speaker's mother is overprotective.

15 What feelings are created by this poem? There are **two** correct answers.

A comfort and security
B warmth and love
C happiness and excitement
D trust and love
E admiration and joy

16 Which statement best describes the ideas in the poem?

A Life is a series of everyday adventures.
B Time with family is time well spent.
C The young learn from the experience of their loved ones.
D The past informs the future.

17 Fa Fa is

A the speaker's grandfather.
B a fisherman.
C a drunk.
D an old man with pigeons.

18 For the speaker, his grandparents are

A inspirational.
B a breath of fresh air.
C daring and exciting.
D alive with knowledge and experience.

It would be a good idea to check your answers to questions 1 to 18 before moving on to the other questions.

Answers and explanations on pages 153–154

Read this biography of David Unaipon and answer questions 19 to 24.

David Unaipon (1872–1967): writer, public speaker and inventor

David Unaipon made significant contributions to science and literature, and to improvements in the conditions of Aboriginal people.

A Ngarrindjeri man, Unaipon was born at the Point McLeay Mission, on the Lower Murray in South Australia, on 28 September 1872, the fourth of nine children of the evangelist James Ngunaitponi and his wife, Nymbulda, both of whom were Yaraldi speakers.

Unaipon received his initial education at the Point McLeay Mission School and as a teenager demonstrated a thirst for knowledge, particularly in philosophy, science and music. An avid reader, he was obsessed with scientific works and inventions and, with no advanced education in mathematics, he researched many engineering problems and devised a number of his own inventions.

In 1909 he patented an improved handpiece for sheep-shearing. Other inventions included a centrifugal motor, a multi-radial wheel and a mechanical propulsion device; he was unable, however, to get financial backing to develop his ideas. He gained a reputation at the time of being 'Australia's Leonardo' for his promotion of scientific ideas. As early as 1914, Unaipon anticipated the helicopter, applying the principle of the boomerang. His search for the secret of perpetual motion lasted throughout his life.

Unaipon, who married Katherine Carter (nee Sumner), a Tangani woman from The Coorong in January 1902, was prominent in public life as a spokesman for Aboriginal people. He was often called upon to participate in royal commissions and inquiries into Aboriginal issues.

As an employee of the Aborigines' Friends' Association for many years, he travelled widely and became well known through south-eastern Australia. While on his travels, Unaipon lectured on his ideas, preached sermons and spoke about Aboriginal legends and customs. He also spoke of the need for 'sympathetic cooperation' between whites and blacks, and for equal rights for both black and white Australians.

Unaipon became the first Aboriginal writer to be published. His earliest published works include an article entitled 'Aboriginals: Their Traditions and Customs' in the Sydney *Daily Telegraph* (2 August 1924). His articles in the *Daily Telegraph* were said to have been written in a prose that showed the influence of Milton, whose poetry he memorised, and Bunyan.

His writings were included in *Myths and Legends of the Australian Aboriginals* (London, 1930). Other articles, poetry and legends were published throughout his life. The hand-written manuscript of his small book on Aboriginal legends, which is reflected in the $50 note, survives in the Mitchell Library in Sydney.

Unaipon was awarded a Coronation Medal in 1953. He died on 7 February 1967 and was buried in Point McLeay cemetery. In 1985, he posthumously won the FAW Patricia Weickhardt Award for Aboriginal writers. He was also honoured in 1988 by the establishment of an annual national David Unaipon Award for unpublished Aboriginal and Torres Strait Islander writers, and an annual Unaipon lecture in Adelaide.

Source: <http://www.polymernotes.org/biographies/AUS_bio_unaipon.htm>. Reprinted with permission.

19 According to the text, which of the following is correct?
A David Unaipon published articles in newspapers during his lifetime.
B David Unaipon had nine children with his wife.
C David Unaipon was a famous painter like Leonardo da Vinci.
D David Unaipon died before his talents were recognised.

20 The words *(nee Sumner)* are in brackets
A because the information was forgotten.
B because this is extra information about the person.
C to draw attention to this information.
D to separate this information from the rest of the sentence.

21 What did Unaipon want to discover, but failed to do so, during his lifetime?
A the origins of humans
B the helicopter
C the secret of perpetual motion
D the myths and legends of the Indigenous people

22 What is the most likely reason for Unaipon desiring *sympathetic cooperation* between whites and blacks?
A As an Aboriginal man he knew the disadvantages faced by Aboriginal people.
B He saw that such cooperation would be the only way forward into an equal society.
C He was unhappy with his life and wanted a change.
D He saw white society as prejudiced against Aboriginal people.

23 *He gained a reputation at the time of being 'Australia's Leonardo'* (paragraph 4) means that
A Unaipon was a painter as well as an inventor.
B Unaipon's inventions were very famous when he was alive.
C Unaipon had brilliant innovative ideas that challenged traditional ways of thinking, just like Leonardo da Vinci.
D Unaipon was a popular man because he worked hard and was creative.

24 To whom did Unaipon get married?
A Katherine Carter
B Nymbulda
C Katherine Tangani
D Carter Unaipon

Answers and explanations on page 154

Year 9 Reading Sample Online-style Test 1

Read *Teenage girls' fear of fatness* and answer questions 25 to 29.

Teenage girls' fear of fatness

"I know this is going to sound weird," Carrie confesses, "but when I eat too much junk food I'm so guilty I actually hate myself. I'm the kind of person who has plenty of self-control in every other area except food. What makes it so hard is that most of the time when I'm cheating by eating bad stuff, I'm with my friends and having fun. When I'm with my family I eat regular meals and it's much easier to be good."

You would think from the words Carrie uses—guilty, bad, cheating, hate—that she was talking about something more immoral or harmful than snacking on potato chips. You would think she was worried about the osteoporosis, anemia, obesity and cardiovascular disease that might be made worse by eating certain foods. You would think at least that she had a weight problem. You would think that, but you'd be wrong.

The statistics tell the story. Although almost 80% of the teenage girls studied in a recent survey fall within the healthy weight range, less than 50% saw their weight as 'about right'. The proportion who wanted to lose weight increased from 69% in 7th grade to 82% in 12th grade … including 49% of underweight girls. In one study more than 30% of nine-year-old girls expressed fear of fatness, increasing in age to over 80% among 18 year olds. More than the dark, more than mice and snakes and scary movies, what most teenage girls fear is growing fat.

Source: http://www.beinggirl.com/en_US/articledetail.jsp?ContentId=ART1028

25 This text is mainly aimed at

A teenagers. **B** parents. **C** adults. **D** young children.

26 Carrie feels guilty eating junk food because

A she is anorexic.
B she is afraid of developing cardiovascular disease.
C she doesn't want to be unhealthy.
D she is afraid of getting fat.

27 The fear girls have of getting fat

A is most noticeable when girls are young.
B increases when they get to Year 7.
C decreases from age 9 to 18.
D increases from age 9 to 18.

The following two questions require you to consider both texts *Teenage girls' fear of fatness* and 'I was only 19' (page 100).

28 For which purposes were these texts written? Choose **two** purposes per text.

	Teenage girls' fear of fatness	**'I was only 19'**
to inform		
to educate		
to engage		

29 Match the features to the text in which they are used.

	Teenage girls' fear of fatness	**'I was only 19'**
statistics		
second-person narrative		
metaphor		
simile		
listing		

Answers and explanations on pages 154–155

Year 9 Reading Sample Online-style Test 1

Read 'I was only 19' and answer questions 30 to 35.

'I was only 19'

The emotion of Redgum's 'I was only 19' drenches me with regret. Each lamenting cry of 'can you tell me doctor why I still can't get to sleep' throws images of him before my eyes. The photograph in which he assists a young Vietnamese boy with a chisel (or is it a screwdriver?) shows him 'young and strong and clean'. His full head of hair is unfamiliar to me but his strong jaw line and gentle eyes are known well. These features stare back at me each morning as I hastily arrange myself for work.

But where is he now?

My imagination drags me two and a half hours south to a small weatherboard cottage on the lip of a river. My mind's eye pulls me by my hand, forcing me inside the rented abode to face my shame with open eyes. He lies alone on a second-hand couch, propped by a yellowing pillow from his bed. On his stomach is a handful of No Frills jelly snakes and on the ground within reaching distance is a cup of lukewarm instant coffee. The telly throws out light and sound. Tiny flecks of data spinning towards us both—me, the real, and he, the imagined. Young men rush towards one another in their weekend war, embracing the ANZAC legend of 'mud and blood and tears'. His attention is full. These men fill his days, his nights, his weeks, his years. Imagining him here, alone in the half-light of early evening, I can't help thinking of the young man he was, walking in the light greens 30 years ago.

Perhaps the Grand Hotel mentioned in the Redgum song was not my dad's watering hole while on rec leave in Vietnam. But it would simply have been the same place under some other name. The same slight, young, brown-skinned women hoping to catch the eye of an Australian soldier: desperation painted with fuchsia lipstick and broken black heels. I must guess at the place of meeting because, as all children of returned soldiers know, there is no asking these questions. There is no talk of the war. She must have been special to attract the eye of my father. Imagination flares again to see a petite dark woman with small hips that less than two years earlier helped her bear a child. The child was, I'm sure, part of the appeal and—I came to learn—the cause of more emotional pain than physical.

In 1972 love, hope and generosity were pitted against homeland security, white Australia policies and fear. Journalists and politicians, smelling blood in the water, used rhetoric to shape a landscape of racism and isolationism:

> *The Vietnamese have taken innocent young Australian lives.*
>
> *Our new ANZACs have died at the hands of these barbaric people.*
>
> *No upstanding Australians should consider accepting a Vietnamese woman or child into their community.*

Confronting these voices, Dad didn't have a choice. She stayed behind. So did the baby.

Dad's weeks are pock-marked with visits to doctors, specialists, dieticians. His months are defaced with frightening dashes to emergency departments. The rash of war comes but I doubt it ever goes. He fills his physical hours watching footy, chatting to his kids and grandkids, crafting vehicles from blocks of wood. He spends his mental hours fighting the war within himself.

And as the daughter of a Vietnam vet, I'm left wondering if (like Frankie) Dad ever did come home.

Answers and explanations on page XXX–XXX

30 Which word best describes the tone of this story? There are **three** correct answers.
A reflective
B frustrated
C humorous
D emotive
E affectionate

31 According to the narrator, her father is
A caring.
B optimistic.
C distracted.
D dangerous.

32 What song prompts the narrator to think about her father?
A Redgum's 'When I was 19'
B Bluegum's 'Where I was at 19'
C Redgum's 'I was only 19'
D Redgum's 'Yesterday'

33 *These features stare back at me each morning as I hastily arrange myself for work* suggests that the narrator
A doesn't see her father much.
B resembles her father.
C has a photograph of her father on her wall.
D thinks her father was handsome.

34 What does the narrator's dad do during the day?
A He watches cricket.
B He plays with guns.
C He chats to his children and grandchildren and crafts vehicles from wood.
D He watches sports shows on television.

35 Highlight **two** metaphors in the last paragraph.

It would be a good idea to check your answers to questions 19 to 35 before moving on to the other questions.

Answers and explanations on page 155

Read *Volcanoes* and answer questions 36 to 41.

Volcanoes

A volcano is an opening in the planet's crust, which allows hot molten rocks, ash and gases to escape from below the surface. A volcano is a mountain that opens downward to a pool of molten rock called magma. Magma is liquid rock inside a volcano.

The word *volcano* comes from the name of Vulcan, who was the god of fire in Roman mythology. The Earth's crust is made up of huge slabs called tectonic plates. These plates fit together like a complicated jigsaw puzzle and sometimes move, shift and crack.

As the plates crash together, pressure within the volcano builds up. It is like shaking a fizzy drink but much worse. The pressure, like a safety valve, needs to escape somewhere so it travels upwards, causing cracks up the main vent/throat until it finally erupts through the top. Once the magma erupts through the Earth's surface it is called lava. Lava is the liquid that flows out of a volcano.

Lava blasts out along with ash, rocks, and a cloud of dust that is very thick. The lava burns down everything in its way as it reaches temperatures ranging from 700 to 1200 °C. The ash and rock crumble to the ground while the lava moves its way down the volcano side. A volcano's structure can be damaged during the explosion as it literally blows its top off.

Definitions:

Parasitic cone—a small cone-shaped volcano formed by an accumulation of volcanic debris

Sill—a flat piece of rock formed when magma hardens in a crack in a volcano

Vent—an opening in the Earth's surface through which volcanic materials escape

Lava—molten rock that erupts from a volcano and solidifies as it cools

Crater—the mouth of a volcano that surrounds a volcanic vent

Conduit—an underground passage that magma travels through

Throat—the entrance of a volcano (the part of the conduit that ejects lava and volcanic ash)

Ash—fragments of lava or rock smaller than two millimetres in size that are blasted into the air by volcanic explosions

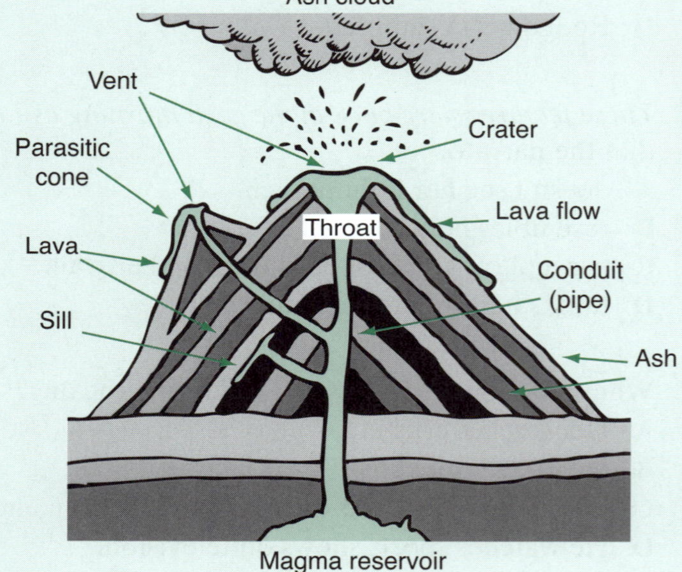

Adapted from <http://www.naturaldisasters.ewebsite.com/page/how-volcanoes-erupt.html>

36 What is magma?
- A liquid rock inside a volcano
- B the liquid that spills out of a volcano
- C rocks inside a volcano
- D the planet's crust

37 What is the purpose of the labelled diagram? There are **two** correct answers.
- A to help the reader better understand the structure of a volcano
- B to show how the lava flows from the volcano
- C to explain the parasitic cone
- D to illustrate the complexities of the volcano's structure

38 Volcanoes may cause massive destruction because
- A they can blow at any time.
- B the lava can be as hot as 1200 °C.
- C they are unpredictable.
- D they are full of magma.

39 The word *volcano* comes from
- A the Latin word for fire.
- B the god of fire, Vulcan, from Roman mythology.
- C the Roman word for fire.
- D the Roman god Volcano.

40 According to the text, the Earth's crust is made up of
- A a series of interlocking islands.
- B a jigsaw puzzle of tectonic plates.
- C huge slabs of rock.
- D a series of volcanoes.

41 What do the definitions beside the diagram suggest about volcanoes?
- A They are highly complex structures.
- B There is a lot to know about volcanoes.
- C They have many different parts.
- D Volcanoes are interesting.

Answers and explanations on page 155

Year 9 Reading Sample Online-style Test 1

Read *The history of mushrooms in Australia* and answer questions 42 to 48.

The history of mushrooms in Australia

The first commercial attempts to grow mushrooms in Australia were in 1933—in open fields in raised beds covered in straw and hessian bags.

The first growing houses of any size were disused railway tunnels in Sydney, including the then incomplete Circular Quay – St James line.

Mushroom growers began outdoor cultivation in the Hills and Hawkesbury districts outside Sydney in the mid-1930s.

These locations were selected because:

- of closeness to a migrant camp for labour supplies and growing expertise;
- raw materials for compost preparation (e.g. straw from the expanding racing industry) could be obtained locally;
- they had access to a large and willing labour force;
- they were close to the burgeoning market of Sydney.

Since then, the industry has become much more sophisticated.

Crops are now produced in sophisticated purpose-built growing rooms and there are farms in many locations across Australia.

Source: <http://www.mushrooms.net.au/PDFs/HistoryMushroomGrowing.pdf>.
Reprinted by permission of the Australian Mushroom Growers' Association.

42 Outdoor cultivation of mushrooms began in
A the mid-1930s. **B** 1933. **C** large railway buildings. **D** the 1940s.

43 According to the text, mushroom farming requires
A migrant labour. **B** compost. **C** straw. **D** hessian bags.

44 This text states that the first mushroom growing houses were
A near migrant camps.
B in the Hills and Hawkesbury districts.
C in disused railway tunnels in Sydney.
D close to the Sydney markets.

45 This information is mainly intended for
A mushroom historians.
B people interested in horticulture.
C gardeners.
D school students.
E people wanting to know about the history of mushroom farming in Australia.

46 The main aim of this information is to
A inform about the origins of mushroom farming in Australia.
B educate people about how to grow mushrooms.
C criticise the early attempts to grow mushrooms.
D celebrate Australia's success in the mushroom farming industry.

47 The word *burgeoning* is closest in meaning to
A large. **B** heavy. **C** growing. **D** small.

48 Why did mushroom growers select the Hills and Hawkesbury districts in the mid-1930s?
A They were closer to the harbour.
B They were close to migrant camps.
C They were very smelly.
D They would be more profitable.

Answers and explanations on page 156

Sample Online-style Test 2

Advanced level

Read this extract from *Alice's Adventures in Wonderland* by Lewis Carroll and answer questions 1 to 6.

Alice's Adventures in Wonderland

Alice was beginning to get very tired of sitting by her sister on the bank, and of having nothing to do; once or twice she had peeped into the book her sister was reading, but it had no pictures or conversations in it, 'and what is the use of a book,' thought Alice, 'without pictures or conversation?'

So she was considering in her own mind (as well as she could, for the hot day made her feel very sleepy and stupid), whether the pleasure of making a daisy-chain would be worth the trouble of getting up and picking the daisies, when suddenly a White Rabbit with pink eyes ran close by her.

There was nothing so very remarkable in that; nor did Alice think it so very much out of the way to hear the Rabbit say to itself, 'Oh dear! Oh dear! I shall be too late!' (when she thought it over afterwards, it occurred to her that she ought to have wondered at this, but at the time it all seemed quite natural); but when the Rabbit actually took a watch out of its waistcoat-pocket, and looked at it, and then hurried on, Alice started to her feet, for it flashed across her mind that she had never before seen a rabbit with either a waistcoat-pocket, or a watch to take out of it, and burning with curiosity, she ran across the field after it, and fortunately was just in time to see it pop down a large rabbit-hole under the hedge.

In another moment Alice went down after it, never once considering how in the world she was to get out again.

The rabbit-hole went straight on like a tunnel for some way, and then dipped suddenly down, so suddenly that Alice had not a moment to think about stopping herself before she found herself falling down a very deep well.

Either the well was very deep, or she fell very slowly, for she had plenty of time as she went down to look about her, and to wonder what was going to happen next. First, she tried to look down and make out what she was coming to, but it was too dark to see anything; then she looked at the sides of the well, and noticed that they were filled with cupboards and pictures hung upon pegs. She took down a jar from one of the shelves as she passed; it was labelled 'orange marmalade', but to her great disappointment it was empty: she did not like to drop the jar for fear of killing somebody, so managed to put it into one of the cupboards as she fell past it.

Year 9 Reading Sample Online-style Test 2

1 Choose the correct **two** options.

For Alice, sitting by her sister on the bank was

A extremely boring.
B not very interesting.
C frustrating.
D making her tired.

2 The main reason that Alice did not make a daisy chain was because

A she was hot and tired.
B she was lazy.
C she couldn't be bothered.
D she saw a white rabbit.

3 *In another moment Alice went down after it, never once considering how in the world she was to get out again.*

This suggests that Alice

A doesn't think about the consequences of her actions.
B may find herself stuck in the hole.
C is a very curious girl.
D is irresponsible.

4 What would be the best way to describe Alice's attitude towards the rabbit?
Two options are correct.

A fascinated B confused C curious D startled

5 *'Oh dear! Oh dear! I shall be too late!'*

What does this suggest about the white rabbit?

A He is scared of something.
B He is anxious about being late.
C He is an unusual character.
D His watch doesn't work.

6 *'and what is the use of a book,' thought Alice, 'without pictures or conversation?'*

What does this suggest about Alice?

A She is easily bored.
B She enjoys adventures.
C She loves being with people.
D She is hard to please.

Answers and explanations on page 156

Read this extract from *Oliver Twist* by Charles Dickens and answer questions 7 to 13.

Oliver Twist

The room in which the boys were fed was a large stone hall, with a copper at one end; out of which the master, dressed in an apron for the purpose, and assisted by one or two women, ladled the gruel at mealtimes. Of this festive composition the boys had one porringer and no more—except on occasions of public rejoicing when he had two ounces and a quarter of bread besides. The bowls never wanted washing. The boys polished them with their spoons till they shone again; and when they had performed this operation (which never took very long, the spoons being nearly as large as the bowls), they would sit staring at the copper, with such eager eyes, as if they could have devoured the very bricks of which it was composed; employing themselves meanwhile, in sucking their fingers most assiduously, with the view of catching up any stray splashes of gruel that might have been cast thereon. Boys have generally excellent appetites. Oliver Twist and his companions suffered the tortures of slow starvation for three months. At last they got so voracious and wild with hunger, that one boy who was tall for his age, hinted darkly to his companions that unless he had another basin of gruel, he was afraid he might some night happen to eat the boy sleeping next to him, who happened to be a weakly youth of tender age. He had a wild, hungry eye and they implicitly believed him. A council was held; lots were cast for who should walk up to the master after supper that evening and ask for more; and it fell to Oliver Twist.

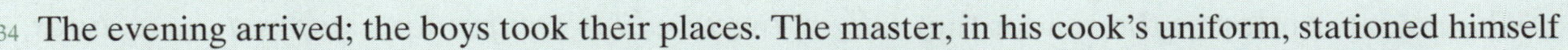

The evening arrived; the boys took their places. The master, in his cook's uniform, stationed himself at the copper; his pauper assistants ranged themselves beside him; the gruel was served out; and a long grace was said over short commons. The gruel disappeared; the boys whispered to each other and winked at Oliver; while his next neighbours nudged him. Child as he was, he was desperate with hunger, and reckless with misery. He rose from the table; and advancing to the master, basin and spoon in hand, said, somewhat alarmed at his own temerity,—

"Please, sir, I want some more."

The master was a fat, healthy man; but he turned very pale. He gazed with stupefied astonishment on the small rebel for some seconds; and then clung for support to the copper. The assistants were paralyzed with wonder, the boys with fear.

"What!" said the master at length, in a faint voice.

"Please, sir," replied Oliver, "I want some more."

The master aimed a blow at Oliver's head with the ladle, pinioned him in his arms, and shrieked aloud for the beadle.

7 For the master, Oliver Twist's request was

A a nasty shock.

B extremely irritating.

C unbelievable.

D sudden and unexpected.

8 The main reason that Oliver Twist asked for more was

A he was the most hungry.

B the boys drew lots as to who would ask for more and Oliver was selected.

C he wasn't afraid of the master.

D the other boys made him.

9 *The master was a fat, healthy man; but he turned very pale.*

This suggests that the master

A couldn't believe that a boy could be so naughty.

B was selfish and ate too much.

C was so surprised by Oliver's request that he lost all colour from his face.

D was feeling unwell.

10 What would be the best way of describing Oliver Twist's decision to ask for more? There are **two** correct answers.

A bold and brave

B foolish and desperate

C incredibly clever

D an act of desperation

E naive and brave

11 *The master aimed a blow at Oliver's head with the ladle, pinioned him in his arms, and shrieked aloud for the beadle.*

What does this suggest about the master?

A He was a cruel man who used physical violence as punishment.

B He lacked compassion and understanding.

C He was outraged by Oliver Twist's rudeness.

D He had anger management issues.

12 The narrator informs the reader that *Oliver Twist and his companions suffered the tortures of slow starvation for three months.*

This suggests that

A the boys were being abused.

B as growing boys they were not being fed enough to sustain them.

C the boys were desperate for more food.

D life is cruel.

13 How did the boys feel towards the master?

A They regarded him as a father figure.

B They would have liked to see him starve the way they were doing.

C They accepted that he had a job to do even if they didn't like it.

D They resented his cruelty and his unwillingness to give them the amount of food they needed to grow and prosper.

Answers and explanations on pages 156–157

Year 9 Reading Sample Online-style Test 2

Read *Waiheke* by Ella Holcombe and answer questions 14 to 18.

Waiheke

for days
we walk the island

broken tennis rackets, tent poles
strange murmurs in the bushes

today is night without the darkness
rain falls like a whisper

we watch a grey mass of cloud
shift across the sky

and smoke damp cigarettes,
hold hands beneath trees

the fish and chip lady sings 'love me tender'
over the splutter of fat

my shoes fill with sand,
we fall asleep on the beach

in the morning we swim
the bluest, coldest sea

Source: <http://www.redroomcompany.org/poet/ella-holcombe/>. Copyright the Red Room Company. Commissioned for the Red Room Company's 'Cabinet of Lost and Found' 2006.

14 *today is night without the darkness*
rain falls like a whisper

These lines suggest that

A the holiday is ruined.
B it is unpleasant on the island.
C the island is quiet and unpopulated.
D there is no one around.

15 *rain falls like a whisper* is best interpreted as

A the rain is soft and quiet.
B the rain cannot be seen or heard.
C the rain is annoying.
D the rain is ruining the holiday.

16 Highlight an example of imagery in the poem.

---

17 The line *broken tennis rackets, tent poles* suggests that

A the couple will not have fun on their holiday.
B the ideal island vacation is over.
C the couple will need to look elsewhere for entertainment.
D material possessions are not as important as relationships.

18 What feelings are created by this poem?

A relaxation and peacefulness
B calm and stillness
C respect for nature and relationships
D reflection and contentment

It would be a good idea to check your answers to questions 1 to 18 before moving on to the other questions.

Answers and explanations on page 157

Year 9 Reading Sample Online-style Test 2

Read this biography of Australian poet Judith Wright and answer questions 19 to 24.

Judith Wright

Judith Wright, born in the early 20th century, was a well-known Australian poet, short-story writer and conversationalist. She was also a highly acclaimed critic of Australian poetry. Apart from this, Wright was an uncompromising campaigner for Aboriginal land rights. She had received honorary degrees from several universities and was also appointed as one of the members of the Australia Council (in 1973–74).

Wright had written numerous poems, literary criticism and letters in her life and strongly believed the fact that a poet should be concerned with national and social problems. Her works have been awarded a number of times and also translated into other languages, including Italian, Japanese and Russian. Wright was also a highly successful literary critic and had edited several collections of Australian verse in her career.

Childhood

Judith Wright was born on the 31st May 1915, in Armidale, New South Wales, Australia. However, Wright spent most of her formative years in Brisbane and Sydney. She was the first child of Phillip Wright and his first wife, Ethel. When she was still in the tender years of her life, Wright went through the frequent ill health of her mother. This was when she started writing poetry, mainly to please her mother and bring her merriment.

Wright was brought up on her family's sheep station, until the death of her mother, in 1927. Thereafter, she was put under the guidance of her grandmother, who also took care of her education. In the year 1929, at the age of 14, Judith Wright was enrolled in New England Girls' School. Her love for poetry was enhanced at the school, as it gave her immense comfort and solace. This was when she decided to become a poet.

Writing style

Judith Wright's writing style was deeply inspired by the places in which she had stayed—New England, New South Wales, the subtropical rainforests of Tamborine Mountain, Queensland, and the plains of the southern highlands (near Braidwood). For Wright, her mission was to connect the human experience with the natural world, through poetry and other works.

Beliefs

Land played an important and influential role for Judith Wright, all her life. This can be seen in her poetry, in which she makes an effort to bridge the gap between nature and man. Wright condemned the educational system and blamed it for failing to teach students the art and pleasure of poetry. For her part, she popularised poetry by encouraging students to read and write poems in schools. However, she also expressed uncertainty about poetry changing the scheme of things.

Being an environmentalist

Judith Wright, together with David Fleay, Kathleen McArthur and Brian Clouston, was a founding member of the Wildlife Preservation Society of Queensland. She was also the president of the society, from 1964 to 1976. She fought to conserve the Great Barrier Reef, when its ecology was threatened by oil drilling, and campaigned against sand mining on Fraser Island. Wright, along with her friends, founded one of the earliest nature conservation movements. She was also an ardent supporter of the Aboriginal land rights movement. Shortly before her death, at 85 years of age, she attended a march in Canberra, for reconciliation between white Australians and the Aboriginal people.

Adapted from <http://www.thefamouspeople.com/profiles/judith-wright-107.php>

19 What is the purpose of this text?
- **A** to inform
- **B** to persuade
- **C** to entertain
- **D** to amuse

20 The words *(near Braidwood)* are in brackets because
- **A** this is the most important information in the sentence.
- **B** this is unnecessary information.
- **C** this is additional information.
- **D** this was forgotten when the text was first written.

21 What first made Judith Wright write poetry?
- **A** her lonely childhood
- **B** her experiences at school
- **C** her mother's ill health
- **D** her love of nature

22 What is the most likely reason for Judith Wright to have founded one of Australia's first nature conservation movements? There are **three** correct answers.
- **A** She grew up in the country and this experience developed her love of the natural world.
- **B** She didn't want to see the environment destroyed by humans.
- **C** She is a passionate person and wanted to be involved in many projects.
- **D** She was passionate about the natural environment and wanted to protect it.
- **E** She was university educated.

23 Choose the **two** correct options. *However, she also expressed uncertainty about poetry changing the scheme of things* (second last paragraph) means that
- **A** poetry is a dying art form.
- **B** she felt that poetry is important but that it may not have the capacity to change the world.
- **C** there are other more effective ways of saving the planet.
- **D** Wright lost faith in the power of poetry as she aged.
- **E** she wasn't confident in her capacity as a poet.

24 To what does the writer attribute Judith Wright's importance as a poet?
- **A** her impressive precision with words
- **B** the large volume of poetry that she produced during her lifetime
- **C** her commitment to both art and nature
- **D** her campaigning for Aboriginal land rights

Answers and explanations on pages 157–158

Year 9 Reading Sample Online-style Test 2

Read *The Rapa Nui culture* and answer questions 25 to 29.

The Rapa Nui culture

This culture is part of the Polynesian cultures. The local language is also called 'Rapa Nui' and is part of the Polynesian language family.

Interestingly, this rare language (which has almost disappeared and is spoken by a little over 4500 ethnic Rapa Nui people) is so unusual that seemingly it has no close connection to any other language.

The religious past is particularly interesting, but unfortunately Roman Catholicism has erased much of the original local beliefs and legends. It is believed that the Moai (the enormous stone heads scattered over the island) have some sort of religious significance, but there are only speculations about what/whom they might represent and why they were erected.

The Rapa Nui people had their own writing: it is called Rongorongo. The locals used this hieroglyphic writing especially to record messages on stones. Many of the carved stones are still intact but the oldest ones date back only to the 17th century, despite the fact that the local population is believed to have lived on the island since 300 AD.

Adapted from <http://www.easterislandquest.com/>

25 It is difficult to learn much about the Rapa Nui religion because

- **A** Roman Catholicism has ensured much of the original beliefs and legends are forgotten.
- **B** the culture died out many years ago.
- **C** there are no survivors of the Rapa Nui peoples.
- **D** the Rapa Nui people hid their beliefs from others.

26 The Rapa Nui are a mysterious people because

- **A** no one knows how or why their culture died out.
- **B** there is no written record of their culture.
- **C** there is only a limited amount of information that can be discovered about these people.
- **D** they carved huge stone heads and put them all over the island.

27 According to the text, why is the Rapa Nui language unusual?

- **A** There are no surviving Rapa Nui people to speak it.
- **B** It has an unusual alphabet.
- **C** It has no close connection to any other language.
- **D** There are many different versions of the language.

The following two questions require you to consider both texts *Waiheke* (page 109) and *The Rapa Nui culture* (above).

28 For which purposes were these texts written?

	to inform	to educate	to entertain
Waiheke			
The Rapa Nui culture			

29 Match the features to the text in which they are used.

	Waiheke	***The Rapa Nui culture***
parentheses		
simile		
factual detail		
third-person narrative		
imagery		

Answers and explanations on page 158

Year 9 Reading Sample Online-style Test 2

Read *Woolworths to phase out cage eggs* and answer questions 30 to 35.

Woolworths to phase out cage eggs

Supermarket giant Woolworths has announced it is phasing out cage eggs.

The chain will slash the number of cage-egg brands it sells to 11, cutting out one of its own lucrative in-house lines in the process.

Woolworths believes the move will increase the popularity of its 28 free-range and barn-laid brands and ultimately make them cheaper.

"(This) will influence our suppliers … and may generate a faster rate of change and that's good," Woolworths general manager Michael Batycki said.

"As demand for free-range and barn-laid increases, through the economies of scale we should see a greater level of affordability."

Free-range hens are currently responsible for 31 per cent of eggs sales, despite 80 per cent of Australia's egg-laying chickens being kept in cages.

The average price for a dozen free-range eggs, $6.50, is $2 more than the same quantity of caged eggs.

But the Australian Egg Corporation warned that while the changes might reduce the cost of free-range brands, they would never be as cheap as the barn variety.

Source: <http://news.ninemsn.com.au/national/849877/woolworths-to-phase-out-cage-eggs>. Reprinted with permission of ninemsn news.

30 The words *phasing out* are closest in meaning to

A becoming obsolete.
B being discontinued.
C never being heard of again.
D being introduced.

31 Highlight in the text the sentence that explains why Woolworths are phasing out cage eggs.

32 In the second paragraph *own lucrative in-house lines* means

A the houses the chickens live in are lucrative.
B Woolworths makes a lot of money from cage eggs.
C brands of eggs owned by Woolworths.
D brands of eggs owned by other big companies.

33 How much more can you expect to pay for a dozen free-range eggs than for a dozen eggs from a caged chicken?

A $5
B $3
C $2
D $1

34 According to the article, free-range hens produce what percentage of eggs sold in Australia?

A 52%
B 31%
C 28%
D 80%

35 How will this move influence suppliers?

A Suppliers will start to sell more cage eggs.
B Suppliers will need to limit the number of cage eggs that they produce and sell to Woolworths.
C Suppliers will lose money if they sell cage eggs.
D Suppliers might fight against the changes.

It would be a good idea to check your answers to questions 19 to 35 before moving on to the other questions.

Answers and explanations on page 158

Read the extract from *The absolutely true diary of a part-time Indian* by Sherman Alexie and answer questions 36 to 41.

The absolutely true diary of a part-time Indian

I was born with water on the brain.

Okay, so that's not exactly true. I was actually born with too much cerebral spinal fluid inside my skull. But cerebral spinal fluid is just the doctors' fancy way of saying brain grease. And brain grease works inside the lobes like car grease works inside an engine. It keeps things running smooth and fast.

But weirdo me, I was born with too much grease inside my skull, and it got all thick and muddy and disgusting, and it only mucked up the works. My thinking and breathing and living engine slowed down and flooded.

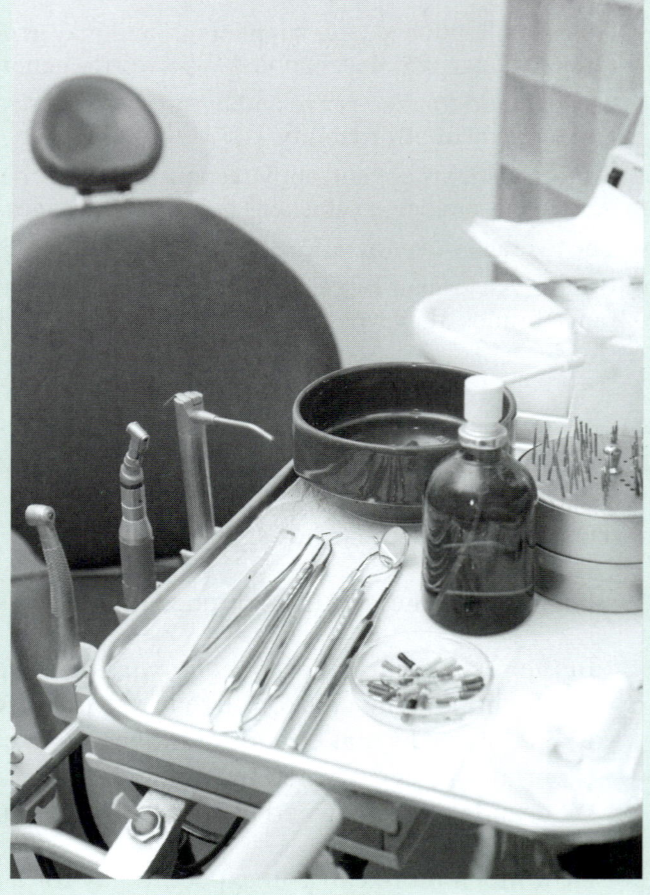

My brain was drowning in grease.

But that makes the whole thing sound weirdo and funny, like my brain was a giant French fry, so it seems more serious and poetic and accurate to say, "I was born with water on the brain."

Okay, so maybe that's not a very serious way to say it, either. Maybe the whole thing is weird and funny.

But, jeez, did my mother and father and big sister and grandma and cousins and aunts and uncles think it was funny when the doctors cut open my little skull and sucked out all that extra water with some tiny vacuum?

I was only six months old and I was supposed to croak during the surgery. And even if I somehow survived the mini-Hoover, I was supposed to suffer serious brain damage during the procedure and live the rest of my life as a vegetable.

Well, I obviously survived the surgery. I wouldn't be writing this if I didn't, but I have all sorts of physical problems that are directly the result of my brain damage.

First of all, I ended up having forty-two teeth. The typical human has thirty-two, right? But I had forty-two.

Ten more than usual.
Ten more than normal.
Ten teeth past human.

My teeth got so crowded that I could barely close my mouth. I went to Indian Health Service to get some teeth pulled so I could eat normally, not like some slobbering vulture. But the Indian Health Service funded major dental work only once a year, so I had to have all ten extra teeth pulled *in one day*.

And what's more, our white dentist believed that Indians felt only half as much pain as white people did, so he gave us only half the Novocain.

Source: <http://www.bookbrowse.com/excerpts/?book_number=2072&The%20Absolutely%20True%20Diary%20of%20a%20Part-Time%20Indian-excerpt>

36 What happened to the narrator when he was six months old?
A He was hit by a car.
B He almost drowned.
C It was discovered that he had water on the brain.
D He had surgery to remove excess cerebral spinal fluid from his brain.

37 In the fifth paragraph the expression *Maybe the whole thing is weird and funny* implies that the narrator
A thinks that having physical health problems is funny.
B accepts that his condition is unusual and tries to look at it positively.
C doesn't see the bad in his condition, only the good.
D is ignorant of the pain and suffering he will face in adulthood.

38 In this extract, the narrator feels
A amazed at his ability to survive his condition.
B sad at being different from everyone else.
C shocked and hurt that people treat him differently.
D surprised that he is alive.

39 Choose the **two** correct options. The mood of this extract is
A angry.
B honest.
C light-hearted.
D humorous.
E serious.

40 Why is it obvious that the narrator didn't die?
A He didn't speak about his death.
B He is too upbeat to be dead.
C He is writing his story and therefore must be alive.
D His story is about his survival.

41 Put these events of the narrator's life in the correct order.
☐ had brain surgery
☐ had ten teeth removed
☐ born with cerebral fluid inside his skull

Answers and explanations on pages 158–159

Year 9 Reading Sample Online-style Test 2

Read *How to throw a boomerang* and answer questions 42 to 48.

How to throw a boomerang

The grip

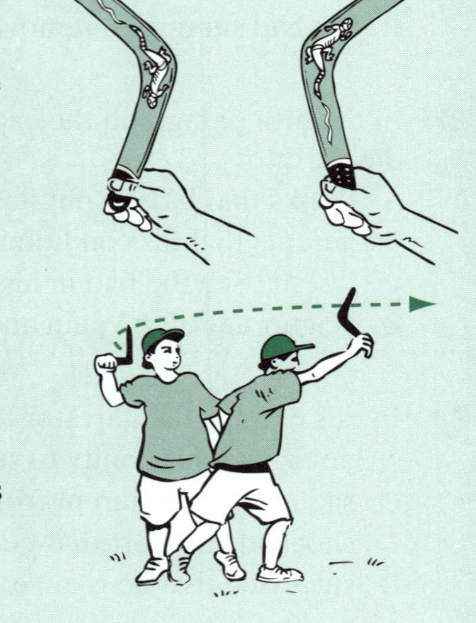

The curved, or decorated, side should always be held towards your body and the flat, unpainted side should always be facing away from you. The easiest way to grip the boomerang is to make a closed fist and slide the boomerang between your thumb and first finger. Make sure to cock the boomerang back for maximum spin. The 'elbow' of the boomerang can be facing either forward or backward as seen in the image to the right. Practice is the best way to find the grip perfect for you.

The throw

Always throw your boomerang in the traditional overarm style. Aim the boomerang at or just above the horizon prior to cocking back. Release the boomerang at the peak height of your throw. When thrown correctly, the boomerang will fly in a circle and reach the apex of its flight at the point furthest away from you. As the boomerang returns it will begin to slow down and hover towards the ground.

Launch angle

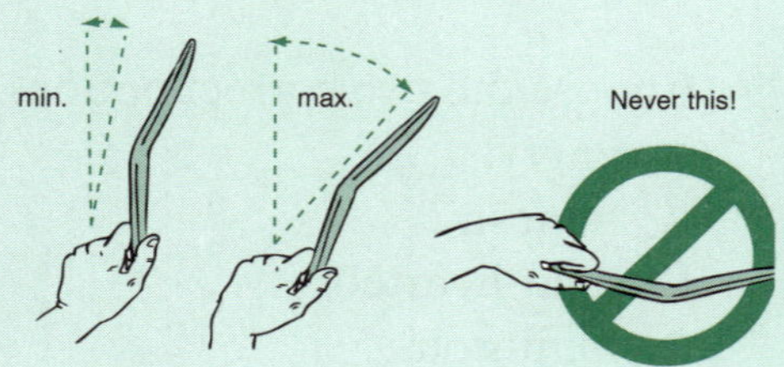

The boomerang should be nearly vertical when released. Increasing the tilt angle makes it fly higher and land further back. Holding the boomerang more vertically will make it fly lower to the ground and land more forward. NEVER hold the boomerang horizontally flat like a frisbee. This will cause the boomerang to fly in dangerous swooping and diving flights.

Adjusting for the wind

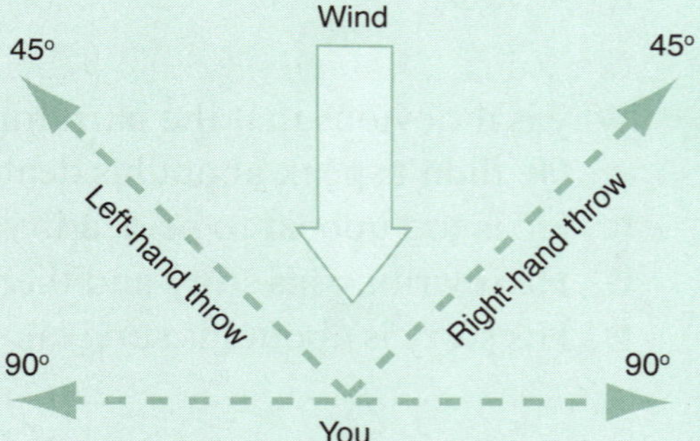

Throw to the right of the wind at an angle between 45 and 90°. Left-handed throwers should throw to the left of the wind between a 45 and 90° angle. Aiming at a 45° angle is usually a good rule of thumb, and will utilize the breeze in your favour to help bring the boomerang back. By standing in the same spot and aiming for an object in the distance, you can adjust the throw angle to the wind.

The catch

Catch the boomerang using both of your hands in a clapping motion, as shown in the diagram to the right. Only attempt to catch the boomerang while it is slowly hovering towards you and is below shoulder height. Aim for the centre section of the boomerang as you catch it, and try to avoid the faster moving wing tips. NEVER try to catch a boomerang that is diving or moving fast.

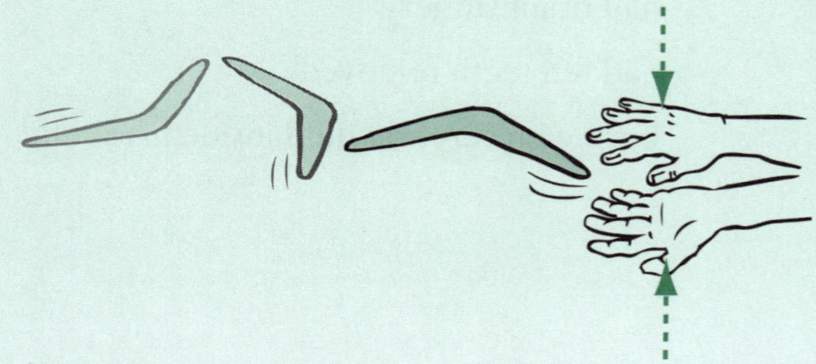

Source: http://www.boomerangs.com/howtothrow.html

42 How should you grip a boomerang?

A with the decorative side towards your body
B at an arm's length away from your body
C tight between both of your hands as if you are praying
D in the middle of the 'elbow' of the boomerang

43 What is the purpose of the labelled diagrams?

A to show the reader how to hold the boomerang
B to help the reader understand how to correctly throw a boomerang
C to demonstrate how easy it is to throw a boomerang
D to make the article more interesting

44 What does this symbol mean?

A Boomerangs are dangerous.
B This is how not to throw the boomerang.
C Don't hold the boomerang.
D Throwing boomerangs this way can kill people.

45 When a boomerang returns to the thrower it should

A land at his or her feet.
B be very fast and powerful.
C be easy to catch between both hands.
D slow down and hover towards the ground.

46 According to the text, to catch a boomerang you should use your hands in a clapping motion and

A let it hit you in the stomach.
B aim for the centre section as you catch it.
C jump towards the boomerang as it flies.
D clasp it between your forefinger and thumb.

47 What do the diagram labels suggest about learning to correctly throw a boomerang?

A It is a complex skill and difficult to master.
B It is quite a simple skill to master.
C There are many important steps to be learnt.
D There are not many steps to be learnt.

48 NEVER is in capitals in the last sentence because

A the editor forgot to change it.
B the writer is yelling.
C it makes it easier to read.
D it highlights the importance of not catching a moving boomerang.

Answers and explanations on page 159

Before you start, make sure you read the Tips for Writing on page 76.

Today you are going to write a persuasive text, often called an exposition.

Television does more harm than good.

What are your thoughts on this idea?

Write to convince your reader of your opinions.

Before you start writing, give some thought to:
- whether you strongly agree or disagree with having pupil-free days
- the way you will present your ideas: clearly list or order your points
- the reasons or evidence for your arguments
- your brief but definite conclusion. In your conclusion list some of your main points—you may add a personal opinion.

Don't forget to:
- plan your writing before you start
- write in correctly formed sentences and take particular care with paragraphing
- choose your words carefully and pay attention to your spelling and punctuation
- write neatly but don't waste time
- quickly check your story once you have finished. Your position must be clear to your reader.

Remember: The stance taken in a persuasive text is not wrong, as long as the writer has evidence to support his or her opinion. How the opinion is supported is as important as the opinion itself.

Start writing here or type your answer on a tablet or computer.

☞ Once you have completed the Writing Test, turn to page147 and use the Marking checklist to check your writing. Also go to pages 169–174 where sample pieces of writing (Standard, Intermediate and Advanced levels) can be used to see at what level you are writing.

Year 9 Writing

Sample Online-style Test 2

Before you start, make sure you read the Tips for Writing on page 79.

Today you are going to write a narrative.

The idea for your narrative is *The cage*. Your narrative might be about discovering a dog trapped in a cage in a local park or diving in a shark cage out in the ocean. It could be about being stuck in a cage with your biggest enemy, your grumpy older sister or an evil magician. Your narrative could be about how people lock away their true emotions or the truth in a cage and what happens when they are let loose.

Before you start writing, give some thought to:

- where your story takes place (the setting)
- the characters and what they do in the story
- the events that take place in the story and the problems that have to be resolved
- how your story begins, what happens in your story, and how your story ends.

Don't forget to:

- plan your story before you begin writing
- write in correctly formed sentences and take care with paragraphing
- choose your words carefully and pay attention to your spelling and punctuation
- write neatly but don't waste time
- quickly check your story once you have finished.

Start writing here or type your answer on a tablet or computer.

☞ **Once you have completed the Writing Test, turn to pages 147–148 and use the Marking checklist to check your writing. Also go to pages 169–174 where sample pieces of writing (Standard, Intermediate and Advanced levels) can be used to see at what level you are writing.**

Mini Test Answers

Standard level questions

SPELLING Mini Test 1

Pages 1–2

1 lightning **2** fierce **3** weird **4** tangle **5** village **6** governor **7** sign **8** faith **9** aching **10** systems **11** fail **12** squad **13** development **14** enthusiasm **15** colour **16** brief **17** fourth **18** notice **19** increases **20** trophy **21** concluded **22** responsible **23** beauty **24** climb **25** eagerly

1 This common noun is often confused with the verb *lightening*. To help tell them apart, use this mnemonic (memory device): even though lightning makes you go 'eeee', there is no ***e*** in *lightning*.

2 The letters ***ie*** combine to make the one sound ***e***. Don't forget the rule '***i*** before ***e***, except after ***c***'.

3 This word has an irregular spelling pattern because ***e*** comes before ***i***. You must memorise the spelling of this word. Try to use a mnemonic such as '***i*** before ***e***, except after ***c***, and *weird* is just weird'.

4 The final sound of this word is often misspelt as ***al*** instead of ***le***. You must memorise the spelling of this word. Try to use a mnemonic such as '*tangle* has an angle'.

5 The final sound in this word is often misspelt as ***adge*** instead of ***age***.

6 The words most people spell wrongly are often longer words. To give yourself a greater chance of spelling success, you must break multi-syllable words into smaller parts by sounding them out into their phonemes. Remember that each syllable contains a vowel (***a***, ***e***, ***i***, ***o***, ***u***) or vowel-sounding letter such as ***y***. For example, the word *governor* becomes *gov-er-nor*.

7 The letters ***ig*** create a long ***i*** sound. To help remember the spelling of this word, think of the word *signature*, which is a derivative of the word *sign*.

8 The letters ***ai*** combine to create an ***ay*** sound in this word and this often causes confusion.

9 Remember that in this word the letters ***ch*** are pronounced as a ***k*** sound.

10 This word has an irregular spelling pattern because the ***y*** in this word has a short ***i*** sound, like the ***i*** in *sing*.

11 The letters ***ai*** combine to create an ***ay*** sound in this word and this often causes confusion. There is no ***e*** at the end.

12 The letters ***qu*** in this word combine to create a ***kw*** sound.

13 This word comprises the root word develop + the suffix ment. When adding a suffix beginning with a consonant to a word ending in a consonant, you simply add the suffix without making any other changes to the root word.

14 The words most people spell wrongly are often longer words. To give yourself a greater chance of spelling success, you must break multi-syllable words into smaller parts by sounding them out into their phonemes. Remember that each syllable contains a vowel (***a***, ***e***, ***i***, ***o***, ***u***) or vowel-sounding letter such as ***y***. For example, the word *enthusiasm* becomes *en-thu-si-a-sm*.

15 Often people misspell this word as they use the American form, *color*. In Australia *colour* is the correct form.

16 The letters ***ie*** combine to make the one sound ***e***. Don't forget the rule '***i*** before ***e*** except after ***c***'.

17 The letters ***our*** combine to create the sound ***or*** in this word. This abstract noun is often confused with the adverb *forth*, which means 'go forward'.

18 This word can become a 'demon' word for both teachers and students. Remember that the ***c*** creates an ***s*** sound.

19 This word comprises the root word *increase* + the suffix ***s***. The letters ***ea*** create a long ***ee*** sound.

20 This is a commonly misspelt word. Remember that the two letters ***ph*** combine to create the ***f*** sound.

21 This word has a single ***l***, not a double ***l***.

22 This word comprises the root word *response* + the suffix ***ible***. When adding a suffix that begins with a vowel to a word ending with an ***e***, the final ***e*** is dropped before adding the suffix. Therefore, *respons**e*** becomes *respons**ible***.

23 This is a commonly misspelt word. The letters ***au*** combine to create the ***oo*** sound.

24 This is a commonly misspelt word. Remember that the final letter, ***b***, is silent—this means you don't pronounce it.

25 This word comprises the root word *eager* + the suffix ***ly***. When adding a suffix beginning with a consonant to a word ending in a consonant, you simply add the suffix without making any other changes to the root word.

Year 9 Literacy Mini Test Answers

SPELLING Mini Test 2

Pages 3–4

1 police **2** average **3** braces **4** Furthermore **5** difficult **6** government **7** whispered **8** mosaics **9** witnessed **10** blackmail **11** points **12** executed **13** paperweight **14** beginning **15** scarecrow **16** descends **17** infuse **18** flower **19** strawberry **20** whipped **21** lifetime **22** inmate **23** Throughout **24** underwear **25** workday

1 The ***c*** in this word makes an ***ss*** sound and can easily be confused with the letter ***s***.

2 The words most people spell wrongly are often longer words. To give yourself a greater chance of spelling success, you must break multi-syllable words into smaller parts by sounding them out into their phonemes. Remember that each syllable contains a vowel (***a***, ***e***, ***i***, ***o***, ***u***) or vowel-sounding letter such as ***y***. For example, the word *average* becomes *av-er-age*.

3 The ***c*** in this word makes an ***ss*** sound and can easily be confused with the letter ***s***.

4 The words most people spell wrongly are often longer words. To give yourself a greater chance of spelling success, you must break multi-syllable words into smaller parts by sounding them out into their phonemes. Remember that each syllable contains a vowel (***a***, ***e***, ***i***, ***o***, ***u***) or vowel-sounding letter such as ***y***. For example, the word *furthermore* becomes *fur-ther-more*.

5 The words most people spell wrongly are often longer words. To give yourself a greater chance of spelling success, you must break multi-syllable words into smaller parts by sounding them out into their phonemes. Remember that each syllable contains a vowel (***a***, ***e***, ***i***, ***o***, ***u***) or vowel-sounding letter such as ***y***. For example, the word *difficult* becomes *diff-i-cult*.

6 This word is frequently misspelt because it is not pronounced the way it is spelt. The ***n*** is often silent and the ***e*** is pronounced as a short ***a***.

7 The opening ***wh*** sound is similar to that in *whale* and *which*.

8 Remember the ***c*** at the end of this word makes a ***k*** sound.

9 This word comprises the root word *witness* + the suffix ***ed***. When adding the suffix ***ed*** to a word ending in a double consonant, you don't need to make any other changes to the root word.

10 This is a compound word made up of the combination of the two root words *black* and *mail*.

11 The letters ***oi*** in this word combine to make an ***oy*** sound.

12 The words most people spell wrongly are often longer words. To give yourself a greater chance of spelling success, you must break multi-syllable words into smaller parts by sounding them out into their phonemes. Remember that each syllable contains a vowel (***a***, ***e***, ***i***, ***o***, ***u***) or vowel-sounding letter such as ***y***. For example, the word *executed* becomes *ex-e-cuted*.

13 This is a compound word made up of the combination of the two root words *paper* and *weight*.

14 This word contains the root word *begin* and the suffix ***ing***. If the suffix you want to add begins with a vowel, use the doubling rule: for a root word ending in a single vowel and a consonant, such as *shop* or *tap*, the consonant at the end of the word must double before adding the suffix.

15 This is a compound word made up of the combination of the two root words *scare* and *crow*.

16 The letters ***sc*** combine to create the ***s*** sound.

17 This word contains the root word *fuse* and the prefix ***in***. A prefix is always spelt in full and does not affect the spelling of the root word.

18 The letters ***er*** combine to create a short ***a*** sound. Remember: There is only one ***l*** in *flower*.

19 This is a compound word made up of the combination of the two root words *straw* and *berry*.

20 The opening ***wh*** sound is similar to that in *whale* and *which*. This word contains the root word *whip* and the suffix ***ed***. If the suffix you want to add begins with a vowel, use the doubling rule: for a root word ending in a single vowel and a consonant, such as *shop* or *tap*, the consonant at the end of the word must double before adding the suffix.

21 This is a compound word made up of the combination of the two root words *life* and *time*.

22 This is a compound word made up of the combination of the two root words *in* and *mate*.

23 This is a compound word made up of the combination of the two root words *through* and *out*.

24 This is a compound word made up of the combination of the two root words *under* and *wear*.

25 This is a compound word made up of the combination of the two root words *work* and *day*.

Year 9 Literacy Mini Test Answers

Intermediate level questions

SPELLING Mini Test 3

Pages 5–6

1 invitation **2** intelligent **3** demonstrate **4** anniversary **5** agriculture **6** commentator **7** fundamental **8** operator **9** reputation **10** established **11** consequence **12** permission **13** persuade **14** acceptable **15** colleagues **16** occupation **17** shortage **18** specialise **19** overwhelming **20** prominent **21** recruits **22** squad **23** praise **24** portrait **25** statistics

1 The letters ***tion*** combine to make the ***shun*** sound.

2 The words most people spell wrongly are often longer words. To give yourself a greater chance of spelling success, you must break multi-syllable words into smaller parts by sounding them out into their phonemes. Remember that each syllable contains a vowel (***a***, ***e***, ***i***, ***o***, ***u***) or vowel-sounding letter such as ***y***. For example, the word *intelligent* becomes *in-tell-i-gent*. Remember that this word has a double ***l***.

3 The words most people spell wrongly are often longer words. To give yourself a greater chance of spelling success, you must break multi-syllable words into smaller parts by sounding them out into their phonemes. Remember that each syllable contains a vowel (***a***, ***e***, ***i***, ***o***, ***u***) or vowel-sounding letter such as ***y***. For example, the word *demonstrate* becomes *de-mon-strate*.

4 The words most people spell wrongly are often longer words. To give yourself a greater chance of spelling success, you must break multi-syllable words into smaller parts by sounding them out into their phonemes. Remember that each syllable contains a vowel (***a***, ***e***, ***i***, ***o***, ***u***) or vowel-sounding letter such as ***y***. For example, the word *anniversary* becomes *ann-i-ver-sa-ry*. This word has a double ***n***.

5 The words most people spell wrongly are often longer words. To give yourself a greater chance of spelling success, you must break multi-syllable words into smaller parts by sounding them out into their phonemes. Remember that each syllable contains a vowel (***a***, ***e***, ***i***, ***o***, ***u***) or vowel-sounding letter such as ***y***. For example, the word *agriculture* becomes *ag-ri-cul-ture*.

6 The words most people spell wrongly are often longer words. To give yourself a greater chance of spelling success, you must break multi-syllable words into smaller parts by sounding them out into their phonemes. Remember that each syllable contains a vowel (***a***, ***e***, ***i***, ***o***, ***u***) or vowel-sounding letter such as ***y***. For example, the word *commentator* becomes *com-men-ta-tor*. Remember that this word has a double ***m***.

7 The words most people spell wrongly are often longer words. To give yourself a greater chance of spelling success, you must break multi-syllable words into smaller parts by sounding them out into their phonemes. Remember that each syllable contains a vowel (***a***, ***e***, ***i***, ***o***, ***u***) or vowel-sounding letter such as ***y***. For example, the word *fundamental* becomes *fun-da-men-tal*.

8 The words most people spell wrongly are often longer words. To give yourself a greater chance of spelling success, you must break multi-syllable words into smaller parts by sounding them out into their phonemes. Remember that each syllable contains a vowel (***a***, ***e***, ***i***, ***o***, ***u***) or vowel-sounding letter such as ***y***. For example, the word *operator* becomes *op-er-a-tor*.

9 The letters ***tion*** combine to create the ***shun*** sound.

10 The words most people spell wrongly are often longer words. To give yourself a greater chance of spelling success, you must break multi-syllable words into smaller parts by sounding them out into their phonemes. Remember that each syllable contains a vowel (***a***, ***e***, ***i***, ***o***, ***u***) or vowel-sounding letter such as ***y***. For example, the word *established* becomes *es-tab-lish-ed*.

11 The letters ***que*** combine to create a ***kwe*** sound. The second letter ***c*** makes an ***ss*** sound.

12 The letters ***ssion*** combine to create a ***shun*** sound. Remember that this word is a combination of the root word *mission* and the prefix ***per***.

13 The letters ***ua*** combine to create a ***way*** sound.

14 The first letter ***c*** creates to hard ***k*** sound. The second letter ***c*** creates the soft ***s*** sound.

15 The letters ***ea*** combine to create a long ***ee*** sound.

16 The letters ***tion*** combine to create a ***shun*** sound.

17 The end of this word is often misspelt as ***adge***. Remember the suffix is ***age***.

18 The letters ***cial*** combine to create a ***shul*** sound.

19 The ***wh*** sound is often misspelt as ***w***.

20 The letter ***i*** makes a short ***a*** sound in this word.

21 The letters ***ui*** combine to create an ***oo*** sound in this word.

22 The letters ***qu*** combine to create a ***kw*** sound in this word.

23 The letters ***ai*** combine to create an ***ay*** sound in this word.

24 The letters ***ai*** combine to create an ***ay*** sound in this word.

25 The words most people spell wrongly are often longer words. To give yourself a greater chance of spelling success, you must break multi-syllable words into smaller parts by sounding them out into their phonemes. Remember that each syllable contains a vowel (***a***, ***e***, ***i***, ***o***, ***u***) or vowel-sounding letter such as ***y***. For example, the word *statistics* becomes *sta-tis-tics*.

SPELLING Mini Test 4

Pages 7–8

1 crucial **2** cautious **3** cease **4** conscious **5** device **6** column **7** amateur **8** protein **9** seize **10** satellite **11** fault **12** maroon **13** integrate **14** headquarters **15** mechanism **16** musician **17** preparation **18** nightmare **19** procrastinate **20** scientific **21** psychological **22** reluctant **23** retirement **24** reasonable **25** revolutionary

1 This word is spelt differently from how it sounds. The letters ***cial*** combine to make the ***shul*** sound.

2 This word is spelt differently from how it sounds. The letters ***tious*** combine to create the ***shus*** sound.

3 This word is spelt differently from how it sounds. The letters ***ea*** combine to create the ***ee*** sound.

4 This word is spelt differently from how it sounds. The letters ***sci*** combine to create the ***sh*** sound.

5 This word is spelt differently from how it sounds. The letter ***c*** creates an ***s*** sound in this word.

6 This word is spelt differently from how it sounds. The letter ***n*** is silent in this word.

7 This word is spelt differently from how it sounds. The letter ***u*** is pronounced ***y*** in this word.

8 This word is spelt differently from how it sounds. The letters ***ei*** combine to create the ***ee*** sound in this word. This is an exception to '***i*** before ***e***, except after ***c***'.

9 This word is spelt differently from how it sounds. The letters ***ei*** combine to create the long ***ee*** sound in this word.

10 This word is spelt differently from how it sounds. The letter ***e*** creates the short ***a*** sound in this word.

11 This word is spelt differently from how it sounds. The letters ***au*** combine to create the short ***o*** sound in this word.

12 This word is spelt differently from how it sounds. The letters ***oon*** are pronounced ***own*** in this word.

13 This word is spelt differently from how it sounds. The letter ***e*** creates the short ***a*** sound in this word.

14 The words most people spell wrongly are often longer words. To give yourself a greater chance of spelling success, you must break multi-syllable words into smaller parts by sounding them out into their phonemes. Remember that each syllable contains a vowel (***a***, ***e***, ***i***, ***o***, ***u***) or vowel-sounding letter such as ***y***. For example, the word *headquarters* becomes *head-quar-ters*.

15 The words most people spell wrongly are often longer words. To give yourself a greater chance of spelling success, you must break multi-syllable words into smaller parts by sounding them out into their phonemes. Remember that each syllable contains a vowel (***a***, ***e***, ***i***, ***o***, ***u***) or vowel-sounding letter such as ***y***. For example, the word *mechanism* becomes *mec-han-ism*.

16 The words most people spell wrongly are often longer words. To give yourself a greater chance of spelling success, you must break multi-syllable words into smaller parts by sounding them out into their phonemes. Remember that each syllable contains a vowel (***a***, ***e***, ***i***, ***o***, ***u***) or vowel-sounding letter such as ***y***. For example, the word *musician* becomes *mu-si-cian*.

17 The words most people spell wrongly are often longer words. To give yourself a greater chance of spelling success, you must break multi-syllable words into smaller parts by sounding them out into their phonemes. Remember that each syllable contains a vowel (***a***, ***e***, ***i***, ***o***, ***u***) or vowel-sounding letter such as ***y***. For example, the word *preparation* becomes *pre-par-a-tion*.

18 This is a compound word. It is created by the combination of the two root words *night* and *mare*.

19 The words most people spell wrongly are often longer words. To give yourself a greater chance of spelling success, you must break multi-syllable words into smaller parts by sounding them out into their phonemes. Remember that each syllable contains a vowel (***a***, ***e***, ***i***, ***o***, ***u***) or vowel-sounding letter such as ***y***. For example, the word *procrastinate* becomes *pro-cras-ti-nate*.

20 The words most people spell wrongly are often longer words. To give yourself a greater chance of spelling success, you must break multi-syllable words into smaller parts by sounding them out into their phonemes. Remember that each syllable contains a vowel (***a***, ***e***, ***i***, ***o***, ***u***) or vowel-sounding letter such as ***y***. For example, the word *scientific* becomes *sci-en-ti-fic*.

21 The words most people spell wrongly are often longer words. To give yourself a greater chance of spelling success, you must break multi-syllable words into smaller parts by sounding them out into their phonemes. Remember that each syllable contains a vowel (***a***, ***e***, ***i***, ***o***, ***u***) or vowel-sounding letter such as ***y***. For example, the word *psychological* becomes *psy-cho-lo-gi-cal*.

22 The words most people spell wrongly are often longer words. To give yourself a greater chance of spelling success, you must break multi-syllable words into smaller parts by sounding them out into their phonemes. Remember that each syllable contains a vowel (***a***, ***e***, ***i***, ***o***, ***u***) or vowel-sounding letter such as ***y***. For example, the word *reluctant* becomes *re-luc-tant*.

23 The words most people spell wrongly are often longer words. This word contains the root word *retire* combined with the suffix *ment*.

24 The words most people spell wrongly are often longer words. This word contains the root word *reason* and the suffix *able*.

25 The words most people spell wrongly are often longer words. This word contains the root word *revolution* and the suffix *ary*.

SPELLING Mini Test 5

Pages 9–10

1 victimise **2** vulnerable **3** substantial **4** tremendous **5** stomach **6** sufficient **7** rough **8** paranoia **9** shortage **10** provision **11** obtain **12** negotiate **13** accusation **14** anxious **15** celebration **16** coverage **17** conservation **18** courageous **19** essentially **20** imagination **21** immigration **22** initially **23** seriously **24** unfortunately **25** virtually

1 This word is made up of the root word *victim* and the suffix ***ise***. Sometimes this word is misspelt 'victimice' but remember that many words ending in ***ise*** are verbs.

2 The words most people spell wrongly are often longer words. To give yourself a greater chance of spelling success, you must break multi-syllable words into smaller parts by sounding them out into their phonemes. Remember that each syllable contains a vowel (***a***, ***e***, ***i***, ***o***, ***u***) or vowel-sounding letter such as ***y***. For example, the word *vulnerable* becomes *vul-ner-a-ble*.

3 This word is made up of the root word *substance* and the suffix ***tial***. For this word the ***ce*** is dropped and replaced with ***tial*** to change it from a noun to an adjective.

4 The letters ***ous*** combine to make the ***us*** sound.

5 The letters ***ch*** combine to create a short ***k*** sound.

6 The letters ***cient*** combine to create a ***shant*** sound.

7 The letters ***gh*** combine to create an ***f*** sound, as in *fish*.

8 The letters ***oi*** in this word make an ***oy*** sound. The letters ***oia*** combine to create an ***oya*** sound.

9 The end of this word is often misspelt ***adge*** because the letters ***age*** combine to create the ***adge*** sound.

10 The letters ***si*** combine to create the ***sh*** sound in this word.

11 The letters ***ai*** in this word make an ***ay*** sound. The letters ***ain*** combine to create an ***ayn*** sound.

12 The letters ***ti*** combine to create the ***sh*** sound in this word.

13 The letters ***ti*** combine to create the ***sh*** sound in this word. This word only has one ***s***.

14 The letters ***xi*** combine to create the ***ksh*** sound in this word.

15 The second ***e*** creates the short ***a*** sound. The letters ***ti*** combine to create the ***sh*** sound in this word.

16 The end of this word is often misspelt ***adge*** because the letters ***age*** combine to create the ***adge*** sound.

17 This word is made up of the root word *conserve* and the suffix ***tion***. The ***e*** of the root word is changed to ***a*** before adding the suffix.

18 This word is made up of the root word *courage* and the suffix ***ous***.

19 This word is made up of the root word *essential* and the suffix ***ly***.

20 This word is made up of the root word *imagine* and the suffix ***tion***. The ***e*** of the root word is changed to ***a*** before adding the suffix.

21 This word is made up of the root word *immigrate* and the suffix ***ion***. The ***e*** of the root word must be dropped before adding the suffix.

22 This word is made up of the root word *initial* and the suffix ***ly***.

23 This word is made up of the root word *serious* and the suffix ***ly***.

24 This word is made up of the root word *fortunate* with the prefix ***un*** and the suffix ***ly***.

25 This word is made up of the root word *virtual* and the suffix ***ly***.

SPELLING Mini Test 6

Pages 11–12

1 except **2** surprised **3** deficit **4** chaos **5** assault **6** cough **7** because **8** thought **9** eager **10** guerilla **11** disappearance **12** loiter **13** furniture **14** debris **15** corps **16** coup **17** doubt **18** receipts **19** solemn **20** autumn **21** asthma **22** knowledge **23** foreigner **24** design **25** resign

Year 9 Literacy Mini Test Answers

1 The ***c*** in this word makes the ***s*** sound.

2 This word is often misspelt because people leave out the first ***r***.

3 The ***c*** in this word makes the ***s*** sound.

4 The letters ***ch*** in this word combine to make the ***k*** sound.

5 The letters ***au*** in this word combine to create the short ***o*** sound.

6 This word is often misspelt as 'coff' because the letters ***ou*** combine to create a short ***o*** sound and the letters ***gh*** combine to create an ***f*** sound.

7 This word is often misspelt as 'becawse'. This is because the letters ***au*** combine to create the ***aw*** sound.

8 This word is not spelt the way it sounds and this makes it difficult to spell. You will have to memorise how this word is spelt.

9 The letters ***ea*** in this word combine to create a long ***ee*** sound. The letters ***er*** combine to create a short ***a*** sound.

10 This word is not spelt the way it sounds and this makes it difficult to spell. You will have to memorise how this word is spelt. Note: *guerrilla* is also an acceptable spelling.

11 This word is made from the root word *appear* plus the prefix ***dis*** and the suffix ***ance***.

12 The ***i*** in this word creates a long ***y*** sound.

13 The end letters of this word (***ture***) are often pronounced ***cha*** and so misspelt.

14 The letter ***s*** is silent in this word.

15 The letters ***p*** and ***s*** are silent in this word.

16 The letter ***p*** is silent in this word. The letters ***ou*** combine to create an ***oo*** sound.

17 The letter ***b*** is silent in this word.

18 The letter ***p*** is silent in this word.

19 The letter ***n*** is silent in this word.

20 The letter ***n*** is silent in this word.

21 The letters ***th*** are silent in this word.

22 The letter ***d*** is silent in this word.

23 The letter ***g*** is silent in this word. The letters ***ei*** combine to create the short ***e*** sound.

24 The letter ***g*** in this word is silent.

25 The letter ***g*** in this word is silent.

Advanced level questions

SPELLING Mini Test 7

Pages 13–14

1 consequence **2** permanent **3** atmosphere **4** imaginary **5** accommodation **6** perspective **7** processor **8** classification **9** exclamation **10** paragraphs **11** vocabulary **12** personification **13** digestion **14** condensation **15** vertebrate **16** circulation **17** laboratories **18** longitude **19** constitution **20** isosceles **21** apparatus **22** deduction **23** clarification **24** hypothesis **25** empirical

1 Break multi-syllable words into chunks to help you spell them correctly. Remember that each syllable contains a vowel (***a***, ***e***, ***i***, ***o***, ***u***) or vowel-sounding letter such as ***y***. For example, the word *consequence* becomes *con-se-quence*.

2 Break multi-syllable words into chunks to help you spell them correctly. Remember that each syllable contains a vowel (***a***, ***e***, ***i***, ***o***, ***u***) or vowel-sounding letter such as ***y***. For example, the word *permanent* becomes *per-ma-nent*.

3 Break multi-syllable words into chunks to help you spell them correctly. Remember that each syllable contains a vowel (***a***, ***e***, ***i***, ***o***, ***u***) or vowel-sounding letter such as ***y***. For example, the word *atmosphere* becomes *at-mos-phere*.

4 Break multi-syllable words into chunks to help you spell them correctly. Remember that each syllable contains a vowel (***a***, ***e***, ***i***, ***o***, ***u***) or vowel-sounding letter such as ***y***. For example, the word *imaginary* becomes *im-ag-in-ar-y*.

5 Break multi-syllable words into chunks to help you spell them correctly. Remember that each syllable contains a vowel (***a***, ***e***, ***i***, ***o***, ***u***) or vowel-sounding letter such as ***y***. For example, the word *accommodation* becomes *a-ccomm-o-da-tion*.

6 Break multi-syllable words into chunks to help you spell them correctly. Remember that each syllable contains a vowel (***a***, ***e***, ***i***, ***o***, ***u***) or vowel-sounding letter such as ***y***. For example, the word *perspective* becomes *per-spec-tive*.

7 Break multi-syllable words into chunks to help you spell them correctly. Remember that each syllable contains a vowel (***a***, ***e***, ***i***, ***o***, ***u***) or vowel-sounding letter such as ***y***. For example, the word *processor* becomes *pro-cess-or*.

8 Break multi-syllable words into chunks to help you spell them correctly. Remember that each syllable contains a vowel (***a***, ***e***, ***i***, ***o***, ***u***) or vowel-sounding letter such as ***y***. For example, the word *classification* becomes *class-if-i-ca-tion*.

9 Break multi-syllable words into chunks to help you spell them correctly. Remember that each syllable contains a vowel (***a***, ***e***, ***i***, ***o***, ***u***) or vowel-sounding letter such as ***y***. For example, the word *exclamation* becomes *ex-clam-a-tion*.

10 Break multi-syllable words into chunks to help you spell them correctly. Remember that each syllable contains a vowel (***a***, ***e***, ***i***, ***o***, ***u***) or vowel-sounding letter such as ***y***. For example, the word *paragraphs* becomes *pa-ra-graphs*.

11 Break multi-syllable words into chunks to help you spell them correctly. Remember that each syllable contains a vowel (***a***, ***e***, ***i***, ***o***, ***u***) or vowel-sounding letter such as ***y***. For example, the word *vocabulary* becomes *vo-cab-u-lar-y*.

12 Break multi-syllable words into chunks to help you spell them correctly. Remember that each syllable contains a vowel (***a***, ***e***, ***i***, ***o***, ***u***) or vowel-sounding letter such as ***y***. For example, the word *personification* becomes *per-son-i-fi-ca-tion*.

13 Scientific words are often difficult to spell. Many are abstract nouns that have been formed from verbs by adding the suffix ***ion*** or ***ation***. This word features the root word *digest* and the suffix ***ion***.

14 Scientific words are often difficult to spell. Many are abstract nouns that have been formed from verbs by adding the suffix ***ion*** or ***ation***. This word is created from the root word *condense* and the suffix ***ation***. When adding a suffix to a word ending in ***e***, drop the letter ***e*** first.

15 Scientific words are often difficult to spell. Many have irregular or difficult spellings. The letter ***e*** in this word makes the ***a*** sound.

16 Scientific words are often difficult to spell. Many are abstract nouns that have been formed from verbs by adding the suffix ***ion*** or ***ation***. This word is created from the root word *circulate* and the suffix ***ion***. When adding a suffix to a word ending in ***e***, drop the letter ***e*** first.

17 Many scientific words have irregular or difficult spellings. If a noun ends in ***y*** preceded by a consonant, change the ***y*** to ***i*** before adding ***es*** to form the plural. For example, *laboratory* becomes *laboratories*.

18 Scientific words are often difficult to spell. You may find it easier to break this multi-syllable word into chunks: *lon-gi-tude*.

19 Scientific words are often difficult to spell. Many are abstract nouns that have been formed from verbs by adding the suffix ***ion*** or ***ation***. This word is created from the root word *constitute* and the suffix ***ion***. When adding a suffix to a word ending in ***e***, drop the letter ***e*** first.

20 Scientific words are often difficult to spell. Many have irregular or difficult endings. The letters ***sc*** create the ***s*** sound and the first ***e*** creates the ***a*** sound.

21 Scientific words are often difficult to spell. Remember that this word contain a double ***p***.

22 Scientific words are often difficult to spell. Many are abstract nouns that have been formed from verbs by adding the suffix ***tion*** or ***ation***. This word is created from the root word *deduce* and the suffix ***tion***. When adding a suffix to a word ending in ***e***, drop the letter ***e*** first.

23 Scientific words are often difficult to spell. Many are abstract nouns that have been formed from verbs by adding the suffix ***ion*** or ***ation***. This word is created from the root word *clarify* and the suffix ***ation***. When adding a suffix to a word ending in ***y***, drop the letter ***y*** and add ***i***.

24 Scientific words are often difficult to spell. This word features the root word *thesis* and the prefix ***hypo***. Remember that a prefix must be spelt in its entirety.

25 Scientific words are often difficult to spell. You may find it easier to break this multi-syllable word into chunks: *em-pi-ri-cal*.

SPELLING Mini Test 8

Pages 15–16

1 orchestral **2** indecision **3** syncopation **4** theatrical **5** generosity **6** tournament **7** quadriceps **8** collage **9** aesthetic **10** preference **11** spectrum **12** disassemble **13** encyclopedia **14** parochial **15** presumably **16** legislation **17** equivalent **18** elsewhere **19** ambassador **20** concede **21** analyst **22** inevitable **23** regime **24** bacterium **25** bureaus

1 Subject-specific words often have complex spelling. This word would likely be used in the subject Music. The letters ***ch*** combine to create a ***k*** sound in this word.

2 Many complex words are multi-syllable words, and so you should break them into sound chunks when trying to spell them. Remember that each syllable contains a vowel (***a***, ***e***, ***i***, ***o***, ***u***) or vowel-sounding letter such as ***y***. For example, the word *indecision* becomes *in-de-ci-sion*.

3 Subject-specific words often have complex spelling. This word would likely be used in the subject Music. The ***y*** in this word makes the short ***i*** sound and the letter ***c*** makes the ***k*** sound.

4 Subject-specific words often have complex spelling. This word would likely be used in the subject Drama. The letter ***e*** makes the long ***ee*** sound in this word.

Year 9 Literacy Mini Test Answers

5 Many complex words are multi-syllable words, and so you should break them into sound chunks when trying to spell them. Remember that each syllable contains a vowel (***a***, ***e***, ***i***, ***o***, ***u***) or vowel-sounding letter such as ***y***. For example, the word *generosity* becomes *gen-er-os-i-ty*.

6 Subject-specific words often have complex spelling. This word would likely be used in English or History. The letters ***our*** combine to create the ***or*** sound in this word.

7 Subject-specific words often have complex spelling. This word would likely be used in Personal Development (PD), Health and Physical Exercise (PE). The letters ***qu*** combine to create the ***kw*** sound in this word and the letter ***c*** creates the ***s*** sound.

8 Subject-specific words often have complex spelling. This word would likely be used in Visual Arts. The ending of this word is irregular—the letters ***age*** combine to create an ***arsh*** sound.

9 Subject-specific words often have complex spelling. This word would likely be used in Visual Arts. The letter ***e*** after the ***a*** is silent in this word.

10 Many complex words are multi-syllable words, and so you should break them into sound chunks when trying to spell them. Remember that each syllable contains a vowel (***a***, ***e***, ***i***, ***o***, ***u***) or vowel-sounding letter such as ***y***. For example, the word *preference* becomes *pre-fer-ence*.

11 Subject-specific words often have complex spelling. This word would likely be used in Photography. The letter ***c*** makes a ***k*** sound in this word.

12 This word features the root word *assemble* and the prefix ***dis***. Remember that prefixes must be spelt in their entirety.

13 The first ***c*** in this word makes the ***s*** sound while the second makes the ***k*** sound. *Encyclopaedia* is also an acceptable spelling.

14 Subject-specific words often have complex spelling. This word would likely be used in History or English. The letters ***ch*** combine to create a ***k*** sound in this word.

15 Many complex words are multi-syllable words, and so you should break them into sound chunks when trying to spell them. Remember that each syllable contains a vowel (***a***, ***e***, ***i***, ***o***, ***u***) or vowel-sounding letter such as ***y***. For example, the word *presumably* becomes *pre-sum-a-bly*.

16 Subject-specific words often have complex spelling. This word would likely be used in Legal Studies. The first letters ***leg*** are actually pronounced ***ledge***, and this is why students often misspell this word. The suffix ***tion*** is pronounced ***shun***.

17 Many complex words are multi-syllable words, and so you should break them into sound chunks when trying to spell them. Remember that each syllable contains a vowel (***a***, ***e***, ***i***, ***o***, ***u***) or vowel-sounding letter such as ***y***. For example, the word *equivalent* becomes *e-qui-va-lent*.

18 This word is a compound word. It is combination of the words *else* and *where*.

19 Subject-specific words often have complex spelling. This word would likely be used in History or Legal Studies. The letters ***ss*** combine to create the ***s*** sound and students often only write one ***s***.

20 Complex words are often those that don't sound the same way they are spelt. The second letter ***c*** creates the ***s*** sound and the first ***e*** creates the ***ee*** sound.

21 Complex words are often those that don't sound the same way they are spelt. The letter ***y*** in this word creates the short ***i*** sound.

22 Many complex words are multi-syllable words, and so you should break them into sound chunks when trying to spell them. Remember that each syllable contains a vowel (***a***, ***e***, ***i***, ***o***, ***u***) or vowel-sounding letter such as ***y***. For example, the word *inevitable* becomes *in-ev-it-a-ble*.

23 Complex words are often those that don't sound the same way they are spelt. This word originates from the French language and therefore the ***g*** is pronounced ***sh***. The letter ***i*** also creates an ***ee*** sound in this word.

24 Many complex words are multi-syllable words, and so you should break them into sound chunks when trying to spell them. Remember that each syllable contains a vowel (***a***, ***e***, ***i***, ***o***, ***u***) or vowel-sounding letter such as ***y***. For example, the word *bacterium* becomes *bac-ter-i-um*.

25 Complex words are often those that don't sound the same way they are spelt. This word originates from the French language and therefore the letters ***eau*** combine to create a long ***o*** sound, like the end of the word *tomato*.

SPELLING Mini Test 9

Pages 17–18

1 pharaoh **2** antique **3** physical **4** comfortable **5** enough **6** answer **7** dinosaurs **8** weather **9** rhyme **10** rough **11** skeleton **12** colleagues **13** succinct **14** nutrients **15** tableau **16** consumed **17** sauce **18** produced **19** corrupting **20** dissolves **21** sacrifice **22** apprentice **23** synchronised **24** formerly **25** appropriate

Year 9 Literacy Mini Test Answers

1 Some words are not spelt the way they sound when spoken. The letters ***ao*** combine to create an ***o*** sound and the letters ***ph*** combine to create an ***f*** sound.

2 Some words are not spelt the way they sound when spoken. The letters ***ique*** combine to create an ***eek*** sound.

3 Some words are not spelt the way they sound when spoken. The letters ***ph*** combine to create the ***f*** sound and the letter ***y*** makes a short ***i*** sound.

4 Some words are not spelt the way they sound when spoken. The middle of this word (***ort***) is not pronounced by many people. Try to break the word into syllables: *com-for-ta-ble*.

5 Some words are not spelt the way they sound when spoken. The letters ***ou*** combine to create the ***a*** sound and the letters ***gh*** combine to create the ***f*** sound.

6 Some words are not spelt the way they sound when spoken. The ***w*** in this word is silent—this means we don't pronounce it when we say the word.

7 Some words are not spelt the way they sound when spoken. The letters ***aur*** combine to create the ***or*** sound in this word.

8 The abstract noun *weather* is often confused with the conjunction *whether*. The letters ***ea*** combine to create the short ***e*** sound.

9 Some words are not spelt the way they sound when spoken. The letters ***hy*** combine to create a long ***i*** sound as in *time*.

10 Some words are not spelt the way they sound when spoken. The letters ***ou*** combine to create the short ***u*** sound and the letters ***gh*** combine to create the ***f*** sound.

11 Some words are not spelt the way they sound when spoken. The second letter ***e*** makes the short ***a*** sound in this word.

12 Some words are not spelt the way they sound when spoken. The letters ***ea*** combine to create the ***ee*** sound. The ***u*** is a silent letter.

13 Some letters combine to make a completely new sound, and this can make these words difficult to spell. The first ***c*** makes the hard ***k*** sound while the second makes the ***s*** sound. The third ***c*** makes the hard ***k*** sound.

14 Some letters combine to make a completely new sound, and this can make these words difficult to spell. The letters ***ie*** combine to create an ***ee*** sound in this word.

15 Some letters combine to make a completely new sound, and this can make these words difficult to spell. The letters ***eau*** combine to create the long ***o*** sound in this word.

16 This word is often misspelt with a double ***s***.

17 Some letters combine to make a completely new sound, and this can make these words difficult to spell. The letters ***au*** in this word combine to create the ***or*** sound.

18 The letter ***c*** in this word creates an ***s*** sound.

19 This word has a double ***r***, not just one ***r***.

20 This word contains the root word *solves* and the prefix ***dis***. Remember that a prefix is always spelt fully.

21 The first ***c*** in this word makes a ***k*** sound and the second ***c*** makes an ***s*** sound.

22 Some letters combine to make a completely new sound, and this can make these words difficult to spell. The ending of this word is often spelt wrongly because the ***c*** makes an ***s*** sound.

23 Some letters combine to make a completely new sound, and this can make these words difficult to spell. The letters ***ch*** combine to create a ***k*** sound and the letter ***s*** creates a ***z*** sound.

24 This word is a homophone and is often confused with *formally*. Remember that the suffix ***ly*** is simply added to the end of the root word *former*.

25 Some letters combine to make a completely new sound, and this can make these words difficult to spell. The letter ***i*** creates the long ***ee*** sound in this word. Remember that this word also has a double ***p***.

SPELLING Mini Test 10

Pages 19–20

1 sincerely **2** unfortunately **3** approximately **4** horizontally **5** governmentally **6** beautifully **7** sequentially **8** technologically **9** consciously **10** deliberately **11** controversially **12** fundamentally **13** suspiciously **14** persuasion **15** outrageous **16** conscience **17** amphibian **18** respiration **19** dispersal **20** inevitable **21** symmetrical **22** imperialism **23** chronological **24** parishioner **25** sanctions

1 To transform a word from an adjective to an adverb, simply add ***ly***. The ***c*** in this word makes an ***s*** sound.

2 To transform a word from an adjective to an adverb, simply add ***ly***. Don't forget that the ***e*** in *unfortunate* remains in this word.

3 To transform a word from an adjective to an adverb, simply add ***ly***. The adjective is *approximate*. Don't forget this word has a double ***p***.

4 To transform a word from an adjective to an adverb, simply add ***ly***. The adjective is *horizontal*. There is only one ***t*** in this word.

5 To transform a word from an adjective to an adverb, simply add ***ly***. This word is often mispronounced as *gov-**a**-mentally* and this causes it to be misspelt. Remember that there is a silent ***n***.

6 To transform a word from an adjective to an adverb, simply add ***ly***. The adjective is *beautiful*. The letters ***au*** in this word create an ***oo*** sound.

7 To transform a word from an adjective to an adverb, simply add ***ly***. There is only one ***n*** in this word.

8 To transform a word from an adjective to an adverb, simply add ***ly***. There is only one ***g*** in *technological*. The letters ***ch*** combine to create a ***k*** sound in this word.

9 To transform a word from an adjective to an adverb, simply add ***ly***. The adjective is *conscious*. The letters ***sci*** combine to create a ***sh*** sound in this word.

10 To transform a word from an adjective to an adverb, simply add ***ly***. Don't forget that the ***e*** in *deliberate* remains in this word.

11 To transform a word from an adjective to an adverb, simply add ***ly***. The adjective is *controversial*. This word is often mispronounced as *contr-**a**-versially*. Remember that it is ***o*** and not ***a***. Also, the letters ***sial*** combine to create a ***shul*** sound in this word.

12 To transform a word from an adjective to an adverb, simply add ***ly***. The adjective is *fundamental*. The words most people spell wrongly are often longer words. To spell this word correctly, break it into smaller chunks (*fun-da-ment-al-ly*).

13 To transform a word from an adjective to an adverb, simply add ***ly***. The adjective is *suspicious*. The letters ***cious*** combine to create the ***shus*** sound in this word.

14 Often complex words are longer words or have irregular spelling patterns. The letters ***ua*** in this word combine to create the ***wa*** sound.

15 Often complex words are longer words or have irregular spelling patterns. The letters ***eous*** combine to create the ***us*** sound in this word.

16 Often complex words are longer words or have irregular spelling patterns. The letters ***sc*** create a ***sh*** sound in this word.

17 Often complex words are longer words or have irregular spelling patterns. The letters ***ph*** combine to create an ***f*** sound in this word.

18 Often complex words are longer words or have irregular spelling patterns. The first ***i*** in this word is often pronounced as a short ***a***.

19 The ending of this word is often misspelt as ***le***.

20 Often complex words are longer words or have irregular spelling patterns. The second ***i*** in this word is often pronounced as a short ***a***.

21 Often complex words are longer words or have irregular spelling patterns. The double ***m*** in this word is often forgotten.

22 Often complex words are longer words or have irregular spelling patterns. The second ***i*** in this word makes an ***ee*** sound.

23 Often complex words are longer words or have irregular spelling patterns. The letters ***ch*** combine to create a ***k*** sound in this word.

24 Often complex words are longer words or have irregular spelling patterns. The letters ***io*** combine to create a short ***o*** sound in this word.

25 Often complex words are longer words or have irregular spelling patterns. The letters ***tion*** combine to create the ***shun*** sound in this word.

Standard level questions

GRAMMAR Mini Test 1

Pages 21–23

1 He **2** him **3** she **4** A **5** A **6** B **7** A **8** C **9** B **10** D **11** B **12** had seen her **13** had lost her **14** will find an **15** B **16** allowed **17** helped **18** conjured **19** D **20** B **21** B **22** C **23** D **24** A **25** C

1 A pronoun is a word that takes the place of a noun or proper noun (e.g. *he*, *she*, *it*, *I*).

2 A pronoun is a word that takes the place of a noun or proper noun (e.g. *him*, *her*, *it*, *me*).

3 A pronoun is a word that takes the place of a noun or proper noun. In this sentence *she* is taking the place of *the teacher*.

4 This question requires you to select the correct demonstrative. Demonstratives (e.g. *that*, *those*, *this*, *these*) are used to point out a particular item. Be sure to use *this* or *that* with singular nouns and *these* or *those* with plural nouns.

5 This question requires you to select the correct reflexive pronoun. A reflexive pronoun is created by adding ***self*** or ***selves*** to a personal pronoun (e.g. *him*, *her*, *them*) and refers back to the subject of a sentence (usually a noun or personal pronoun). The subject is *he* and so the correct reflexive pronoun is *himself*.

Year 9 Literacy Mini Test Answers

6 This question requires you to identify the correct articles. The definite article *the* refers to a specific object, group or person that has been previously mentioned. The indefinite articles *a* and *an* refer to an unknown or unspecified object, group or person. There is only one private sector so we must use the definite article. Note that *an* is used before words beginning with a vowel and *a* is used before words beginning with a consonant.

7 To determine if a text is written in the present (e.g. *walk*), future (*will walk*) or past (*walked*) tense, look at the verbs and the use of participles. In this text the verbs are in the present tense (e.g. *looks*, *is*), indicating that the action is occurring now.

8 To help identify what narrative voice a text is written in, look for *you* (indicating the second person), *I* (indicating the first person) or a character's name (indicating the third person).

9 Italics can be used to show added emphasis in a sentence, to indicate the title of a text or to show that a word is from another language. In this case italics are used to indicate a title of a text.

10 Italics can be used to show added emphasis in a sentence, to indicate the title of a text or to show that a word is from another language. In this case italics are used to indicate that a word is from another language.

11 *Should* is a modal verb meaning 'ought to'. It is used as a 'helper' verb before the main verb (*look*).

12 *Seen* is the past participle of the irregular verb *see* and it needs a 'helper' verb. The main verb (*knew*) shows the sentence is in the past tense and that this event is even further in the past. Therefore *had* is the correct helper verb, not *has*.

13 With *lost* (the past participle of the irregular verb *lose*) you need a 'helper'—another verb to 'help' it. The main verb (*noticed*) shows the sentence is in the past tense and that this event is even further in the past. Therefore *had* is the correct helper verb, not *has*.

14 Note that the sentence is written in the future tense. The verb *find* is complemented by the 'helper' verb *will* to show that the action will occur in the future.

15 With *gone* (past participle of the irregular verb *go*) you need a 'helper'—another verb to 'help' it. *Have*, *has* and *had* can be helping verbs. The helper verb *would* is used here to indicate future when the sentence is in the past tense.

16 A verb is an action word (e.g. *run*, *jump*, *hop*). In this sentence the word *allowed* is the past tense form of the verb *allow*.

17 A verb is an action word (e.g. *run*, *jump*, *hop*). In this sentence the word *helped* is the simple past tense form of the verb *help*.

18 A verb is an action word (e.g. *run*, *jump*, *hop*). In this sentence the word *conjured* is the simple past tense form of the verb *conjure*.

19 *Slowly* is an adverb and adds meaning to the past tense verb *dug*.

20 To determine if a text is written in the present (e.g. *walk*), future (*will walk*) or past (*walked*) tense, look at the verbs and the use of participles. In this text the verbs are written in either the simple past tense (e.g. *dug*, *sat*) or are complemented by 'helper' verbs to show that the actions occurred in the past (e.g. *had been*).

21 To help identify what narrative voice a text is written in, look for *you* (indicating the second person), *I* (indicating the first person) or a character's name (indicating the third person).

22 An adjective is a word used to describe a noun. In this sentence the adjectives are *fat* and *steep*.

23 A common noun is the word for a person, place or thing. In this sentence the thing is the film, and the person is the child. A proper noun is the name for something; in this sentence *E.T.* is a proper noun.

24 The word *is* is the present tense form of the verb *be*. It indicates that the action or event is occurring in the present tense. Singular nouns need singular verbs. There is one shark and so the correct verb is the singular *is*, not the plural *are*.

25 This sentence is written in the present tense and therefore the simple present tense of the word *celebrate* is needed. The word *celebrating* also indicates the present tense, but requires a 'helper' such as *am* or *are* to help it make sense.

Intermediate level questions

GRAMMAR Mini Test 2

Pages 24–26

1 would have **2** has not had **3** has not **4** They're **5** we've **6** B **7** A **8** D **9** A **10** D **11** since **12** down, up **13** inside **14** upon **15** on **16** on **17** in **18** D **19** D **20** A **21** A **22** A **23** B **24** B **25** A

1 With *been* (the past participle of the irregular verb *be*) you need a 'helper'—another verb to 'help' it. *Have*, *has* and *had* can be helping verbs. The helper verb *would* is used to indicate the future as the sentence is in the past tense.

2 The expression is *have a cold* and the past participle of the irregular verb *have* is *had*. With a past participle you need a 'helper'—another verb to 'help' it. *Have*, *has* and *had* can also be helping verbs and in this case the singular verb *has* is required. The negative *not* is needed so that the sentence makes sense.

3 With the verb *washed* (the past participle of *wash*) you need a 'helper'—another verb to 'help' it. *Have*, *has* and *had* can be helping verbs. Sometimes the helper verb is separated from the verb by another word: in this case *not* separates *has* and *washed*.

4 The word *they're* is a contraction of the pronoun *they* and the verb *are*. The apostrophe takes the place of the missing letter ***a***.

5 The word *we've* is a contraction of the pronoun *we* and the verb *have*. The apostrophe takes the place of the missing letters ***ha***.

6 This question requires you to identify tautology. Tautology is the repeating of words or phrases that have a similar meaning. In this example the word *free* is unnecessary because all gifts are free.

7 The sentence is written in the present tense; therefore, the simple present *spend* is needed.

8 The preposition *of* after the gap shows that the word before it must be a noun or pronoun and so the noun *cause* is correct. The verb forms *caused* and *causing* are incorrect.

9 Plural nouns require plural verbs. In this case the noun *foods* is plural and therefore requires the plural verb *are* and not the singular verb *is*.

10 The word *shown* is the past participle of the irregular verb *show* and needs a 'helper'—another verb to 'help' it. *Have*, *has* and *had* can be helping verbs. The helper *been* is needed to indicate passive voice (Australians did not show something; something was shown about Australians).

11 Prepositions put events in position in time or place. The correct word is the preposition *since*.

12 Prepositions put events in position in time or place. The correct words are the prepositions *down* and *up*.

13 Prepositions put events in position in time or place. The correct word is the preposition *inside*.

14 Prepositions put events in position in time or place. The correct word is the preposition *upon*.

15 Prepositions put events in position in time or place. The correct word is the preposition *on*.

16 Prepositions put events in position in time or place. The correct word is the preposition *on*.

17 Prepositions put events in position in time or place. The correct word is the preposition *in*.

18 Prepositions put events in position in time or place. In everyday speech certain prepositions regularly tend to go with certain words. We use *in* with places (e.g. habitat) in order to show where an event occurs. The correct word is the preposition *in*.

19 Plural nouns must have plural verbs. In this case the plural noun *sites* requires the plural noun *are*, not *is* or *was*.

20 With the verb *granted* (past participle of *grant*) you need a 'helper'—another verb to 'help' it. The helpers *will be* indicate that the event will happen in the future.

21 The verb *become* is complemented by the 'helper' verb *will* to show that the action will occur in the future.

22 To determine if a text is written in the present (e.g. *walk* or *walking*), future (*will walk*) or past (*walked*) tense, look at the verbs. In this sentence the main verb is *was* (the past tense of the verb *be*).

23 To determine if a text is written in the present (e.g. *walk* or *walking*), future (*will walk*) or past (*walked*) tense, look at the verbs. In this sentence the verb (*are*) is in the present tense.

24 To determine if a text is written in the present (e.g. *walk* or *walking*), future (*will walk*) or past (*walked*) tense, look at the verbs and the use of participles. In this text the verbs are in the present tense (*comes*, *means*, *have*).

25 *Have* is a plural verb. In this example it indicates that octopuses possess eight arms.

GRAMMAR Mini Test 3

Pages 27–29

1 B **2** D **3** C **4** B **5** B **6** D **7** D **8** D **9** D **10** A **11** is **12** have **13** puts **14** are **15** have no precise **16** captures **17** will look **18** was **19** is **20** that have made **21** who were there **22** C **23** B **24** C **25** D

1 The verb *should* means 'ought to' and after it we use the simple form of the verb for the present tense (e.g. *should make*) and *have* with the past participle to indicate the past tense. The past participle of the irregular verb *make* is *made*.

2 To indicate the future tense we use the simple form of the verb (*want*) with *will* or *shall*.

3 With *been* (the past participle of the verb *be*) you need a 'helper'—another verb to 'help' it. *Have*, *has* and *had* can be helping verbs.

4 The word *he's* is a contraction of *he is* and the word *his* is a possessive pronoun to show ownership.

5 The past participle of the irregular verb *bring* is *brought*.

6 This text is written in the past tense; therefore, the past tense *could* is needed.

7 This text is written in the past tense and Haty was thinking of the past (past in the past), and so *had* is correct, not *has*. With *had* we use the past participle, not the present participle.

8 This text is written in the past tense and so *was* is needed. Singular verbs require singular nouns—the subject noun in this sentence (*father*) is singular; therefore, the verb must be singular (*was* and not *were*).

9 This text is written in the past tense; therefore, the simple past tense *expected* is needed.

10 This text is written in the past tense, but Haty was thinking about the future. To form the future in the past, the helper verb *would* (past tense of *will*) must be used.

11 Singular nouns require singular verbs. The singular noun *Jabberwocky* requires the singular verb *is*.

12 Plural nouns require plural verbs. The plural noun *words* require the plural verb *have*.

13 Singular nouns require singular verbs. The singular subject *main character, Alice* requires the singular verb *puts*.

14 Plural nouns require plural verbs. The plural pronoun *they* requires the plural verb *are*.

15 Plural nouns require plural verbs. The plural noun *words* requires the plural verb *have*.

16 Singular nouns require singular verbs. The pronoun *that* stands for the singular noun *activity* and so requires the singular verb *captures*.

17 As the sentence is referring to the future, the future tense is needed.

18 Singular nouns require singular verbs. The singular noun *Ashley* requires the singular noun *was*. The sentence is in the past tense, as shown by the verb *yawned*.

19 Singular nouns require singular verbs. The singular noun *Jupiter* requires the singular verb *is*. The present tense is needed in this sentence.

20 The novels and films were made in the past and so the past tense is needed. The past participle of the irregular verb *make* is *made*.

21 This clause refers to *people* and this requires *who*, not *that*, as *that* refers to things. Plural nouns require plural verbs. The plural noun *people* requires the plural verb *were*, and not the singular verb *was*.

22 In this sentence the verbal noun *eating* is the subject of the sentence. The other options are verbs and so are incorrect.

23 An adjective is a descriptive word used to describe nouns and pronouns. In this example the adjective *dramatic* describes the situation. Nouns are things that we can touch, think or feel. In this example the noun is *drama*.

24 To determine the tense of a sentence you should look at the form that the verbs take. In this sentence the main verb is *will be* and so the sentence is in the future tense.

25 Verbs require a 'helper' verb to indicate the future tense. In this case it is the word *will*.

Advanced level questions

GRAMMAR Mini Test 4

Pages 30–32

1 violently, swiftly **2** effortlessly **3** nervously **4** silly **5** tiny, refugee **6** phenomenal **7** light **8** really quickly **9** hastily thrusting **10** the illusion appeared **11** A **12** C **13** D **14** C **15** A **16** B **17** B **18** A **19** B **20** B **21** B **22** C **23** A **24** D **25** B

1 Adverbs usually describe a verb. They often end in ***ly***. The adverb *violently* is use to describe the verb *fell* and the adverb *swiftly* describes the verb *rushed*.

2 Adverbs usually describe a verb. They often end in ***ly***. The adverb *effortlessly* is used to describe the action of lifting off the ground.

3 Adverbs usually describe a verb. They often end in ***ly***. The adverb *nervously* describes the verb *walked*.

4 An adjective is a word used to describe a noun. In this example the adjective *silly* is used to describe the joke.

5 An adjective is a word used to describe a noun. In this example the adjective *tiny* describes the corridor and the adjective *refugee* describes the families.

6 An adjective is a word used to describe a noun. In this example the adjective *phenomenal* describes the light display.

7 An adjective is a word used to describe a noun. In this example the adjective *light* is used to describe the breeze.

8 Adverbs usually describe a verb or sometimes an adjective. They often end in ***ly***. The word *quickly* is an adverb used to describe the verb *threw*; *really* is an adverb describing the adverb *quickly*.

9 Adverbs usually describe a verb or sometimes an adjective. They often end in ***ly***. The word *hastily* is an adverb used to describe the verb *thrusting*. *Thrusting* is a present participle form of the verb *thrust*.

10 The order of words in a sentence can vary but the succession of definite article (*the*), noun (*illusion*) and main verb (*appeared*) is a commonly used pattern.

11 A phrase is a group of words that add information to an independent clause. The correct phrase to complete this sentence is *new teacher, who is French,*

12 A phrase is a group of words that add information to an independent clause. The correct phrase to complete this sentence is *the stars shine brightly.*

13 Adverbs usually describe a verb. They often end in ***ly***. The adverb *delicately* is used to describe the action of touching.

14 An adjective is a word used to describe a noun. In this example the adjective *sandy* is used to describe the boy's hair.

15 Only the same sorts of things can be compared. My typing skills can only be compared to Holly's typing skills, not to Holly.

16 A phrase is a group of words that add information to an independent clause. The correct phrase to complete this sentence is *ordinary electric guitar*.

17 The word *the* is referred to as the definite article. This is because when used it refers to a specific object or person meaning it is *definitely* this object or person and not another one. The helper verb *had* is required to indicate 'past in the past'.

18 Adjectives have three degrees of comparison. These degrees are used to describe one thing or to compare two things, or three or more things. In this case more than three things are being compared (all the hats in the parade) and, therefore, *biggest* is the correct word to use.

19 The sentence is in the past tense and is referring to an event still further in the past, and so the helper verb *had* is used.

20 The text is written in the past tense and so *was* is the correct verb. Having explained what happened last year the writer has now moved to *This year*.

21 You need to recognise the correct order of words. An adjective (*ordinary*) usually goes before a noun. As the first word after the gap is the participle *intensified*, the last word in the answer should be a helper verb, in this case *has*.

22 You need to recognise the correct order of words. A sentence often begins with an article (*the*, *a* or *an*) followed by a noun. The first word after the gap is an adjective (*powerful*) and in this case the adverb *so* is used to describe it.

23 You need to recognise the correct order of words. The definite article *The* must be followed by a noun, in this case *discoveries*, which is the plural of the abstract noun *discovery*. The first word after the gap is the verb *revealed*, and the helper verb *have* can come before it.

24 Adjectives have three degrees of comparison. These degrees are used to describe one thing or to compare two things, or three or more things. In this case more than three things are being compared and, therefore, *best* is the correct word to use.

25 Adverbs describe a verb. They often end in ***ly***. The words *swiftly*, *quickly* and *hastily* are all adverbs ending in ***ly***. The adverb *fast* is unusual as it does not end in ***ly*** but it is also used to describe verbs (e.g. *she ran fast*).

GRAMMAR Mini Test 5

Pages 33–36

1 what **2** In Germany I came into contact with what **3** them **4** B **5** C **6** A **7** D **8** C **9** A **10** D **11** A **12** B **13** A **14** it **15** rock, dangerous, straight **16** simple, smooth **17** but **18** potential **19** found, associated **20** A **21** C **22** B **23** C **24** C **25** B, C

1 *What* is a pronoun that refers to people or things in general.

2 This question required you to recognise a correctly formed sentence. *What* is a relative pronoun and refers to people or things in general, in this case the spirit of a great land.

3 *Them* is a plural pronoun referring to people. It is used as the object of a verb or preposition.

4 An adjectival clause functions just like an adjective in that it gives extra information to a noun or noun group. In this example it is the Kombi that is being described further. The adjectival clause *that was 34 years old* gives extra information about the Kombi.

5 The word *as* is used as a conjunction in this sentence. It establishes the relationship between the dependent clause (*as a means of camouflage*) and the rest of the sentence.

6 The word *but* is a conjunction. The conjunction *but* indicates a connection between two independent clauses in the one sentence when the second clause somehow contradicts the first.

7 *That* is used here as an adjective referring to the new boy. It can be used with singular or plural nouns. *This* can only be used with singular nouns and *those* can only be used with plural nouns.

8 A sentence must have a main verb, in this case *believe*.

9 This is the only sentence with a subject (*John*) and a main verb (*opened*) in the active voice that describes an action and who performed it. B, C and D are in the passive voice and do not specify who performed the action (this is either unknown, unimportant or obvious).

10 This question required you to recognise a correctly formed sentence, with the verb agreeing with the subject.

11 This question required you to recognise a correctly formed sentence, with the verb agreeing with the subject of the sentence as well as being in the correct tense.

12 The relative pronoun *who* is used to refer to people; *that* or *which* is used for things. You also need to recognise that *they* is used for the subject of a verb and *them* for the object of a verb or preposition.

13 The word *because* is a conjunction. It establishes the relationship between the dependent clause and the rest of the sentence.

14 A pronoun is a word that takes the place of a noun or a proper noun (e.g. he, she, it, me). *It* is a pronoun and it stands in place of the word *canyoning*.

15 An adjective is a word used to describe a noun. In this example the adjectives are *rock*, *dangerous* and *straight*.

16 An adjective is a word used to describe a noun. In this example the adjectives are *simple* and *smooth*.

17 Conjunctions join ideas in a sentence. The conjunction *but* indicates a connection between the independent and dependent clauses.

18 An adjective is a word used to describe a noun. In this example the adjective is *potential*.

19 Look at the ending or form of verbs to identify their tense. In this sentence the past-tense verbs are *found* and *associated*.

20 To determine what tense a text is written in, pay attention to the form that the verbs take. In this example the simple past tense verbs *zoomed*, *instructed* and *reminded* indicate that this text is written in the past tense.

21 Third-person narrative is indicated by the use of *he*, *she*, *they* and the names of characters.

22 A metaphor is a non-literal description of an object, person or thing. In this example Belinda's eyes are described as zooming and falling on her husband's face, even though this does not literally occur.

23 A simile is a comparison between two things using *like* or *as*. In this example Belinda compares her exhaustion during childbirth to that felt by a marathon runner.

24 Personification is the attributing of human characteristics to non-human things. In this example the trees are given the human characteristics of dancing and waving.

25 Second-person narrative is indicated by the use of *you* and *your*.

Standard level questions

PUNCTUATION Mini Test 1

Pages 37–40

1 A **2** D **3** B **4** A **5** D **6** D **7** A **8** A, D **9** C, D **10** B **11** C **12** A **13** A **14** A **15** A, C **16** A **17** B **18** A **19** C **20** B **21** B **22** A **23** colon **24** colon **25** colon

1 The comma comes after the introductory clause and before the speech marks.

2 A capital letter is used at the beginning of proper nouns (names of places or people) and at the beginning of sentences. A capital letter must also be used for the title of a novel.

3 This sentence is a question and must have a question mark at the end.

4 This is an example of indirect speech. No actual words are spoken and so speech marks are not needed. No question is actually asked and so no question mark is needed.

5 The actual words spoken are enclosed in the speech marks (inverted commas). There is no comma needed after the spoken words as an exclamation mark is used to complete the sentence. A capital letter is not used at the start of the dialogue tag.

6 A capital letter is always used at the beginning of a sentence. *November* is a proper noun and must begin with a capital letter.

7 The comma comes after the phrase *After eating breakfast* to indicate that this is an adverbial phrase. An adverbial phrase describes when, where, how or why an action has taken place.

8 This is an example of indirect speech. No actual words are spoken and so speech marks are not needed. The tone of the sentence is apologetic; therefore, an exclamation mark is not needed.

9 Only the actual words spoken are enclosed in the speech marks (inverted commas). A comma after the spoken words and before the closing speech marks indicates that the dialogue tag is part of the sentence.

10 The word *it's* is a contraction of *it is* and therefore requires an apostrophe between ***t*** and ***s*** to indicate the missing ***i***. The noun *brothers* is a plural and does not require an apostrophe.

11 Remember: *it's* is a contraction of *it is*. Imagine that the apostrophe is a tiny letter ***i*** and this should help you to remember that *it's* is short for *it is*.

12 When something belongs to an individual (or thing), ownership is shown with ***'s***. In this case, global warming owns the impact on Earth.

13 Remember: *it's* is a contraction of *it is*. Imagine that the apostrophe is a tiny letter ***i*** and this should help you to remember that *it's* is short for *it is*.

14 *Don't* requires an apostrophe because it is a contraction of *do not*. The other options are second-person singular verbs and do not require an apostrophe: *belongs*, *likes*, *sits*.

15 Only the actual words spoken are enclosed in the speech marks (inverted commas). The dialogue tag, *exclaimed Tarma*, does not require speech marks.

16 *Jamie's* requires an apostrophe because it shows possession. *Its* does not require an apostrophe because it is showing possession and not a contraction of *it is*, which is spelt *it's*.

17 This is an example of indirect speech. No actual words are spoken and so speech marks are not needed. No question is actually asked and so no question mark is needed.

18 Only the actual words spoken are enclosed in the speech marks (inverted commas). A comma after the spoken words and before the closing speech mark indicates that the dialogue tag is part of the sentence. A comma must also come after the dialogue tag to indicate that the second part of the dialogue is still part of the one sentence.

19 There are two contractions in this statement that must be indicated by an apostrophe (*wouldn't* and *didn't*). There is no direct question asked and so a question mark is not needed.

20 This is an example of changing from direct to indirect speech. No actual words are spoken and so speech marks are not needed. The sentence is a statement and therefore does not require a question mark.

21 This is an example of changing from direct to indirect speech. No actual words are spoken and so speech marks are not needed.

22 This is an example of changing from direct to indirect speech. No actual words are spoken and so speech marks are not needed. The exclamation mark indicated that this statement was made with a tone of surprise and therefore a reference to the action of exclaiming is needed.

23 A colon (**:**) is used to indicate the introduction of a list (*the following items*). Commas are used to divide items in a list.

24 A colon (**:**) is used to indicate the introduction of a list.

25 A colon (**:**) is used to indicate the introduction of a list.

Intermediate level questions

PUNCTUATION Mini Test 2

Pages 41–44

1 A **2** B **3** C **4** C **5** A **6** A **7** A **8** D **9** B **10** A **11** D **12** D **13** B **14** B **15** C **16** C **17** A **18** C **19** C **20** A, C **21** A, C **22** …, Dr Johnston, … **23** *Surfache* **24** A, C **25** C, D

1 This is an example of direct speech. The comma comes after the introductory clause and before the speech marks.

2 This is an example of direct speech. The comma comes after the introductory clause and before the speech marks.

3 This is an example of direct speech. Only the actual words spoken are enclosed in the speech marks (inverted commas). The comma comes before the final speech mark and before the dialogue tag (*gasped Tabitha*).

4 This is an example of direct speech. Only the actual words spoken are enclosed in the speech marks (inverted commas). The comma comes before the final speech mark and before the dialogue tag (*proclaimed the politician*).

5 This is an example of direct speech. Only the actual words spoken are enclosed in the speech marks (inverted commas). The comma comes after the introductory clause (*Ashley asked*) and before the speech marks.

6 This is an example of indirect speech. No actual words are spoken and so speech marks are not needed.

7 This is an example of indirect speech. No actual words are spoken and so speech marks are not needed.

8 This is an example of indirect speech. No actual words are spoken and so speech marks are not needed.

9 This is a complex sentence and requires a comma to indicate a pause between the two parts of the sentence. A comma comes before the conjunction *but* to indicate a pause. Remember that proper nouns require capital letters.

10 This is an example of indirect speech. No actual words are spoken and so speech marks are not needed.

11 This is an example of direct speech. Only the actual words spoken are enclosed in the speech marks (inverted commas). The comma comes after the introductory clause (*With emotion in his voice, he cried*) and before the speech marks.

12 This is an example of direct speech. Only the actual words spoken are enclosed in the speech marks (inverted commas). The comma comes after the introductory clause (*Softly she whispered*) and before the speech marks.

13 This is an example of direct speech. Only the actual words spoken are enclosed in the speech marks (inverted commas). The comma comes before the final speech marks and before the dialogue tag (*declared the student passionately*).

14 This is an example of direct speech. Only the actual words spoken are enclosed in the speech marks (inverted commas). The comma comes before the final speech marks and before the dialogue tag (*apologised Ellie*).

15 This is an example of direct speech. The actual words spoken are enclosed in the speech marks (inverted commas). The comma comes after the introductory clause (*Quickly she admitted*) and before the speech marks.

16 This is an example of direct speech. Only the actual words spoken are enclosed in the speech marks (inverted commas). There are two complete sentences as part of this dialogue. The first sentence ends with the full stop after the dialogue tag.

17 This is an example of direct speech. Only the actual words spoken are enclosed in the speech marks (inverted commas). There are two complete sentences as part of this dialogue. The first sentence ends with the full stop after the dialogue tag.

18 This is an example of direct speech. Only the actual words spoken are enclosed in the speech marks (inverted commas). Remember that this is one complete sentence and, therefore, a capital letter is used only at the beginning of the sentence and for proper nouns (*Annie*).

19 The contraction *they'd* requires an apostrophe because it is a contraction of *they had*. Option A should be *were* and options B and C should be *their*.

20 A non-defining adjectival clause functions just like an adjective in that it gives extra information about a noun or a noun group. It is separated from the rest of the sentence by commas. In this example it is the Kombi van that is being described.

21 A non-defining adjectival phrase functions just like an adjective in that it gives extra information about a noun or a noun group. It is separated from the rest of the sentence by commas. In this example it is Eddie Mabo who is being described.

22 In this sentence the commas are placed on either side of *Dr Johnston* to indicate that this is the name of the dentist being discussed.

23 Italics can be used to show added emphasis in a sentence, to indicate the title of a text or to show that a word is from another language. In this case italics are used to indicate the title of a text. In this example it is the novel *Surfache* that is being described.

24 In Option A the commas are placed on either side of *John* to indicate this is additional information that could be deleted from the sentence without altering the meaning of the sentence. Similarly, in option C the comma is placed before *the man with the kindest heart* to indicate that this adjectival phrase is additional information to describe John which could be deleted without altering the meaning of the sentence.

25 In option C the commas are placed on either side of *Mr Anderson* to indicate that this adjectival phrase is additional information to describe the writer's fourth-grade teacher. In option D the commas are placed either side of *the teacher with bushy eyebrows* to indicate this is additional information about Mr Anderson.

PUNCTUATION Mini Test 3

Pages 45–48

1 A **2** B **3** C **4** D **5** B **6** C **7** C **8** C **9** D **10** A **11** A **12** B **13** D **14** semicolon **15** semicolon **16** semicolon **17** D **18** A, C **19** A, C **20** Easter is celebrated with chocolate; for many the origins of the holiday are being forgotten. **21** Jessie was unforgettable; her sister Ann was equally memorable. **22** Every night I have trouble getting to sleep; every morning I am tired. **23** Last night I watched four episodes; I've got two more to go. **24** A, B **25** A, C

Year 9 Literacy Mini Test Answers

1 If the direct speech comes first, the comma must be placed before the closing speech mark. You need to pay close attention to where a sentence begins and ends. This is only one sentence and a capital letter is used only for the beginning of the sentence and for the beginning of proper nouns (e.g. the speaker *Mrs McLeod*). A capital letter is not required for the beginning of the second half of the direct speech (*but*) as it is still part of the one sentence.

2 If the direct speech comes first, the comma must be placed before the closing speech mark. You need to pay close attention to where a sentence begins and ends. This is only one sentence and a capital letter is used only for the beginning of the sentence and for the beginning of proper nouns (e.g. the speaker *Bandy*). A capital letter is not required for the beginning of the second half of the direct speech (*although*) as it is still part of the one sentence.

3 If the direct speech comes first, the comma must be placed before the closing speech mark. You need to pay close attention to where a sentence begins and ends. This is only one sentence and a capital letter is used only for the beginning of the sentence and for the beginning of proper nouns (*Dad*). A capital letter is not required for the beginning of the second half of the direct speech (*so*) as it is still part of the one sentence.

4 If the direct speech comes first, the comma must be placed before the closing speech mark. You need to pay close attention to where a sentence begins and ends. This is only one sentence and a capital letter is used only for the beginning of the sentence. A capital letter is not required for the beginning of the second half of the direct speech (*because*) as it is still part of the one sentence.

5 If the direct speech comes first, the comma must be placed before the final speech mark. You need to pay close attention to where a sentence begins and ends. This is only one sentence and a capital letter is used only for the beginning of the sentence. A capital letter is not required for the beginning of the second half of the direct speech (*yet*) as it is still part of the one sentence.

6 If the direct speech comes first, the comma must be placed before the final speech mark. Just as in all sentences, capital letters must only be used at the beginning of a sentence or for the beginning of a proper noun. You need to pay close attention to where a sentence begins and ends.

7 If the direct speech comes first, the comma must be placed before the closing speech mark. Just as in all sentences, capital letters must only be used at the beginning of a sentence or for the beginning of a proper noun (*Sara*). You need to pay close attention to where a sentence begins and ends. This is only one sentence but as the second half of the direct speech begins with the pronoun *I*, it has a capital in this case.

8 Semicolons are used to separate pieces of information that are different, yet related. You should imagine that the semicolon is replacing a conjunction such as *and*.

9 Semicolons are used to separate pieces of information that are different, yet related. You should imagine that the semicolon is replacing a conjunction such as *and*.

10 Semicolons are used to separate pieces of information that are different, yet related. You should imagine that the semicolon is replacing a conjunction such as *and*.

11 A colon (:) is used to indicate the beginning of a list of items (*a large meal*). A semicolon is used to separate complete ideas and commas are used to separate items in a list.

12 A colon (:) is used to indicate the beginning of a list of items (*the following cities*). A semicolon is used to separate complete ideas and commas are used to separate items in a list.

13 If the direct speech comes first, the comma must be placed before the closing speech mark. You need to pay close attention to where a sentence begins and ends. This is only one sentence and a capital letter is used only for the beginning of the sentence and for the name of the speaker (*Claudia*). A capital letter is not required for the beginning of the second half of the direct speech (*but*) as it is still part of the one sentence.

14 Semicolons are used to separate pieces of information that are different, yet related. You should imagine that the semicolon is replacing a conjunction such as *and*.

15 Semicolons are used to separate pieces of information that are different, yet related. You should imagine that the semicolon is replacing a conjunction such as *and*.

16 Semicolons are used to separate pieces of information that are different, yet related. You should imagine that the semicolon is replacing a conjunction such as *and*.

17 Semicolons are used to separate pieces of information that are different, yet related. You should imagine that the semicolon is replacing a conjunction such as *and*.

18 Speech marks are used to enclose the words actually spoken in the sentence (*It's absolutely unbelievable! Where did you find it?*).

19 Speech marks are used to enclose the words actually spoken in the sentence (*I'm ashamed to admit it but I'm a chocoholic*).

20 Semicolons are used to separate pieces of information that are different, yet related. You should imagine that the semicolon is replacing a conjunction such as *and*.

21 Semicolons are used to separate pieces of information that are different, yet related. You should imagine that the semicolon is replacing a conjunction such as *and*.

22 Semicolons are used to separate pieces of information that are different, yet related. You should imagine that the semicolon is replacing a conjunction such as *and*.

23 Semicolons are used to separate pieces of information that are different, yet related. You should imagine that the semicolon is replacing a conjunction such as *and*.

24 A colon (**:**) is used to indicate the introduction of a list.

25 Only the actual words spoken are enclosed in speech marks (inverted commas). A comma after the spoken words and before the closing speech mark indicates that the dialogue tag (*pointed out Dad*) is part of the sentence. Sentence C is in indirect speech. No speech marks (inverted commas) are required as the actual words spoken are not recorded.

Advanced level questions

PUNCTUATION Mini Test 4

Pages 49–52

1 A **2** A **3** C **4** B **5** C **6** A **7** D **8** C **9** C **10** D **11** A **12** B **13** C **14** A **15** B **16** should've **17** could've **18** Isn't **19** would've **20** dashes **21** We're **22** I've **23** D **24** A, B **25** A, D

1 Only the actual words spoken are enclosed in speech marks (inverted commas). A comma after the spoken words and before the closing speech mark indicates that the dialogue tag (*the detective informed shocked Amanda*) is part of the sentence. Just as in all sentences, capital letters must only be used at the beginning of a sentence or for the beginning of a proper noun.

2 Only the actual words spoken are enclosed in speech marks (inverted commas). A comma after the spoken words and before the closing speech mark indicates that the dialogue tag (*whined Jessie*) is part of the second sentence. Just as in all sentences, capital letters must only be used at the beginning of a sentence or for the beginning of a proper noun.

3 If the sentence has an introductory clause before the direct speech (*In an authoritative tone, Professor Hewes informed the students*), a comma must follow this clause. Just as in all sentences, capital letters must only be used at the beginning of a sentence or for the beginning of a proper noun. *Psychology* is a proper noun as it is the name of a subject.

4 Speech marks come after the question mark. Just as in all sentences, capital letters must only be used at the beginning of a sentence or for the beginning of a proper noun.

5 Capital letters are used to begin sentences (e.g. *Upon*). Proper nouns are the names of particular people, places or things and always begin with a capital letter. Titles (e.g. *Detective*) also require a capital letter. Cities (e.g. *Washington DC* and *London*) must also begin with a capital letter.

6 Sentences begin with a capital letter. Proper nouns are the names of particular people, places or things and always begin with a capital letter.

7 Commas are placed after the word *boy* and the word *pyjamas* to indicate that this is an adjectival phrase that can be removed from the sentence without destroying the main meaning. An adjectival phrase functions just like an adjective in that it gives extra information about a noun or a noun group. In this sentence it is the little boy who is being described.

8 Commas can be used to separate a noun or phrase from the rest of the sentence. In this sentence the phrase *even the clever kids* provides extra information about the class but it can be removed from the sentence without affecting the main meaning.

9 Commas can be used to indicate where a main clause begins if a sentence starts with a subordinate clause or phrase. In this sentence the comma separates the adjectival phrase *Cycling as fast as his legs would move* from the main clause, *Harry sped down the hill*.

10 Commas can be used to indicate where a main clause begins if a sentence starts with a subordinate clause or phrase. In this sentence the comma separates the adjectival phrase *Thinking only of himself* from the main clause, *Peter began eating the chocolates in the box*.

11 There are two contractions in this statement that must be indicated by an apostrophe. A comma is incorrect in this sentence as the final clause, *who wasn't registered as a professional*, is defining which surgeons I wouldn't trust.

12 Only the actual words spoken are enclosed in speech marks (inverted commas). A comma after the spoken words and before the closing speech mark indicates that the dialogue tag is part of the sentence.

13 A semicolon is used to connect two complete sentences that have closely linked ideas.

14 The first sentence is an exclamation and must end with an exclamation mark. This does not require a comma. A full stop is used after *Ms Peters* to indicate the end of the first sentence.

15 This sentence is in indirect speech. No speech marks (inverted commas) are required as the actual words spoken are not recorded.

16 Apostrophes can be used to show a contraction or abbreviation. When two words are combined to make one shorter word by dropping some letters the apostrophe is used to illustrate where this contraction has occurred. Many students confuse the contraction *should've* with the two words *should of*. Remember that *should've* is a contraction of *should have*.

17 Apostrophes can be used to show a contraction or abbreviation. When two words are combined to make one shorter word by dropping some letters the apostrophe is used to illustrate where this contraction has occurred. Many students confuse the contraction *could've* with the two words *could of*. Remember that *could've* is a contraction of *could have*.

18 Apostrophes can be used to show a contraction or abbreviation. When two words are combined to make one shorter word by dropping some letters the apostrophe is used to illustrate where this contraction has occurred. *Isn't* is a contraction of *Is not*.

19 Apostrophes can be used to show a contraction or abbreviation. When two words are combined to make one shorter word by dropping some letters the apostrophe is used to illustrate where this contraction has occurred. *Would've* is a contraction of *would have*.

20 Dashes can be used to separate a phrase or clause from the main sentence. This phrase or clause often gives extra information. A sentence should be able to stand independently of the dashes.

21 Apostrophes can be used to show a contraction or abbreviation. When two words are combined to make one shorter word by dropping some letters the apostrophe is used to illustrate where this contraction has occurred. *We're* is a contraction of the two words *We are*.

22 Apostrophes can be used to show a contraction or abbreviation. When two words are combined to make one shorter word by dropping some letters the apostrophe is used to illustrate where this contraction has occurred. *I've* is a contraction of the two words *I have*.

23 Semicolons are used to connect pieces of information that are different, yet related.

24 Proper nouns require capital letters.

25 A phrase is a group of words that add information to an independent clause. Commas must be used to separate phrases from independent clauses.

PUNCTUATION Mini Test 5

Pages 53–55

1 B **2** A **3** A **4** B **5** A **6** A **7** B **8** B **9** performers **10** spectators **11** Joneses **12** where **13** who's **14** they're **15** couldn't **16** A **17** B **18** A **19** A **20** C **21** D **22** B **23** A **24** C **25** A

1 The word *car* is a noun and has direct ownership of its faulty accelerator and this is shown through the use of the possessive apostrophe. The word *deaths* is the plural form of the noun *death* and does not require an apostrophe.

2 The word *Japan* is a noun and has direct ownership of its forces and this is shown through the use of the possessive apostrophe. The words *forces, series* and *victories* are all plural nouns and do not require an apostrophe.

3 The word *laboratory* is a noun and has direct ownership of its equipment and this is shown through the use of the possessive apostrophe. The word *seeds* is the plural form of the noun *seed* and does not require an apostrophe.

4 The word *James* is a proper noun and has direct ownership of his parents and this is shown through the use of the possessive apostrophe. The words *parents* and *movies* are the plural forms of the nouns *parent* and *movie* and do not require an apostrophe.

5 The word *CSIRO* is a proper noun and has direct ownership of the partnership and this is shown through the use of the possessive apostrophe. The words *advances* and *technologies* are plural nouns and do not require an apostrophe. The word *numerous* is an adjective and adjectives never have an apostrophe.

Year 9 Literacy Mini Test Answers

6 The word *Craig* is a proper noun and has direct ownership of his ideas and this is shown through the use of the possessive apostrophe. The word *centres* is the plural form of the noun *centre* and does not require an apostrophe.

7 The word *school* is a noun and has direct ownership of its agriculture project and this is shown through the use of the possessive apostrophe. The word *deliveries* is the plural form of the noun *delivery* and does not require an apostrophe.

8 The word *individual* is a noun and has direct ownership of the decisions and this is shown through the use of the possessive apostrophe. The words *doctors* and *decisions* are plurals and do not require an apostrophe.

9 Apostrophes are used to indicate a contraction or possession. Plurals do not require apostrophes. In this sentence the word *performers* is the plural form of the noun *performer*.

10 Apostrophes are used to indicate a contraction or possession. Plurals do not require apostrophes. In this sentence the word *spectators* is the plural form of the noun *spectator*.

11 Apostrophes are used to indicate a contraction or possession. Plurals do not require apostrophes. In this sentence the word *Joneses* is the plural form of the proper noun *Jones*.

12 The word *where* is a homophone. It sounds the same as *wear* but has a different meaning.

13 Apostrophes can be used to show a contraction or abbreviation. When two words are combined to make one shorter word by dropping some letters the apostrophe is used to illustrate where this contraction has occurred. In this sentence the words *who* and *is* have been contracted to make the word *who's*.

14 Apostrophes can be used to show a contraction or abbreviation. When two words are combined to make one shorter word by dropping some letters the apostrophe is used to illustrate where this contraction has occurred. The words *they* and *are* have been contracted to create the word *they're*.

15 Apostrophes can be used to show a contraction or abbreviation. When two words are combined to make one shorter word by dropping some letters the apostrophe is used to illustrate where this contraction has occurred. In this sentence the words *could* and *not* have been contracted to make the word *couldn't*.

16 Semicolons are used to connect pieces of information that are different, yet related. You should imagine that the semicolon is replacing a conjunction such as *and*. Using a comma here is incorrect as it creates a 'comma splice'.

17 Semicolons are used to connect pieces of information that are different, yet related. You should imagine that the semicolon is replacing a conjunction such as *and*. Using a comma here is incorrect as it creates a 'comma splice'.

18 Dashes (**—**) are used to give added emphasis to the following information, or to indicate an interruption or an abrupt change of thought.

19 Dashes (**—**) are used to replace commas and parentheses to indicate that the words they enclose are extra information.

20 Ellipsis points (**...**) are used to indicate an interruption or missing information, or when a person's dialogue trails off.

21 Semicolons are used to separate pieces of information that are different, yet related. You should imagine that the semicolon is replacing a conjunction such as *and*. Using a comma here is incorrect as it creates a 'comma splice'.

22 Commas can be used to indicate where a main clause begins if a sentence starts with a subordinate clause or phrase. In this sentence the comma separates the adjectival phrase *With his heart beating fast* from the main clause, *Ryo pulled open the door*.

23 Commas can be used to indicate where a main clause begins if a sentence starts with a subordinate clause or phrase. In this sentence the comma separates the adjectival phrase *Dancing with glee* from the main clause, *the tiny girl accepted her certificate*.

24 Commas can be used to separate a noun or phrase from the rest of the sentence. In this sentence the phrase *even the very hot one last year* provides more information about the summers, but it is separated from the rest of the sentence as it is extra information that is not essential to the meaning.

25 Commas can be used to indicate where a main clause begins if a sentence starts with a subordinate clause or phrase. In this sentence the comma separates the adverbial phrase *Swiftly and softly* from the main clause, *Smaug the dragon flew over the mountain*.

Year 9 Literacy Mini Test Answers

Standard level questions

READING Mini Test 1: Narrative

Pages 56–57

Go to the **inside back cover** for a guide to question types.

1 C **2** D **3** C **4** A **5** D **6** A, D **7** C **8** D

1 This is a **fact-finding type of question**. The answer is a fact in the text. The text informs you that *A nursing home at night is a strange place, full of seemingly unearthly sounds* (e.g. see line 22).

2 This is a **judgement type of question**. You read that *there was still the possibility of a nurse walking down to his ward, doing the final checks before leaving for a warm meal and comfortable bed* (see lines 16–20) and then combine that information with your own knowledge that when the nurses leave no-one else will be around.

3 This is a **fact-finding type of question**. The answer is a fact in the text. The text informs you that *A nursing home at night is a strange place* (see line 22).

4 This is a **fact-finding type of question**. The answer is a fact in the text. The text informs you that *He had been working here for six months. During this time he had become accustomed to the eeriness of his environment and the fact that one must always expect the unexpected* (see lines 32–33).

5 This is a **fact-finding type of question**. The answer is a fact in the text. The text informs you that *Sitting at his small desk and studying the roster for the coming week, JT was startled by a new sound. Shuffling. Putting down his handful of papers, he turned his attention to the hallway behind him* (see lines 26–27).

6 This is a **judgement type of question**. You read that JT was feeling unsure in his workplace because it was creepy (see lines 22–25) and then combine this with your own knowledge that suspense and the unknown are appealing to many people.

7 This is an **inferring type of question**. To find the answer you have to 'read between the lines'. You read *He knew this place and the way it made his heart beat a little faster. He expected his breath to catch in his throat at the smallest sound* (see lines 7–13) and then combine this information with your own knowledge of how people feel unsure about the unknown and yet become accustomed to unusual occurrences.

8 This is a **fact-finding type of question**. The answer is a fact in the text. The text informs you that *During this time he had become accustomed to the eeriness of his environment and the fact that one must always expect the unexpected* (see lines 32–33).

READING Mini Test 2: Procedure

Pages 58–59

1 B **2** A **3** C **4** C, D **5** C **6** A **7** B **8** D

1 This is **a judgement type of question**. The text is a series of instructions on how to make a paper plane, and you combine that with your own knowledge that instructions help people to learn.

2 This is a **fact-finding type of question**. The answer is a fact in the text: *Take an A4 sheet of paper and fold it in half* (see step 1).

3 This is a **fact-finding type of question**. The answer is a fact in the text. You read that *This will produce a 45 degree angle* (see step 2).

4 This is a **judgement type of question**. You read the instructions about how to create a paper plane, and you combine that with your own knowledge that people who want to learn read instructional texts.

5 This is a **judgement type of question**. Step 4 says *Do (3) again for both sides* and you combine that with your own knowledge that *do again* means 'repeat' and that *(3)* refers to step 3.

6 This is a **judgement type of question**. You read in step 2 *Fold the short edge of one side down to the first fold* and combine that with your understanding that the second diagram is showing how to fold the shorter edge down.

7 This is a **fact-finding type of question**. The answer is a fact in the text. You must count the number of times you fold the paper.

8 This is an **inferring type of question**. To find the answer you have to 'read between the lines'. You are told *Now throw!* (see step 6) and need to combine this with your own knowledge that paper planes are thrown in order to make them fly.

Intermediate level questions

READING Mini Test 3: Procedure

Pages 60–61

1 B **2** A **3** A, E **4** C **5** B **6** A **7** D **8** D

1 This is a **fact-finding type of question**. The answer is a fact in the text. Step 4 tells you that *If the wheel will not come free, it could be that corrosion has caused the wheel to stick* (see lines 22–23).

2 This is a **judgement type of question**. Step 1 tells you to *make sure you pull over in a safe area, clear of passing traffic (see lines 2–3)*. Combine this information with your own knowledge that changing a tyre on a busy road could result in an accident.

3 This is an **inferring type of question**. To find the answer you have to 'read between the lines'. You are told that you may need to *give the wheel a kick in order to free it (see line 24)*. Combine this information with your own knowledge that tyres are often difficult to change.

4 This is an **inferring type of question**. To find the answer you have to 'read between the lines'. You are told that when removing a jack you must *keep a straight arm and back, and with the wheel brace horizontal to the ground, use the weight of your body to tighten all of the wheel nuts (see lines 34–35)*. Combine this with your own understanding that such detailed instructions are *specific*.

5 This is a **judgement type of question**. Look at the third image. It shows a wheel brace placed on a wheel nut. Combine this information with your own knowledge that the wheel nuts must be loosened using the wheel brace.

6 This is a **judgement type of question**. In step 2 you are given very specific instructions on where to place the jack: *look for small notches or grooves on the underside of your car (see line 8)*. Combine this information with your own knowledge that such specific instructions are given when people find a task difficult.

7 This is a **judgement type of question**. You are given a series of five images to support the written text. Each image shows a different step in the procedure of changing a car tyre. Combine this information with your own knowledge that images can help people better understand a procedure.

8 This is a **judgement type of question**. In step 1 you are told to *pull over in a safe area (see lines 2–3)*, in step 2 you are told how to place the jack in the right spot *(see lines 8–9)* and in step 6 you are told to *use the weight of your body to tighten all of the wheel nuts (see lines 34–35)*. Combine this information with your own knowledge that this procedure is full of important steps that must be followed to successfully change a car tyre.

READING Mini Test 4: Response

Pages 62–63

1 B 2 D 3 A 4 B 5 B 6 A 7 C 8 A, B

1 This is an **inferring type of question**. To find the answer you have to 'read between the lines'. You are told that the speaker thinks *the fate of our Indigenous people* is *not really funny (see lines 5–6)*. Combine this information with your own knowledge that the word *fate* means 'destiny', and your understanding that the Guringai people were killed or fled their homeland.

2 This is a **judgement type of question**. The speaker says that *We are the future of our nation and we must work together to remember and celebrate those who came before us (see lines 29–30)*. Combine this information with your own knowledge that young people are the future of a country.

3 This is an **inferring type of question**. To find the answer you have to 'read between the lines'. You are told that Bungaree *sailed with Matthew Flinders, around the entire coast of Australia*, after which the speaker asks *How cool is that? (see lines 22–23)*.

4 This is a **judgement type of question**. At the end of the speech the speaker says, *So, how can you help to celebrate the traditional custodians of our land? (see line 27)*. Combine this information with your own knowledge that questions are asked by speakers to prompt their audience to think about what is being asked.

5 This is an **inferring type of question**. To find the answer you have to 'read between the lines'. You are told that *I want to share with you some of the beautiful stories of the traditional custodians of the land (see lines 7–8)* and you need to combine that with your own knowledge that stories are part of the Guringai culture and your understanding that individuals refer to something as *beautiful* when they value it.

6 This is a **judgement type of question**. The phrase *the giants of the sea (see lines 15–16)* is a metaphor used to describe whales and sharks. A metaphor is an example of figurative language.

7 This is an **inferring type of question**. To find the answer you have to 'read between the lines'. The speaker asks *How cool is that? (see line 23)* and you need to combine your own knowledge that the word *cool* means 'great' and your understanding that individuals only refer to something as *cool* when they are impressed by it.

8 This is an **inferring type of question**. To find the answer you have to 'read between the lines'. The speaker asks *how can you help to celebrate the traditional custodians of our land? (see line 27)*.

Combine this information with your own knowledge that young people are responsible for the future and your understanding that the speaker's call to action is asking for young people to remember the Guringai people.

READING Mini Test 5: Poem

Pages 64–65

1 B **2** C **3** C **4** B **5** D **6** A **7** Answers will vary **8** D

1 This is an **inferring type of question.** To find the answer you have to 'read between the lines'. You are told that despite the king being powerful when he was alive, now *Nothing beside remains (see line 12)*. Combine this information with your own knowledge that all humans must die and that artworks can survive many years longer than humans.

2 This is a **judgement type of question**. The poet tells you that the *sculptor well those passions read (see line 6)* and you need to combine that with your knowledge that *passions* is often used to mean 'temper'.

3 This is an **inferring type of question**. To find the answer you have to 'read between the lines'. You need to know that the word *lifeless (see line 7)* means 'without power' and combine that with your understanding that in death all individuals are powerless.

4 This is a **judgement type of question**. The poet describes the *shattered visage* that is *half sunk* in the sand *(see line 4)*. You need to know that a visage is a face and that *shattered* means 'broken'.

5 This is a **judgement type of question**. The poet describes the *wrinkled lip and sneer of cold command (see line 5)* as well as the statue being a *colossal wreck (see line 13)*. Combine this information with your own knowledge that individuals are often amazed by large things and contemplative of how these come to be destroyed.

6 This is a **judgement type of question**. The poet tells you that *Nothing beside remains (see line 12)* of this king and his kingdom other than the statue created by a sculptor who knew the king well. Combine this information with your own knowledge that human beings are mortal and that art can be immortal.

7 This is a **judgement type of question**. Combine your knowledge of figurative language with your reading of the text to work out the answer. Figurative language is the use of metaphor, simile or personification to create imagery. Possible correct answers include: *two vast and trunkless legs of stone (line 2), stamped on these lifeless things (line 7), the hand that mocked them and the heart that fed (line 8).*

8 This is a **judgement type of question**. The poet uses the metaphor *The hand that mocked them and the heart that fed (see line 8)* to describe the temperament of the king. Combine this information with your own knowledge that a metaphor is comparing two different things for effect.

READING Mini Test 6: Narrative

Pages 66–67

1 D **2** A **3** D **4** D **5** D **6** D **7** Answers will vary **8** A

1 This is an **inferring type of question.** To find the answer you have to 'read between the lines'. You are told that the boy's sister Gemma spilt orange juice on the doona and that his mother was angry as a result *(see lines 3–4)*. Combine this information with your own knowledge that people only get angry when something they value is ruined and your understanding that the boy knows his mother is angry because of the spill on the doona.

2 This is a **fact-finding type of question**. The answer is a fact in the text. It says that *the fever broke during the night (see lines 9–10)*.

3 This is an **inferring type of question.** To find the answer you have to 'read between the lines'. You are told that the doona is old and has a *yellow stain at the bottom (see line 3)*. Combine this information with your own knowledge that people often think old things should be thrown away and your understanding that young people like new things.

4 This is an **inferring type of question.** To find the answer you have to 'read between the lines'. You are told that the boy has suffered from a bad fever that caused him to collapse and spend 24 hours in bed. The boy tells you that *I realise that life is a light I don't want to let go of for a long, long time (see lines 43–44)*. Combine this information with your own knowledge that very high fevers can be fatal and your understanding that people who come close to death often appreciate life more.

5 This is a **judgement type of question**. In the second paragraph the narrator describes his bedroom—*Glancing around my haven I see that over the years I've accumulated some pretty cool stuff (see lines 8–9)*—and later he informs you that he has come to a *moment of rumination (see line 42)*. Combine this information with your own knowledge that people often become reflective when they survive a major illness.

6 This is a **judgement type of question**. The narrator describes his room—*In here it's dark and stuffy* (see line 7)—and says *The thick doona has kept me warm and secure for the last 12 hours* (see lines 1–2). Combine this information with your own knowledge that people's bedrooms are often safe places to retreat to and you can work out that the detailed description of the boy's bedroom helps to build an atmosphere of security and familiarity.

7 This is a **judgement type of question**. Combine your knowledge of figurative language with your reading of the text to work out the answer. Figurative language is the use of metaphor, simile or personification to create imagery. Possible correct answers include: *my whole room's a bit of an exhibition of me* (lines 4–5), *the birds are tiring of their morning songs* (line 7), *since the darkness dropped* (lines 28–29), *one massive contraction of aching and throbbing muscles* (lines 31–32) and *life is a light that I don't want to let go of* (line 43).

8 This is a **judgement type of question**. The narrator suffers a very serious fever and comes close to death: *the darkness dropped* (see line 29). Combine this information with your own knowledge that life-threatening illness can affect young people.

Advanced level questions

READING Mini Test 7: Poem

Pages 68–69

1 D **2** D **3** B **4** A **5** 4, 5, 7, 1, 3, 6, 2 **6** A **7** C **8** C

1 This is an **inferring type of question**. To find the answer you have to 'read between the lines'. You are told that a young man is *sighing like furnace* (see line 10). Combine this information with your own knowledge that furnaces are hot like people in love, and your understanding that people become flustered when they are in love and find it difficult to express themselves.

2 This is a **judgement type of question**. When you read the last line of the poem you notice the word *sans* is repeated four times in the one line (see line 28) and that this is the only example of repetition of this type in the poem. Combine this information with your own knowledge that repetition forces people to pay attention to particular ideas.

3 This is a **judgement type of question**. When you read the poem you notice that Shakespeare is listing the seven stages that individuals experience in life. Combine this information with your own knowledge that reflecting on life and death can be difficult.

4 This is an **inferring type of question**. To find the answer you have to 'read between the lines'. You are told that the soldier seeks *the bubble reputation / Even in the cannon's mouth* (see lines 14–15) and need to combine that with your own knowledge that bubbles are temporary and your understanding of the desires that many young men have to be well known and respected whatever the cost.

5 This is a **fact-finding type of question**. The answer is in the text. You read: *the infant, Mewling* [crying baby] (lines 5–6); *whining* [complaining] *school-boy* (line 7); *the lover* (line 9); *a soldier* (line 11); *the justice* (line 15); *the lean and slipper'd pantaloon…sound* [old man] (lines 20–25); *second childishness… sans teeth, sans eyes…* [second childhood] (line 27). (*Sans* means 'without'.)

6 This is an **inferring type of question**. To find the answer you have to 'read between the lines'. You are told that *All the world's a stage, / And all the men and women merely players* (see lines 1–2). Combine this information with your own knowledge that actors must perform many different roles and your understanding that people act in certain ways at different times of their lives.

7 This is a **judgement type of question**. When you read the extract you notice that Shakespeare describes the young boy as *creeping like snail / Unwillingly to school* (see lines 8–9) and the lover as *Sighing like furnace, with a woeful ballad, / Made to his mistress' eyebrow* (see lines 10–11). Combine this information with your own understanding that young boys walk very slowly when going to school and that young men are silly when they're in love.

8 This is an **inferring type of question**. To find the answer you have to 'read between the lines'. You are told that *one man in his time plays many parts* and *Last scene of all, / That ends this strange eventful history* (see lines 4 and 25–26). Combine this information with your own knowledge that each of these stages of man is a fairly accurate picture of man's life and your understanding that human behaviour often intrigues creative people.

READING Mini Test 8: Visual text

Pages 70–71

1 A **2** (possible answer) The boy is unhappy, confused and unsure. **3** B **4** B **5** A, E **6** D **7** A **8** (possible answers) Young people like technology. Young people dress casually. Young people experience problems with relationships.

Year 9 Literacy Mini Test Answers

1 This is an **inferring type of question**. To find the answer you have to 'read between the lines'. You read that the first boy feels he can't be friends with the second boy because he doesn't *know how much common ground we have now (see frame 1)*. Combine this information with your own knowledge that *common ground* means 'things people have in common' and your understanding that the iPhone is something the two will have in common soon.

2 This is a **judgement type of question**. In the first frame the second boy says *OUCH* and then says nothing for two frames. Combine this information with your own knowledge that people are often silent when they are unsure or confused.

3 This is an **inferring type of question**. To find the answer you have to 'read between the lines'. You are told that the first boy is finding it hard to find *common ground (see frame 1)* with the second boy and then he becomes excited when the second boy states *I'm getting an iPhone (see frame 4)*. Combine this information with your own knowledge that often technology is a common ground for young people and your understanding that having the same phone means that the two boys can talk about the same thing.

4 This is a **judgement type of question**. After the first boy says that he doesn't think he can be friends with the second boy, the second boy replies *OUCH (see frame 1)*. Combine this information with your own knowledge that it is painful to lose a friend over something trivial.

5 This is a **judgement type of question**. The facial expressions of the second boy lack emotion, despite the fact that he is possibly losing his friend, and the facial expression of the first boy when he discovers that his friend is also getting an iPhone is an exaggerated smile *(see frame 4)*. Combine this information with your own knowledge that young people bond over trivial things like iPhones and your understanding adults are often cynical about what they perceive to be the superficiality of teenagers' friendships and love of technology.

6 This is an **inferring type of question**. To find the answer you have to 'read between the lines'. Frames 2 and 3 are identical, with both boys staring at each other expressionlessly. Combine this information with your own knowledge that the boys are not talking because their friendship may be ending and your understanding that ending a friendship can be tense.

7 This is an **inferring type of question**. To find the answer you have to 'read between the lines'. You are shown three frames with the boy expressionless *(see frames 1–3)*. These are in contrast to the final frame where he is smiling because he has discovered his friend is also getting an iPhone. Combine this information with your own knowledge that young people often base their relationships on things they have in common.

8 This is a **judgement type of question**. There are a number of possible answers to this question. The cartoonist draws both boys wearing casual clothes. He also shows the difficulty of establishing a relationship that isn't based on similar material possessions. Combine this information with your own knowledge that these are not true of all young people and are simply generalisations.

READING Mini Test 9: Poem

Pages 72–73

1 (possible answers) I wandered lonely as a cloud, Fluttering and dancing in the breeze, Continuous as the stars that shine, Tossing their heads in sprightly dance, The waves beside them danced, They flash upon that inward eye, then my heart with pleasure fills, / And dances with the daffodils
2 A **3** D **4** 4, 2, 1, 3 **5** B **6** C **7** C **8** A

1 This is a **judgement type of question**. There are a number of correct answers for this question as this poem features many examples of figurative language. Poets use figurative language to create images of how they see the world. Combine this information with your own knowledge of the definitions of simile, metaphor and personification to identify an example of figurative language in the poem.

2 This is an **inferring type of question**. To find the answer you have to 'read between the lines'. You are told that the poet is *lonely as a cloud (see line 1)* and then he is *gay, / In such a jocund company (see lines 15–16)*. Combine this information with your own knowledge that often lonely people are sad and your understanding that being in the company of other people (or in this case nature) can make people happy.

3 This is an **inferring type of question**. To find the answer you have to 'read between the lines'. You are told that the poet is lonely *(see line 1)* but later feels happy in the presence of the flowers in real life and in his imagination *(see lines 15–16 and 23)*. Combine this information with your own knowledge that being lonely is not something people desire and your understanding that poets often spend time alone but seek inspiration from nature.

4 This is a **fact-finding type of question**. The answer is in the text. You read that the poet was *lonely* (line 1) *When all at once I saw a crowd, … of golden daffodils* (lines 3–4); *Ten thousand I saw* (line 11); *A poet could not but be gay* (line 15); *when on my couch I lie…And then my heart with pleasure fills* (lines 19–23).

5 This is an **inferring type of question**. To find the answer you have to 'read between the lines'. You are told that the daffodils *flash upon that inward eye* (see line 21) and combine that with your knowledge that the imagination is thought to be in the mind's eye and your understanding that the poet's memory of the daffodils is powerful so that they appear to him even when he isn't thinking of them.

6 This is a **judgement type of question**. The first three stanzas describe the poet watching the daffodils: *The waves beside them danced; but they / Out-did the sparkling waves in glee* (see lines 13–14). However, the last stanza is describing the poet at home, remembering the daffodils, *when on my couch I lie / In vacant or in pensive mood* (see lines 19–20). Combine this information with your own knowledge that remembering an event requires an individual to be reflective.

7 This is a **judgement type of question**. Compare the first line *I wandered lonely as a cloud* with the line *A poet could not but be gay / In such a jocund company* (see lines 15–16). Combine this information with your own knowledge that being alone and being in the company of something beautiful can alter a person's mood.

8 This is an **inferring type of question**. To find the answer you have to 'read between the lines'. You are told that the daffodils are *jocund company* (see line 16). Combine this information with your own knowledge that the word *gay* means 'happy' and your understanding that the beauty of nature can make people feel happy.

READING Mini Test 10: Narrative

Pages 74–75

1C 2A 3C 4D 5C 6A 7D 8A

1 This is a **judgement type of question**. You read the narrator's description of *the mysterious, far-reaching hair-line trail, the absence of sun from the sky, the tremendous cold, and the strangeness and weirdness of it all* (see lines 31–32). Combine this information with your own knowledge that these things are often seen as obstacles to human survival.

2 This is an **inferring type of question**. To find the answer you have to 'read between the lines'. You are told about the difficult weather conditions and natural landscape the man is faced with. Combine this information with your own knowledge that these things can be obstacles to human survival.

3 This is an **inferring type of question**. To find the answer you have to 'read between the lines'. You are told that there seemed to be *an intangible pall over the face of things* (see line 5). Combine that with your own knowledge that *intangible* means 'cannot be touched' and a pall is the covering over a coffin and your understanding that both suggest bad things.

4 This is a **judgement type of question**. You read that the man was travelling along *a dim and little traveled trail* by himself (see line 2). Combine this information with your own knowledge that travelling alone in remote places can be dangerous.

5 This is a **judgement type of question**. You read that *He was quick and alert to the things of life, but only in the things, and not in the significances* (see lines 34–35). Combine this information with your own knowledge that being alone and enduring great physical hardships often lead people to consider the purpose of their existence.

6 This is an **inferring type of question**. To find the answer you have to 'read between the lines'. You are told that *North and south, as far as his eye could see, it was unbroken white* (see lines 19–21). Combine this information with your own knowledge that humans find it difficult to survive in such cold conditions and your understanding that nature's power is impressive.

7 This is an **inferring type of question**. To find the answer you have to 'read between the lines'. You are told that *It had been days since he had seen the sun* (see line 7). Combine this information with your own knowledge that the sun is circular and your understanding that the sun is desired by those walking through snow.

8 This is a **judgement type of question**. You are told *he paused for breath at the top, excusing the act to himself by looking at his watch* (see lines 3–4). Combine that with your own knowledge that people get tired walking in difficult terrain and would require a rest, and your understanding that someone who has to excuse stopping to himself would not like to admit he needs to rest.

Year 9 Literacy Mini Test Answers

WRITING Mini Test 1: Persuasive text

Page 77

Marking checklist for a persuasive text

Tick each correct point.
Read the student's work through once to get an overall view of their response.

Focus on general points

- ☐ Did it make sense?
- ☐ Did it flow? Were the points logical and relevant?
- ☐ Did the points arouse any reactions?
- ☐ Was the body of the writing mainly in the third person?
- ☐ Did you want to read on?
- ☐ Were the arguments convincing?
- ☐ Has the writer been assertive (e.g. *is* is used rather than a less definite term)?
- ☐ Was the handwriting readable?
- ☐ Was the writing style suitable (i.e. objective, and not casual or dismissive) for a persuasive text?

Now focus on the detail. Read each of the following points and find out whether the work has these features.

Focus on content

- ☐ Did the opening sentence(s) focus on the topic?
- ☐ Was the writer's point of view established early in the writing?
- ☐ Did the writer include any evidence to support his or her opinion?
- ☐ Did the writer include information relevant to his or her experiences?
- ☐ Were the points/arguments raised by the writer easy to follow?
- ☐ Did the writing follow the format with an introduction, the body of the text and a conclusion?
- ☐ Were personal opinions included?
- ☐ Was the concluding paragraph relevant to the topic?

Focus on structure, vocabulary, grammar, spelling and punctuation

- ☐ Was there a variety of sentence lengths, types and beginnings?
- ☐ Was a new paragraph started for each additional argument or point?
- ☐ Has the writer used any similes (e.g. *as clear as crystal*) to stress a point raised?
- ☐ Did the writer avoid approximations such as *probably*, *perhaps* and *maybe*?
- ☐ Did the writer use such phrases as *I know* … and *It is important to* …?
- ☐ Did the writer refer to the question in the points raised? (A good way to do this is to use the keywords from the question in the introduction.)
- ☐ Has the writer used any less common words correctly?
- ☐ Was indirect speech used correctly?
- ☐ Were adjectives used to improve descriptions (e.g. *expensive buildings*)?
- ☐ Were adverbs used effectively (e.g. *firstly*)?
- ☐ Were capital letters used where they should have been?
- ☐ Was punctuation correct?
- ☐ Was the spelling of words correct?

Writing samples

Go to **pages 160–162** for Standard, Intermediate and Advanced Writing samples for Mini Test 1.

WRITING Mini Test 2: Narrative text

Page 79

Marking checklist for a narrative text

Tick each correct point.
Read the student's work through once to get an overall view of their response.

Focus on general points

- ☐ Did it make sense?
- ☐ Did it flow?
- ☐ Did the story arouse any feeling?
- ☐ Did you want to read on?
- ☐ Did the story create suspense?
- ☐ Was the handwriting readable?

Now focus on the detail. Read each of the following points and find out whether the work has these features.

Focus on content

- ☐ Did the opening sentence(s) 'grab' the reader's attention?
- ☐ Was the setting established (i.e. where the action takes place)?
- ☐ Was the reader told when the action takes place?
- ☐ Was it clear who the main character(s) is/are? (The story can be in the first person using *I*.)
- ☐ Was there a 'problem' to be solved early on in the writing?
- ☐ Was a complication or unusual event introduced?
- ☐ Did descriptions refer to any of the senses (e.g. *cold air*, *strange smell*)?
- ☐ Was there a climax (a more exciting part near the end)?
- ☐ Was the conclusion (resolution of the problem) believable?

Year 9 Literacy Mini Test Answers

Focus on structure, vocabulary, grammar, spelling and punctuation

- ☐ Was there a variety of sentence types, lengths and beginnings?
- ☐ Was a new paragraph begun for each change in time, place or action?
- ☐ Were conversations or direct speech in separate paragraphs for each change of speaker?
- ☐ Was a range of *said* words used for speech?
- ☐ Were any similes used (e.g. *as clear as glass*)?
- ☐ Were less common words used correctly?
- ☐ Were adjectives used to improve descriptions (e.g. *careful steps*)?
- ☐ Were adverbs used to make actions more interesting (e.g. *shook his head sadly*)?
- ☐ Were capital letters used where they should have been?
- ☐ Was punctuation correct?
- ☐ Was the spelling correct?

Writing samples

Go to **pages 163–165** for Standard, Intermediate and Advanced Writing samples for Mini Test 2.

WRITING Mini Test 3: Recount text

Page 81

Marking checklist for a recount

Tick each correct point.
Read the student's work through once to get an overall view of their response.

Focus on general points

- ☐ Did it make sense?
- ☐ Did it flow?
- ☐ Did the recount arouse any feeling?
- ☐ Did you want to read on? (Were the events interesting?)
- ☐ Was the handwriting readable?

Now focus on the detail. Read each of the following points and find out whether the work has these features.

Focus on content

- ☐ Did the opening sentence(s) introduce the subject of the recount?
- ☐ Was the setting established (i.e. where the action took place)?
- ☐ Was the reader told when the action took place?
- ☐ Was it clear who the main character(s) was/were?
- ☐ Were personal pronouns used (e.g. *I*, *we*, *our*)?
- ☐ Were the events recorded in chronological (time) order?
- ☐ Was the recount in the past tense?
- ☐ Did the writing include some personal comments on the events (e.g. *feeling cold*, *disappointed*)?
- ☐ Did descriptions make any reference to any of the senses (e.g. *loud commentary*, *salty air*)?
- ☐ Were interesting details included?
- ☐ Was the conclusion satisfactory?

Focus on structure, vocabulary, grammar, spelling and punctuation

- ☐ Was there a variety of sentence lengths and beginnings?
- ☐ Was a new paragraph begun for every change in time, place or action?
- ☐ Were subheadings used (optional)?
- ☐ Were adjectives used to improve descriptions (e.g. *frozen ground*)?
- ☐ Were adverbs used to make actions more interesting (e.g. *swam strongly*)?
- ☐ Were adverbs used for time changes (e.g. *later*, *soon*, *then*)?
- ☐ Were similes used (e.g. *as clear as glass*)?
- ☐ Were less common words used correctly?
- ☐ Was direct and indirect speech used appropriately?
- ☐ Were capital letters used where they should have been?
- ☐ Was punctuation correct?
- ☐ Was the spelling correct?

Writing samples

Go to **pages 166–168** for Standard, Intermediate and Advanced Writing samples for Mini Test 3.

CONVENTIONS OF LANGUAGE

Pages 83–86

Sample Test 1

1 D **2** A **3** C **4** D **5** A **6** A **7** A **8** C **9** C **10** D **11** C **12** D **13** A **14** about **15** on **16** ellipsis **17** him **18** The fortnightly inspection, which was designed to detect faulty wiring, was a complete success. **19** *No Country for Old Men* **20** they **21** bitter **22** Correct punctuation: Each December we pack up our car and head north. **23** weight, protein, foods **24** B, D **25** her, one **26** queen **27** guard **28** piling **29** safari **30** alpha **31** country **32** eternity **33** burglar **34** permission **35** officially **36** dramatic **37** easily **38** canoes **39** wonderful **40** thrive **41** causeway **42** bedtime **43** carnival **44** parcel **45** pigtails **46** disregard **47** department **48** catch **49** heroic **50** encourage

1 A comma comes before the second speech mark in direct speech. A full stop is not used at the end of spoken words if the dialogue tag follows, as it is all part of one sentence. Remember that proper nouns must have capital letters.

2 With the verb *brought* (the past participle of the irregular verb *bring*) you need a 'helper'—another verb to 'help' it. *Have, has* and *had* can be helping verbs.

3 This question requires you to select the correct reflexive pronoun. A reflexive pronoun is created by adding ***self*** or ***selves*** to a personal pronoun (*him, her, them*) and refers back to the subject of a sentence. In this example the subject is *She* and so the correct reflexive pronoun is *herself.*

4 The actual words spoken are enclosed in the speech marks (inverted commas). A comma is not needed because a question mark has been used. The question mark comes inside the speech marks.

5 This is an example of direct speech. Only the actual words spoken are enclosed in the speech marks (inverted commas). Proper nouns require a capital letter.

6 Conjunctions are words that connect sentences or parts of sentences. In this example the conjunction *even though* connects the dependent clause *we had no money for the bond* to the independent clause *We began looking for a new place to live.*

7 In direct speech a comma comes after the introductory dialogue tag and before the speech marks. An exclamation mark is used to indicate the distress of the speaker.

8 Italics can be used to show added emphasis in a sentence, to indicate the title of a text or to show that a word is from another language. In this case italics are used to emphasise the adjective *only*.

9 The helper verb *can* shows ability to do something. In this case it is used with the verb *affect*.

10 Conjunctions join ideas in a sentence. The conjunction *and* indicates a connection between two independent clauses in the one sentence. The subject (*People*) and the helper verb *must* are understood from the first part of the sentence and so the correct form of the verb is *put*.

11 The preposition *over* must be followed by a noun or pronoun and so the correct word is the verbal noun *having.*

12 Italics can be used to show added emphasis in a sentence, to indicate the title of a text or to show that a word is from another language. In this case italics are used to indicate that a word is from another language.

13 In this sentence the word *Yesterday* is an adverbial phrase and is separated from the independent clause *I went to the promenade for a stroll* by a comma.

14 Prepositions show the relationship between a noun or pronoun and another word. In this example the preposition *about* shows the relationship between *recycling* and *question.*

15 Prepositions show the relationship between a noun or pronoun and another word. In this example the preposition *on* shows the relationship between *playing board games* and *rainy evening.*

16 Ellipsis points (**...**) are used to indicate an interruption, missing information or when a person's dialogue trails off.

17 A pronoun is a word that takes the place of a noun or a proper noun (e.g. he, she, it, me). *Him* is a pronoun and it refers to the *weatherman.*

18 A non-defining adjectival clause functions just like an adjective in that it gives extra information about a noun or a noun group. It is separated from the rest of the sentence by commas. In this example it is the inspection that is being described.

Year 9 Literacy Sample Online-style Test Answers

19 Italics can be used to show added emphasis in a sentence, to indicate the title of a text or to show that a word is from another language. In this case italics are used to indicate the title of a text.

20 A pronoun is a word that takes the place of a noun or a proper noun (e.g. he, she, it, me). *They* is a pronoun and it refers to the two women Alison and Jade.

21 Adjectives are words used to describe nouns. The adjective *bitter* describes the noun *wind*.

22 The word *December* is a proper noun, and requires a capital letter. This is a statement, and should end with a full stop.

23 A noun is a word used to refer to people, places or things. In this sentence there are three nouns: *foods*, *protein* and *weight*.

24 In sentence D the cause is *Josh was afraid of being burnt* and the effect is *he threw the burning stick into the fire really quickly*. In sentence B the cause is *rain was falling very hard on the roof of our car* and the effect is *giving me a headache*.

25 A pronoun is a word that takes the place of a noun or a proper noun (e.g. he, she, it, me). *Her* is a pronoun and it refers to Kathy. *One* is a pronoun and refers to a monkey.

26 The letters ***qu*** in this word combine to create a ***kw*** sound.

27 The letters ***ua*** combine to create a long ***a*** sound.

28 This word is made up of the root word *pile* and the suffix ***ing***. Remember that you must drop the ***e*** before adding ***ing***.

29 To give yourself a greater chance of spelling success, you must break multi-syllable words into smaller parts by sounding them out into their phonemes. For example, the word *safari* becomes *sa-fa-ri*. The ***f*** sound is not created using the ***ph*** letter pattern.

30 In this word the letters ***ph*** combine to create the ***f*** sound.

31 The letters ***oun*** combine to create an ***un*** sound in this word.

32 Be careful to pronounce words correctly. Remember that this word contains an ***i*** near the end.

33 Be careful to pronounce words correctly. Remember that this word has only two syllables, *burg-lar*.

34 Remember that this word has a double ***s***. The letters ***ssion*** create the ***shun*** sound.

35 The words most people spell wrongly are often longer words. To give yourself a greater chance of spelling success, you must break multi-syllable words into smaller parts. This word is made up of the root word *official* plus the suffix ***ly***.

36 This word is made up of the root word *drama* and the suffix ***tic***.

37 The ***i*** is often pronounced ***a*** and so this word can be misspelt. There is only one ***s***, not two.

38 The ending of this word is tricky for some spellers. However, it is a simple plural—you just add ***s*** to the noun *canoe*.

39 This word is made up of the root word *wonder* and the suffix ***ful***. Remember that the suffix ***ful*** has only one ***l***.

40 The ***i*** in this word is a long-sounding ***i***.

41 This word is made up of two separate words: *cause* and *way*. There is no need to alter the spelling of either word.

42 This is a compound word, made up of the combination of the two root words *bed* and *time*.

43 Remember to pronounce words correctly. This word ends in ***val***, not ***vool***.

44 This is a commonly misspelt word. The letter ***c*** creates the ***s*** sound, and the two letters ***el*** combine to create the ***al*** sound.

45 This is a compound word, made up of the combination of the two root words *pig* and *tails*.

46 This word contains the root word *regard* and the prefix ***dis***.

47 This word comprises the root word *depart* and the suffix ***ment***. When adding a suffix beginning with a consonant to a word ending in a consonant, you simply add the suffix without making any other changes to the root word.

48 This word is spelt differently from how it sounds—the first ***c*** is the hard ***k*** sound and the letters ***tch*** combine to create the ***ch*** sound.

49 To give yourself a greater chance of spelling success, you must break multi-syllable words into smaller parts. For example, the word *heroic* becomes *he-ro-ic*.

50 The end of this word is often misspelt ***adge***. Remember that the suffix is ***age***.

Year 9 Literacy Sample Online-style Test Answers

CONVENTIONS OF LANGUAGE

Pages 87–90

Sample Test 2

1 B **2** D **3**.D **4** B **5** D **6** A **7** B **8** B **9** C **10** C **11** A, C **12** A **13** C **14** he, himself **15** They're **16** its, its **17** her **18** it's **19** I, it, you, me **20** black, angry, grim **21** but **22** of, from, with **23** A, C **24** A, D **25** Alfred **26** frequency **27** bandage **28** massacre **29** accelerator **30** mediocre **31** particle **32** literary **33** receiver **34** dangerous **35** relief **36** predators **37** advertisement **38** respiration **39** surrounding **40** reservoir **41** reluctant **42** mosquito **43** addiction **44** Initial **45** insignificance **46** lightening **47** acclaim **48** antique **49** advice **50** arbitrary

1 The word *that* is applied to things, in this case to the phoenix.

2 Prepositions show the relationship between a noun or pronoun and another word. They show the position of something, in this example the preposition *near* shows the position of the phoenix in relation to the well.

3 The conjunction *and* joins the phrase *and sing beautiful songs* to the phrase *to bathe in the water of the well*, and so the infinitive form *(to) sing* is needed to parallel *to bathe*.

4 The present participle *smelling* is used with *sweet* to describe how the wood smelled at that time.

5 This sentence is written in the past tense as shown by the verb *cooled* and therefore requires the simple past tense verb, *arose*.

6 The word *who* is applied to people, in this case to the poet John Donne.

7 This question requires you to identify a noun and a verb. The suffix *er* changes the verb *listen* (an action) into the noun *listener* (someone who listens).

8 A semicolon can be used to join two sentences instead of a conjunction. In this sentence it replaces the conjunction *and*.

9 This is a grammar question. A verb is a doing word; in this example back means 'support'.

10 Brackets are used to separate a phrase or clause from the main sentence. This phrase or clause gives extra information. A sentence should be able to stand independently of the words in the brackets.

11 Commas are placed after the word *house* and the word *dilapidated* to indicate that this is an adjectival phrase. An adjectival phrase functions just like an adjective in that it gives extra information to a noun or a noun group. In this example it is the house that is being described further.

12 This question requires you to sequence three sentences in the correct order. The first sentence becomes an adverbial clause to indicate when the other two events occurred.

13 A prefix attaches to the beginning of a word to modify its meaning.

14 A pronoun is a word that takes the place of a noun or a proper noun. In this sentence the pronouns *he* and *himself* stand for Holden Caulfield.

15 The word *they're* is a contraction of the pronoun *they* and the verb *are*. The apostrophe takes the place of the missing letter ***a***.

16 The word *it's* is a contraction of *it is* and therefore requires an apostrophe between the ***t*** and ***s*** to indicate the missing ***i***. The word *its* indicates possession and is appropriate in both spaces as it refers to the lizard owning its tongue and mouth.

17 A pronoun is a word that takes the place of a noun or a proper noun. In this sentence the pronoun *her* stands for Janie.

18 The word *it's* is a contraction of *it is* and therefore requires an apostrophe between the ***t*** and ***s*** to indicate the missing ***i***. The noun *mums* is a plural and does not require an apostrophe.

19 A pronoun is a word that takes the place of a noun or a proper noun (e.g. he, she, it, me).

20 An adjective is a word used to describe a noun. In this example the adjectives are *black*, *angry* and *grim*.

21 Conjunctions join ideas in a sentence. The conjunction *but* indicates a connection between the independent and dependent clauses.

22 Prepositions show the relationship between a noun or pronoun and another word. They show the position of something, in this example the prepositions *of* and *from* show the relationship between the team and Davidson High School. The preposition *with* shows the relationship between the team and the song *Waltzing Matilda*.

23 Quotation marks are not only used to indicate direct speech and the title of texts, they can also be used to indicate when a word or phrase shouldn't be taken literally. In A, Jay-Jay has claimed to be sick, but he was not really. The quotation marks indicate that he should not be believed. In C, Mark claims not to want to wear the school shoes because they are too cool. The quotation marks indicate that he believes the opposite to be true about the shoes.

Year 9 Literacy Sample Online-style Test Answers

24 In A the adverbial phrase *After breaking her vase* indicates the boys' responsibility. In D the independent clause *The boys broke a vase* indicates their responsibility.

25 A proper noun is the name of a particular person, place, organisation, or thing. Proper nouns begin with a capital letter. In this sentence the only proper noun is *Alfred*.

26 Subject-specific words often have complex spelling. This word would likely be used in technology and the applied sciences. The letters ***qu*** in this word combine to create a ***kw*** sound.

27 The end of this word is often misspelt as ***adge***. Remember that the suffix is ***age***.

28 Many complex words are multi-syllable words. To give yourself a greater chance of spelling success, you must break these words into sound chunks. For example, the word *massacre* becomes *mass-a-cre*. Note that the final two letters (***re***) combine to create the short ***a*** sound.

29 The words most people spell wrongly are often longer words. To give yourself a greater chance of spelling success, you must break multi-syllable words into smaller parts by sounding them out into their phonemes. Remember that each syllable contains a vowel (***a***, ***e***, ***i***, ***o***, ***u***) or a vowel-sounding letter such as ***y***. For example, the word *accelerator* becomes *ac-cel-er-a-tor*. This word has a double ***c***.

30 Break multi-syllable words into chunks to help you spell them correctly. For example, this word becomes *me-di-o-cre*. Note that the last three letters (***cre***) combine to create the ***ka*** sound.

31 Subject-specific words often have more complex spelling. This word would likely be used in Science. The letters ***le*** combine to create the ***al*** sound in this word.

32 Remember to break multi-syllable words into smaller parts by sounding them out. For example, the word *literary* becomes *lit-er-a-ry*. The ***e*** in this word is often pronounced as a short ***a***.

33 This word has an irregular spelling pattern because the ***e*** comes before the ***i***. Remember the rule '***i*** before ***e*** except after ***c***'.

34 This is a commonly misspelt word. The letters ***ou*** combine to create the short ***u*** sound.

35 The letters ***ie*** combine to make the one sound, ***e***. Don't forget the rule '***i*** before ***e*** except after ***c***'.

36 The words most people spell wrongly are often longer words. Remember to break multi-syllable words into smaller parts by sounding them out. For example, the word *predators* becomes *pre-da-tors*. There is only one ***d*** in this word.

37 The words most people spell wrongly are often longer words. This word contains the root word *advertise* combined with the suffix ***ment***.

38 Scientific words are often more complex to spell. Many have irregular or difficult spellings. The letters ***tion*** in this word make a ***shun*** sound.

39 This word is made up of the root word *surround* and the suffix ***ing***. The ***d*** does not need to be doubled in this word.

40 Some letters combine to make a completely new sound, and this can make a word difficult to spell. The letters ***oir*** in this word combine to create a ***wah*** sound. The second ***e*** creates the short ***a*** sound.

41 The letter ***c*** makes a hard ***k*** sound in this word. Sound the word out into parts to make sure you spell it correctly: *re-luc-tant*.

42 This word is frequently misspelt. There is no ***c*** in *mosquito*. The ***key*** sound is created by the letters ***qui***.

43 This word is made up of the root word *addict* and the suffix ***ion***. The letters ***tion*** combine to create a ***shun*** sound.

44 This word is spelt differently from how it sounds. The letters ***tial*** combine to make the ***shul*** sound.

45 Break multi-syllable words into chunks to help you spell them correctly. For example, the word *insignificance* becomes *in-sig-nif-i-cance*. The first ***c*** creates the hard ***k*** sound and the second ***c*** creates the soft ***s*** sound.

46 This verb is often confused with the common noun *lightning*. The verb means 'lighten', so try to remember that the word *verb* has an ***e*** and so does the verb form *lightening*.

47 The letters ***ai*** combine to create an ***ay*** sound in this word.

48 This word is spelt differently from how it sounds. The letters ***qu*** create the hard ***k*** sound in this word and the letter ***i*** creates the long ***e*** sound.

49 The ***c*** in this word makes an ***s*** sound and can be confused with the letter ***s***. Remember: The noun is *advice* and the verb is *advise*.

50 Break this word down into its syllables to help you spell it correctly. The word becomes *ar-bi-tra-ry*.

READING Sample Test 1

Go to the **inside back cover** for a guide to question types.

The llama

Pages 91–92

1 B **2** A **3** C **4** B **5** A, D **6** False

1. This is a **judgement type of question**. You read that the llama is *bred way up on the bleak plateaus of the Andes* (see line 8) and combine this with your knowledge that the word *bleak* means lacking vegetation and exposed to the elements which makes life hard.
2. This is **a judgement type of question**. You read that *The llama is a really interesting and unusual animal. It originates from South America, and is a member of the camel family, known as lamoids* (see lines 1–2) and combine this with your knowledge that factual information on animals is usually consulted by people interested in them.
3. This is a **fact-finding type of question**. The answer is a fact in the text. You read that *A female llama gives birth to one young following a gestation period of 11 months* (see lines 4–5).
4. This is a **fact-finding type of question**. The answer is a fact in the text. You read that *A single llama can carry a load of up to 60 kilograms, and they can travel a long way each day—between 25 and 30 kilometres* (see lines 12–13).
5. This is a **fact-finding type of question**. The answer is a fact in the text. You read that *unlike camels, lamoids do not have humps. Llamas can be identified by their long legs and necks, small heads* (see lines 2–3).
6. This is a **judgement type of question**. You read that *The llama and alpaca have similar dispositions, as they can be gentle but they also have a tendency to kick and spit if they are unhappy* (see lines 16–17). You combine this information with your knowledge that small children are at risk of being injured by animals and infer that a llama would not be a good pet for them.

A little cloud

Pages 93–94

7 B **8** *all that minute vermin-like life and under the shadow of the gaunt spectral-like mansions in which the old nobility of the Dublin had roistered* **9** C **10** A **11** A **12** C **13** B

7. This is an **inferring type of question**. To find the answer you have to 'read between the lines'. You are told *Little Chandler's thoughts ever since lunch-time had been of his meeting with Gallaher and (as always happened when he thought of life) he became sad* (see lines 6, 26–27) and you then combine that information with your own knowledge that a dull life makes you sad and your understanding that doing something new can make you happy.
8. This is a **judgement type of question**. You read in the second-last sentence: *all that minute vermin-like life and under the shadow of the gaunt spectral-like mansions in which the old nobility of the Dublin had roistered* (*lines 43–45*). Using your own knowledge you can identify these words as imagery. Imagery is a description which can be used to help readers imagine a sight, smell, taste, feeling or sound. It is often created using figures of speech like similes or metaphors.
9. This is a **judgement type of question**. You read the sentence *A gentle melancholy took possession of him* (lines 27–28) and combine it with your knowledge of literary devices to work out that this is an example of personification; in this case the quality of melancholy is given the human ability to take possession.
10. This is a **judgement type of question**. You read that *Few fellows had talents like his, and fewer still could remain unspoiled by such success* (see line 3) and then combine that information with your own knowledge that talented people who are unspoiled are often admired.
11. This is a **fact-finding type of question**. The answer is a fact in the text. You read *he sat at his desk in the King's Inns* (line 14).
12. This is a **judgement type of question**. You read that *He picked his way deftly through all that minute vermin-like life and under the shadow of the gaunt spectral mansions in which the old nobility of Dublin had roistered* (see lines 42–45) and then combine this with your own knowledge that shadows are often associated with emptiness.
13. This is a **judgement type of question**. You read that *A horde of grimy children populated the street ... Little Chandler gave them no thought* (see lines 39–42) and combine that with your own knowledge that such an image is shocking and to ignore it means it must be a familiar sight.

My Grandfather's Ice Pigeons

Pages 95–96

14 A **15** A, E **16** C **17** A **18** D

14. This is an **inferring type of question**. To find the answer you have to 'read between the lines'. You are told *She ordered me to stay away from the crabs / reminding me why Uncle Eric lost his finger, / besides they could snap a clothes prop in two* (see lines 10–12) and then you need to

combine that with your own knowledge that crab bites hurt and your understanding that mothers like to protect their children from being hurt.

15 This is a **judgement type of question**. You read that *I stayed / a week and my grandmother showed me / what to do (see lines 13–15)* and then combine that with your own knowledge that learning from relatives creates feelings of comfort and security. You also read that *the river postman saw him through the mist/one morning, balancing on net-boards at the stern/of his boat, singing aloud, throwing pigeons at the sky (lines 31–33)* and combine that with your knowledge that singing creates joy and enjoying work is admirable.

16 This is a **judgement type of question**. You read that *my grandmother showed me / what to do* and *it was my job to ride my bike / into town (see lines 11–15 and 24–25)* and then combine that information with your own knowledge that being given responsibilities helps young people to learn.

17 This is an **inferring type of question**. To find the answer you have to 'read between the lines'. You read that *He'd send the ice to my grandfather next morning / on the mail boat. They talk about the time / Fa Fa got drunk up the river at Spencer (see lines 28–30)* and combine that with your understanding that *Fa Fa* would be what the poet called his grandfather.

18 This is a **judgement type of question**. You read that *my grandmother showed me / what to do* and *My grandfather would leave / again for his next catch (see lines 14–15 and 20–21)* and then combine that with your own knowledge that older people often are full of knowledge and experience.

David Unaipon (1872–1967)

Pages 97–98

19 A **20** B **21** C **22** B **23** C **24** A

19 This is a **fact-finding type of question**. The answer is a fact in the text. The text informs the reader that *His earliest published works include an article entitled 'Aboriginals: Their Traditions and Customs' in the Sydney* Daily Telegraph *(see lines 33–34)*.

20 This is a **judgement type of question**. You read that Unaipon *married Katherine Carter (nee Sumner) (see line 25)* and then combine that with your own knowledge that brackets are used to separate additional information from a sentence.

21 This is a **fact-finding type of question**. The answer is a fact in the text. The text informs the reader that *His search for the secret of perpetual motion lasted throughout his life (see line 24)*.

22 This is an **inferring type of question**. To find the answer you have to 'read between the lines'. You are told *he spoke of the need for 'sympathetic cooperation' between whites and blacks, and for equal rights (see lines 30–31)* and then you need to combine that with your own knowledge that *cooperation* means 'working together' and your understanding that cooperation between people is beneficial for society.

23 This is an **inferring type of question**. To find the answer you have to 'read between the lines'. You read Unaipon *devised a number of his own inventions (see lines 13–14)* and combine that with your own knowledge that Leonardo refers to the Italian inventor Leonardo da Vinci and your understanding that inventors are innovative and challenge traditional ways of thinking.

24 This is a **fact-finding type of question**. The text informs the reader that: *Unaipon, who married Katherine Carter (line 25)*.

Teenage girls' fear of fatness

Page 99

25 B **26** D **27** D **28** *Teenage girls' fear of fatness*: to inform, to educate; '*I was only 19'*: to educate, to engage **29** *Teenage girls' fear of fatness:* statistics, second-person narrative and listing; '*I was only 19'*: metaphor, listing, simile.

25 This is an **inferring type of question**. To find the answer you have to 'read between the lines'. You read that *what most teenage girls fear is growing fat (see line 19)* and then combine that with your own knowledge that parents are responsible for the care of teenagers and your understanding that no parent wants to see their child unwell.

26 This is a **fact-finding type of question**. The answer is a fact in the text. The text informs the reader that *You would think from the words Carrie uses ... that she was talking about something more immoral or harmful than snacking on potato chips ... but you'd be wrong ... what most teenage girls fear is growing fat (see lines 8–13 and line 19)*.

27 This is a **judgement type of question**. In *Teenage girls' fear of fatness* you read *The statistics tell the story,* followed by lots of facts *(paragraph 3)*. The article informs and educates the reader about concerns about body image in young girls. In '*I was only 19'* you read *He spends his mental hours fighting the war within himself (lines 40-41)*. The short story engages the reader in a narrative about a father who is a Vietnam veteran. It also educates the reader about the effect of the Vietnam War on the veterans and their families.

28 This is a **judgement type of question**. In *Teenage girls' fear of fatness* you read *The statistics tell the story,* followed by lots of facts (paragraph 3). The article informs and educates the reader about concerns about body image in young girls. In '*I was only 19*' you read *He spends his mental hours fighting the war within himself* (lines 40-41). The short story engages the reader in a narrative about a father who is a Vietnam veteran. It also educates the reader about the effect of the Vietnam War on the veterans and their families.

29 This is a **judgement type of question**. In *Teenage girls' fear of fatness* you read lots of statistics in paragraph 3. It uses the second person in *You would think* (line 8). In '*I was only 19*' you read descriptions such as *desperation painted with fuchsia lipstick and broken black heels* (lines 22–23). Combine this reading with your knowledge of language and literary devices.

'I was only 19'

Pages 100–101

30 A, D, E **31** A **32** C **33** B **34** C **35** Possible answers are: *The rash of war, Dad's weeks are pock-marked with visits to doctors.*

30 This is a **judgement type of question**. You read the text and combine this with your knowledge that tone is the attitude of a piece of writing. Sentences such as *And as the daughter of a Vietnam vet, I'm left wondering if … Dad ever did come home* (lines 42–43) which show a reflective, emotive and affectionate tone.

31 This is a **judgement type of question**. You read that *The child was, I'm sure, part of the appeal* (see lines 26–27) and then combine that your own knowledge that a man who wants to be with a woman to help with her child is caring and thoughtful.

32 This is a **fact-finding type of question** because the answer is a fact in the text. The text informs the reader that *The emotion of Redgum's 'I was only 19' drenches me with regret* (see line 1).

33 This is an **inferring type of question**. To find the answer you have to 'read between the lines'. You are told *These features stare back at me each morning as I hastily arrange myself for work* (see lines 5–6) and then combine that with your own knowledge that people getting ready for work look in a mirror and your understanding that children often have similar features to their parents.

34 This is a **fact-finding type of question** because the answer is a fact in the text. The text informs the reader that *He fills his physical hours watching footy, chatting to his kids and grandkids, crafting vehicles from blocks of wood* (see lines 39–40).

35 This is a **judgement type of question**. You read the paragraph and combine this with your knowledge that a metaphor is a direct comparison between two things to work out the possible answers are: *The rash of war* (line 38), *Dad's weeks are pock-marked with visits to doctors* (line 37).

Volcanoes

Pages 102–103

36 A **37** A, D **38** B **39** B **40** B **41** A

36 This is a **fact-finding type of question**. The answer is a fact in the text. The text informs the reader that *Magma is liquid rock inside a volcano* (see line 3).

37 This is a **judgement type of question**. You see that the labelled diagram shows the parts of a volcano and then combine that with your own knowledge that sometimes diagrams are used to help people understand written text.

38 This is a **judgement type of question**. You read that *The lava burns down everything in its way as it reaches temperatures ranging from 700 to 1200 °C* (see lines 11–12) and then combine that with your own knowledge that lava burning down everything would result in massive destruction.

39 This is a **fact-finding type of question**. The answer is a fact in the text. The text informs the reader that *The word* volcano *comes from the name of Vulcan, who was the god of fire in Roman mythology* (see line 4).

40 This is a **fact-finding type of question**. The answer is a fact in the text. The text informs the reader that *Earth's crust is made up of huge slabs called tectonic plates. These plates fit together like a complicated jigsaw puzzle* (see lines 5–6).

41 This is a **judgement type of question**. You read the diagram and its related definitions (see lines 15–34) and then combine that with your own knowledge that structures that require many definitions are often complex.

The history of mushrooms in Australia

Page 104

42 B **43** B **44** C **45** E **46** A **47** C **48** B

42 This is a **fact-finding type of question**. The answer is a fact in the text. The text informs the reader that *The first commercial attempts to grow mushrooms in Australia were in 1933 (see lines 1–2)*.

43 This is a **fact-finding type of question**. The answer is a fact in the text. The text informs the reader that locations were selected for *raw materials for compost preparation (see line 10)*.

44 This is a **fact-finding type of question**. The answer is a fact in the text. The text informs the reader that the *first growing houses of any size were disused railway tunnels in Sydney (see lines 3–4)*.

45 This is a **judgement type of question**. You read that the title of the text is *The history of mushrooms in Australia* and then combine that with your own knowledge that people who read information do so because they are interested in the topic.

46 This is a **judgement type of question**. You read that *The first commercial attempts to grow mushrooms in Australia were in 1933* and *Mushroom growers began outdoor cultivation ... in the mid-1930s (see lines 1–2 and lines 5–6)* and combine that with your own knowledge that the word *began* means the same as *origins*.

47 This is a **judgement type of question**. You may know that the word *burgeoning* means 'make large or grow', or you could read that *they were close to the burgeoning market of Sydney (see line 13)* and then combine that with your own knowledge that the market of Sydney would be growing.

48 This is a **fact-finding type of question**. The answer is a fact in the text. You read *These locations were selected because: of closeness to a migrant camp (lines 7–8)*.

READING Sample Test 2

Alice's Adventures in Wonderland

Pages 105–106

1 A, B **2** A **3** A **4** A, C **5** B **6** A

1 This is an **inferring type of question**. To find the answer you have to 'read between the lines'. You are told *Alice was beginning to get very tired of sitting by her sister on the bank (see line 1)* and then you need to combine that with your own knowledge that getting tired of something means you want to stop doing it and your understanding that Alice found her sister's activities boring.

2 This is a **fact-finding type of question**. The answer is a fact in the text. The text informs the reader that *she was considering in her own mind (as well as she could, for the hot day made her feel very sleepy and stupid) whether the pleasure of making a daisy-chain would be worth the trouble of getting up and picking the daisies (see lines 4–9)*.

3 This is an **inferring type of question**. To find the answer you have to 'read between the lines'. You are told *In another moment Alice went down after it, never once considering how in the world she was to get out again (see lines 29–31)* and combine that with your own knowledge that going down the hole could be quite a dangerous activity and your understanding that often people who do dangerous things don't consider the consequences of their actions.

4 This is a **fact-finding type of question**. The answer is a fact in the text. You are told Alice sees the rabbit and then *burning with curiosity, she ran across the field after it (see lines 24–26)*.

5 This is a **judgement type of question**. You are told the rabbit said *Oh dear! Oh dear! I shall be too late! (see line 14)* and you need to combine that with your own knowledge that being late often makes people anxious or worried.

6 This is an **inferring type of question**. To find the answer you have to 'read between the lines'. You are told that Alice is only interested in books with pictures or conversations *(see line 3)* and then you need to combine that with your own knowledge that young children are often engaged by pictures and your understanding that Alice is like most young children.

Oliver Twist

Pages 107–108

7 A **8** B **9** C **10** B, D **11** A **12** B **13** D

7 This is an **inferring type of question**. To find the answer you have to 'read between the lines'. You are told *The master ... turned very pale (see line 41)* and then combine that with your own knowledge that losing colour happens when a person is shocked.

8 This is a **judgement type of question**. You read that *lots were cast for who should walk up to the master after supper that evening and ask for more; and it fell to Oliver Twist (see lines 30–33)* and then combine that with your own knowledge that the casting of lots is a way to select someone.

9 This is an **inferring type of question**. To find the answer you have to 'read between the lines'. You are told that *The master was a fat, healthy man; but he turned very pale* (see line 41) and then you combine that with your own knowledge that people lose the colour in their face when they are shocked and your understanding that a master does not expect his charges to confront him.

10 This is an **inferring type of question**. To find the answer you have to 'read between the lines'. You are told *Child as he was, he was desperate with hunger, and reckless with misery* (see lines 37–38) and then you combine that with your own knowledge that Oliver is starving and your understanding that people take risks when they are desperate.

11 This is an **inferring type of question**. To find the answer you have to 'read between the lines'. You are told *The master aimed a blow at Oliver's head with the ladle, pinioned him in his arms, and shrieked aloud for the beadle* (see lines 46–47) and combine that with your own knowledge that often people use physical punishment to make people follow their orders and your understanding that the master is unhappy with Oliver's request.

12 This is an **inferring type of question**. To find the answer you have to 'read between the lines'. You are told *Oliver Twist and his companions suffered the tortures of slow starvation for three months* (see lines 18–20) and combine that with your own knowledge that young boys require a large amount of food to sustain them and your understanding that starvation only occurs when food is withheld from a person for some reason.

13 This is a **judgement type of question**. You read that *The assistants were paralyzed with wonder, the boys with fear* (see lines 42–43) and then combine that with your own knowledge that people are only afraid of someone if they feel that person is cruel and a threat.

Waiheke

Page 109

14 C **15** A **16** Possible answers: *rain falls like a whisper, the splutter of fat, a grey mass of cloud* **17** C **18** B

14 This is an **inferring type of question**. To find the answer you have to 'read between the lines'. You read *today is night without the darkness / rain falls like a whisper* (see lines 5–6) and combine that with your own knowledge that night time is quiet and your understanding that people are usually asleep or indoors at night time.

15 This is a **judgement type of question**. You read that *rain falls like a whisper* (see line 6) and combine that with your own knowledge that a whisper is quiet and soft.

16 This is a **judgement type of question**. You must read the poem and combine your reading with your knowledge that imagery is language which conjures an image in the mind of the reader. The possible answers are: *rain falls like a whisper* (line 6), *the splutter of fat* (line 12), *a grey mass of cloud* (line 7).

17 This is an **inferring type of question**. To find the answer you have to 'read between the lines'. You are told there are *broken tennis rackets, tent poles* (see line 3) on the island and then you combine that with your own knowledge that people are usually active on island holidays and your understanding that broken sporting equipment will impact on the couple's ability to have fun.

18 This is a **judgement type of question**. You read that *we fall asleep on the beach / in the morning we swim / the bluest, coldest sea* (see lines 14–16) and then combine that with your own knowledge that sleep and swimming are relaxing activities.

Judith Wright

Pages 110–111

19 A **20** C **21** A **22** A, B, D **23** B **24** C

19 This is a **judgement type of question**. This is an article about a poet, which provides information about her life and writing style. Combine this with your own knowledge to work out the purpose is to inform.

20 This is a **judgement type of question**. You read that she was *deeply inspired by ... the plains of the southern highlands (near Braidwood)* (see lines 25–27) and then combine that with your own knowledge that brackets are often used to contain additional information.

21 This is an **inferring type of question**. To find the answer you must 'read between the lines'. You are told *Wright condemned the educational system* (lines 30–31) and *at 85 years of age, she attended a march in Canberra* (lines 39–40) and then you combine this with your own knowledge that people who fight for what they believe in are both passionate and determined.

22 This is a **judgement type of question**. You read that *her mission was to connect the human experience with the natural world* (see lines 27–28) and then combine that with your own knowledge that people who love nature often desire to protect it.

23 This is a **judgement type of question**. You read that *she also expressed uncertainty about poetry changing the scheme of things (see line 33)* and then combine that with your own knowledge that *the scheme of things* means 'the way the world is'.

24 This is an **inferring type of question**. To find the answer you have to 'read between the lines'. You are told *in her poetry ... she makes an effort to bridge the gap between nature and man (see lines 29–30)* and then you combine that with your own knowledge that poets write about what is important to them and your understanding that a valuing of nature is seen as important.

The Rapa Nui culture

Page 112

25 A **26** C **27** C **28** *Waiheke*: to entertain; *The Rapa Nui culture*: to inform, to educate **29** *Waiheke*: imagery, simile; *The Rapa Nui culture:* parentheses, factual detail, third-person narrative.

25 This is a **fact-finding type of question**. The answer is a fact in the text. The text informs the reader that *Roman Catholicism has erased much of the original local beliefs and legends (see lines 6–7)*.

26 This is an **inferring type of question**. To find the answer you have to 'read between the lines'. You are told *there are only speculations about what/whom they might represent (see lines 9–10)* and then combine that with your own knowledge that *speculation* means that people are guessing and your understanding that not knowing much about a culture can make it seem mysterious.

27 This is a **fact-finding type of question**. The answer is a fact in the text. The text informs the reader that *this rare language ... is so unusual that seemingly it has no close connection to any other language (see lines 3–5)*.

28 This is a **judgement type of question**. You read in the poem *Waiheke* images of a trip to an island. You can use your own experience to work out that its purpose is to entertain. In *The Rapa Nui culture* you read about the history of the Rapa Nui people. You can work out its purposes are to inform and educate.

29 This is a **judgement type of question**. You read the texts and combine this reading with your knowledge of language and literary devices. You read in the poem *Waiheke* the simile *like a whisper (line 6)*. In *The Rapa Nui culture* you read parentheses on lines 3–4 and 8–9, factual detail such as *4500 ethnic Rapa Nui people (line 4)* and third-person narrative.

Woolworths to phase out cage eggs

Page 113

30 B **31** Woolworths believes the move will increase the popularity of its 28 free-range and barn-laid brands and ultimately make them cheaper. **32** B **33** C **34** B **35** B

30 This is a **judgement type of question**. You read *The chain will slash the number of cage-egg brands (line 3)*. You have to combine your understanding of the text to make an informed guess that *phasing out* in this context means the eggs will no longer be sold.

31 This is a **judgement type of question**. You read *Woolworths believes the move will increase the popularity of its 28 free-range and barn-laid brands and ultimately make them cheaper (lines 5–7)*. You must combine this with your understanding that a large company is concerned with increased market demand for its products.

32 This is an **inferring type of question**. To find the answer you have to 'read between the lines'. You are told the chain will be *cutting out one of its own lucrative in-house lines in the process (see line 4)* and then combine that with your own knowledge that *lucrative* means 'profitable' and *in-house* refers to Woolworths' own brand.

33 This is a **fact-finding type of question**. The answer is a fact in the text. The text informs the reader that *The average price for a dozen free-range eggs, $6.50, is $2 more than the same quantity of caged eggs (see line 14)*.

34 This is a **fact-finding type of question**. The answer is a fact in the text. The text informs the reader that *Free-range hens are currently responsible for 31 per cent of eggs sales (see line 12)*.

35 This is a **judgement type of question**. You read that *(This) will influence our suppliers ... and may generate a faster rate of change and that's good (see lines 8–9)* and then combine that with your own knowledge that suppliers must give their buyers what they want.

The absolutely true diary of a part-time Indian

Pages 114–115

36 D **37** B **38** A **39** B, D **40** C **41** 2, 3, 1

36 This is a **fact-finding type of question**. The answer is a fact in the text. The text informs the reader that *I was only six months old and I was supposed to croak during the surgery (see lines 24–25)*.

Year 9 Literacy Sample Online-style Test Answers

37 This is an **inferring type of question**. To find the answer you have to 'read between the lines'. You are told *Maybe the whole thing is weird and funny* (see lines 17–18) and then combine that with your own knowledge that having life-threatening surgery and disabilities is not something that is often laughed at and your understanding that people who can laugh at their problems are positive people.

38 This is a **judgement type of question**. You read that *I was supposed to croak during the surgery* (see lines 24–25) and then combine that with your own knowledge that speaking lightly of a life-threatening experience is remarkable.

39 This is a **judgement type of question**. You read that *Maybe the whole thing is weird and funny* (see lines 17–18) and then combine that with your own knowledge that laughing at a terrible situation shows a positive outlook on life.

40 This is a **fact-finding type of question**. The answer is a fact in the text. The text informs the reader that *Well, I obviously survived the surgery. I wouldn't be writing this if I didn't* (see lines 30–31).

41 This is a **fact-finding type of question**. The answer are facts in the text. You have to read the text closely and identify which events took place first, second and third. You first read *I was actually born with too much cerebral spinal fluid* (line 2), then *the surgery* (line 25) and *I had to have all ten extra teeth pulled* (line 41).

How to throw a boomerang

Pages 116–117

42 A **43** B **44** B **45** D **46** B **47** A **48** D

42 This is a **fact-finding type of question**. The answer is a fact in the text. The text informs the reader that *The curved, or decorated, side should always be held towards your body* (see lines 1–2).

43 This is a **judgement type of question**. You read that throwing a boomerang is complicated, with many steps (*The grip*, *The throw*, *Launch angle*, *Adjusting for the wind* and *The catch*) and then combine that with your own knowledge that diagrams help to explain a process.

44 This is an **inferring type of question**. To find the answer you have to 'read between the lines'. You are shown an image of a caution circle over a boomerang being held and then combine that with your own knowledge that there is a specific way to hold a boomerang and your understanding that caution circles inform people of danger.

45 This is a **fact-finding type of question**. The answer is a fact in the text. The text informs the reader that *Only attempt to catch the boomerang while it is slowly hovering towards you and is below shoulder height* (see lines 33–35).

46 This is a **fact-finding type of question**. The answer is a fact in the text. The text informs the reader that you should *Aim for the centre section of the boomerang as you catch it* (see lines 36–37).

47 This is an **inferring type of question**. To find the answer you have to 'read between the lines'. You are shown a series of diagrams supported by labels such as *Left-hand throw* and *Right-hand throw* and then combine that with your own knowledge that there are many steps involved in throwing a boomerang, and your understanding that diagrams are designed to help understand a difficult topic or process.

48 This is an **inferring type of question**. The text says: *NEVER try to catch a boomerang that is diving or moving fast* (lines 38–39). You must read between the lines to work out that catching a moving boomerang is dangerous; therefore the capital letters serve as a warning to the reader.

WRITING Sample Tests 1 and 2

Pages 118–119

Go to **pages 169–174** for Standard, Intermediate and Advanced Writing samples for Sample Tests 1 and 2.

Go to **pages 152–153** for Marking checklists for Sample Tests 1 and 2:

- Persuasive text (page 147)
- Narrative text (pages 147–148).

White chocolate is better than milk chocolate

Chocolate is tasty and everyone loves it. Milk chocolate is heaps yummier than white chocolate. But white chocolate isn't even chocolate because it doesn't have cocoa in it, plus it's not good for you like milk chocolate and it can't be used in lots of different recipies. This is why milk chocolate is better.

White chocolate isn't even chocolate. It hasn't got any cocoa liquor in it and only has cocoa paste in it. This means it can't be called chocolate at all so it can't be as good as milk chocolate that does have cocoa liquor in it. White chocolate is mostly just sugar and milk. Milk chocolate is much tastier too.

White chocolate isn't good for you but milk chocolate is. White chocolate has lots of fat and sugar in it. Milk chocolate is better because it has cocoa and cocoa is good for your heart and can stop cancer. Because of this people should choose milk chocolate and not white chocolate to eat.

Milk chocolate can be used in way more recipies than white chocolate and this means it can be eaten more and more. White chocolate doesn't melt well and goes all funny which makes the food not taste very good. Milk chocolate doesn't do this and can be used in lots of recipies like cakes and biscuits. You can eat it more which is a good thing

White chocolate is tasty but milk chocolate is better. It has good stuff for your health, you can cook lots of recipies with it and it's got cocoa liquor in it and this makes it real chocolate. Milk chocolate gets my vote as being the best.

Structure

Audience

Outlining of the writer's position—that milk chocolate is superior—is simplistic.

The writer attempts to outline reasons to support the argument.

Persuasive techniques

The writer tries to use a variety of persuasive techniques, including emotive words and high modal words.

Text structure

The writer attempts to correctly structure the persuasive text, including introduction, supporting paragraphs and conclusion. The conclusion and/or introduction may be missing.

Paragraphing

The writer attempts to use a new paragraph to introduce an idea.

Cohesion

Connectives are used infrequently. Supporting lines of argument lack detail.

Language and Ideas

Vocabulary

The writer attempts to use language appropriate to the purpose—to persuade.

The writer uses simple verbs and adjectives.

Sentence structure

The writer uses mostly simple sentences with some compound sentences.

Ideas

Ideas are simple and reasons given to support the persuasive argument are basic.

Punctuation

Simple punctuation is used. Sometimes punctuation is missing or incorrect.

Spelling

Most words are frequently used words with regular spelling. Some words are spelt incorrectly.

These writing samples have been analysed based on the marking criteria used by markers to assess the NAPLAN Writing Test.

Intermediate level — Sample of Persuasive Writing

White chocolate is better than milk chocolate

Chocolate has been enjoyed for many years. Chocolate brings smiles to the faces of children around the world and brings peace to their parents. White chocolate is a fake. Some claim that this so-called 'chocolate' is better than milk chocolate. How can this be? There are three reasons why. White chocolate is not even chocolate, it isn't as healthy as milk chocolate and finally, it lacks the versatility of milk chocolate. Because of this, milk chocolate is superior to white chocolate.

White chocolate is not actually chocolate. White chocolate does not contain cocoa liquor. The cocoa bean is grown in places like Indonesia and Malaysia. It is roasted and ground to make cocoa paste. This paste is melted into liquor and used to make chocolate. How is it possible for something to be called 'chocolate' when it doesn't have the ingredient essential to chocolate? White chocolate is made from sugar, milk and cocoa butter. Cocoa butter is just one part of cocoa and lacks the full flavour and colour of milk chocolate.

Also, white chocolate isn't as healthy as milk chocolate. White chocolate has a lot of sugar and fat. Milk chocolate has a lot of sugar and fat too but it also contains cocoa liquor and this can improve an individual's heart health and even stop them getting cancer! White chocolate doesn't have much cocoa in it and can't fight illness. People should choose milk chocolate over white chocolate if they want to be healthy.

Finally, you can make more things from milk chocolate than you can from white chocolate. Milk chocolate can be added to many different dishes, including savoury dishes. White chocolate goes bad when it is melted and this makes it hard to cook with. Milk chocolate doesn't have this problem because it is made with cocoa liquor. Milk chocolate can be made into drinks, biscuits, cakes and lots of other tasty treats. If it can be used more, it can be eaten more and this has to be a good thing!

In conclusion, white chocolate is tasty, but it's easy to see why milk chocolate is better. White chocolate isn't made with cocoa liquor and this means it is less tasty, not as good for you and less versatile. Milk chocolate is the better choice by far.

Please note that this sample has not been written under test conditions. However, it gives you a standard to aim for.

Structure

Audience

An attempt is made to alert the reader to the writer's position—that milk chocolate is superior.

Emotive phrases engage the emotions of the reader.

Persuasive techniques

The writer tries to use a variety of high modal words to enforce his or her position. Rhetorical questions encourage thought in the reader.

Text structure

The text is correctly structured for a persuasive text, including introduction, supporting paragraphs and conclusion.

Paragraphing

A new paragraph is used to introduce a new idea.

Cohesion

Basic connectives are used to show connections between ideas and enhance argument. Each paragraph features reasons to support the argument.

Language and Ideas

Vocabulary

Language choices are appropriate to the purpose—to persuade.

The writer uses strong verbs and adjectives.

The writer attempts to use a combination of everyday and more complex vocabulary.

Sentence structure

The text contains a variety of simple and compound sentences.

Ideas

The writer uses good ideas that are relevant to the argument and are explained in the body of the text to support the persuasive argument.

Punctuation

Correct punctuation is used throughout the argument.

The punctuation used is simple.

Spelling

All words are correctly spelt.

Some difficult and challenging words are included.

Writing Mini Test 1

White chocolate is better than milk chocolate

Chocolate is a treat that has been enjoyed for centuries. Sweet and smooth, chocolate brings smiles to the faces of children around the world and brings peace to their parents. All true lovers of chocolate know that it is the humble cocoa bean that is transformed daily into liquid velvet and shaped into pyramids of desire. Yet an imposter has entered the chocolate arena—white chocolate. Some claim that this so-called 'chocolate' is superior to milk chocolate. How can this be? That white chocolate is better than milk chocolate is an impossible position to adopt for three reasons. White chocolate is a fraud—it's not even chocolate, it lacks the health benefits of milk chocolate and, finally, it lacks the versatility of milk chocolate. For these reasons it is clear that milk chocolate is superior to white chocolate.

The claim that white chocolate is actually chocolate is fraudulent. Why is it fraudulent? White chocolate does not contain cocoa liquor. Cocoa liquor is the very heart of chocolate. The cocoa bean, grown lovingly in countries including Indonesia and Malaysia, is roasted and ground to make a bitter and fragrant cocoa paste. This pure paste is melted into liquor, which is eventually used to manufacture chocolate as we know and love it. How is it possible for a confectionary to label itself as 'chocolate' when it lacks the very ingredient essential to chocolate, cocoa liquor? White chocolate is made primarily from sugar, milk and cocoa butter. Cocoa butter is simply a product of cocoa production and lacks the full flavour and colour that is a favourite feature of milk chocolate.

Not only is white chocolate a fraud, it also lacks the health benefits with which milk chocolate is endowed. White chocolate is high in sugar and fat, with few nutritional benefits. Milk chocolate is also high in sugar and fat, but because it is truly chocolate and contains cocoa liquor it can improve an individual's cardiovascular health. Consuming cocoa has been scientifically proven to lower rates of heart disease and cancer. White chocolate is made from the less potent form of cocoa, cocoa butter, and lacks its healing properties. For their own health, individuals owe it to themselves to choose milk chocolate over white chocolate.

Furthermore, the versatility of milk chocolate makes it superior to white chocolate. Chocolate is a favourite ingredient of chefs all over the world because of its ability to be used in a diverse range of dishes. It is milk chocolate, not white chocolate, that can be added to both sweet and savoury dishes. As mentioned above, white chocolate is manufactured from cocoa butter and as a result this makes it unsuitable for cooking in most dishes. When heated, cocoa butter splits and becomes oily. Milk chocolate does not split because it is derived from cocoa liquor. Milk chocolate can be melted to add to drinks and cakes. Milk chocolate can be used to make sauces and cakes. This versatility of milk chocolate means it can be enjoyed more often and in more exciting ways. More chocolate more often? No one could deny the superiority of this idea!

White chocolate is tasty—there's no denying that. But when it comes to choosing between white chocolate and milk chocolate, the choice is easy. White chocolate lacks one key ingredient that makes its darker brother much more attractive—cocoa liquor. This ingredient ensures that milk chocolate is tasty, good for us and versatile. Milk chocolate is the better choice by far.

Structure

Audience

The reader is immediately alerted to the writer's position—that milk chocolate is superior.

Emotive phrases engage the emotions of the reader.

Persuasive techniques

High modal words enforce the writer's position. Rhetorical questions encourage thought in the reader. Repetition emphasises the writer's point.

Text structure

The text has the correct structure for a persuasive text, including introduction, supporting paragraphs and conclusion. This structure assists in the development of the writer's position.

Paragraphing

A new paragraph is used to introduce a new idea.

Cohesion

Connectives and referring words show connections between ideas and enhance the argument. All supporting lines of argument are articulated fully and supported by evidence and/or reasons.

Language and Ideas

Vocabulary

Language choices are appropriate to the purpose—to persuade.

The writer uses strong verbs, adverbs and adjectives.

Sentence structure

All sentences are grammatically correct, well structured and meaningful.

Ideas

Well-selected and relevant ideas are elaborated in the body of the text to support persuasive argument.

Punctuation

Correct complex punctuation is used throughout the argument.

Spelling

All words are correctly spelt.

Difficult and challenging words are frequently included.

Please note that this sample has not been written under test conditions. During a test you might not have the time to produce such a polished piece of writing. However, this sample gives you a standard to aim for.

Writing Mini Test 2

Standard level — Sample of Narrative Writing

An accident

The rain is heavy and falling on the windscreen of the car. Sitting in his car, Miro stares at the wiper-blades. He has been stuck in the traffic for a long time. The rain has been falling for three days.

Earlier that day Miro's old car wouldn't work. Miro had tried to make the car start but it wouldn't. Miro was forced to take his wife's car that was a yellow car. She didn't want to drive it because the brakes were bad. She had taken the bus to work.

So here Miro sits in a car too small for him and stuck in terrible traffic and the heavy rain. He feels uncomfortable because he ate old pizza for breakfast and his pants are digging in to his stomach. His hair has gone all fuzzy.

The lights change and he can move forward, but only two car spaces. Miro looks at the other drivers and sees that some are angry. Others just seem to be staring into space. The rain does strange things to people. As he moves through the lights they go orange and he tries to stop. The brakes won't work and his car crashes into the car in front. Bang.

The driver of the other car is really mad. He gets out of his car and walks over to Miro's car. Miro gets his wallet and takes out his drivers' licence. He then gets out and greets the man, knowing that this acident would cost him money.

Structure

Audience

There is a lack of sensory detail to engage the imagination of the reader. Some adjectives and verbs maintain audience interest.

Character and setting

The writer attempts to create believable characters but fails to use descriptive language. Character and setting are simplistic.

Text structure

The first paragraph is the story's orientation.

The complication of the story is less easily identified.

The resolution is obvious.

Paragraphing

The writer attempts to use a new paragraph to introduce a new thought or situation.

Cohesion

Connectives are used infrequently. The perspective may change within the narrative.

Language and Ideas

Vocabulary

The writer attempts to use simple verbs and adjectives.

Sentence structure

The writer uses mostly simple sentences and compound sentences.

Ideas

The story has simplistic ideas. No clear theme is established.

Punctuation

Simple punctuation is used. Sometimes punctuation is missing or incorrect.

Spelling

Most words are frequently used words with regular spelling. Some words are spelt incorrectly.

These writing samples have been analysed based on the marking criteria used by markers to assess the NAPLAN Writing Test.

Writing Mini Test 2

An accident

Rain falls rhythmically on the windscreen of the car, only to be flicked aside by the overworked wipers. Miro watched the blades as he stops at the 13th set of red traffic lights. The rain has been falling for three days.

That morning Miro's '74 Beetle had refused to start. Turning the key and whispering encouraging words, the bug coughed and wheezed then sat still. Admitting defeat, Miro ran inside and grabbed the keys for his wife's Getz. His wife hadn't driven the car in weeks, telling Miro that the brakes were as unreliable as Miro was. She had taken the bus.

So here Miro sits, in a car too small for a child, fighting through three lanes of traffic. His grey suit pants are tight and he begins to regret having eaten pizza for breakfast. His hair has turned to fuzz in the damp air. The lights change to green and Miro's car moves two car lengths forward. Since the rain began Miro has been watching other people in their cars. Most sit looking angry. Others seem to stare into nothingness.

The next set of lights are orange and Miro puts his foot on the brake to slow down. But they would not do as they were supposed to do and Miro found himself out of control and heading towards another car. The crunch of metal tells Miro that he has hit the other car. The owner is furious and immediately exits his car and heads towards Miro. The rain keeps coming down hard and makes the man look more intimidating. Quickly, Miro searches his pockets and finds his wallet. Taking out his driver's licence and grabbing a pen from his other pocket, Miro got out of the car.

Structure

Audience

Attempts are made to engage the audience through strong verbs and description of the rain.

Character and setting

Personification of the car is used.

Miro's character is established through description.

Text structure

The first paragraph is the story's orientation.

The complication of the story—the car doesn't work—is easily identified.

The resolution is a cliff-hanger.

Paragraphing

A new paragraph is used to introduce a new thought or situation.

Cohesion

Connectives are used to enhance the story.

There is continuity of ideas throughout the story—the focus is on Miro's perspective.

Language and Ideas

Vocabulary

The writer uses strong verbs, adverbs and adjectives.

Attempts are made to use a variety of everyday and more complex vocabulary.

Sentence structure

The writer uses a variety of simple, compound and complex sentences.

Ideas

The story has good ideas. Focus is on the idea of an accident.

Punctuation

Correct punctuation is used throughout the story.

Simple punctuation is used.

Spelling

All words are correctly spelt.

Some words with irregular spelling patterns are included.

Please note that this sample has not been written under test conditions. During a test you might not have the time

Writing Mini Test 2

Structure

Audience

Figurative language—simile and personification—is used to create imagery for the reader.

Character and setting

Personification of the car continues, suggesting that it will feature significantly in the narrative.

Use of parenthesis creates a humorous and personal voice for the main character.

Text structure

The first paragraph is the story's orientation.

The descriptive language establishes the setting.

The complication of the story is easily identified—the car brake doesn't work.

The resolution is a cliff-hanger.

Paragraphing

A new paragraph is used to introduce a new thought or situation.

Cohesion

Connectives are used appropriately to enhance the reading. There is continuity of ideas throughout the story—the focus is on Miro's perspective.

An accident

Heavy fat drops fall rhythmically on the windscreen of the groaning car, only to be unceremoniously flicked aside by the overworked wipers. The dance of the blades mesmerise Miro as he stops at the thirteenth set of red traffic lights. Drop. Flick. Drop. Flick. The rain has been falling for three days.

That morning Miro's 74 Beetle (toffee apple red with black racing stripes) had refused to start. He had tried to get it going, turning the key and whispering encouraging words like a mother cajoling a child to swallow bitter medicine, but the bug coughed and wheezed and then sat silently still. Admitting defeat, and with no other option, Miro ran inside and grabbed the keys for his wife's Getz (fake banana yellow). His wife hadn't driven the car in weeks, having protested loudly that the brakes were as unreliable as Miro himself. She had taken the bus.

So here Miro sits: in a car too small for a child, fighting through three lanes of dense traffic as the sky slowly releases a constant barrage of water. His grey suit pants are tight around his stomach and he begins to regret having eaten the leftover super-supreme for breakfast. Tight black curls on his head turn to spirals of fuzz as the air moistens. Finally the lights flick to the glory of green and Miro is rewarded for his patience, edging two car lengths forward. Stopped again. Since the rain began Miro has been surprised by what he sees others do in their cars. Most sit with a concentrated look of barely contained rage. Others seem to drift into a trance, hypnotised by the low lullaby of the rain splattering the metal and plastic bubble surrounding them. A bubble that separates these workers – these humans – from nature and from each other.

The next set of lights greets Miro with amber and with a squeeze of the brake he attempts to comply with its command to slow. Unfortunately the brakes are as defiant as bored school children and refuse to oblige. Encased in his own bubble of metal and plastic Miro races towards the barely contained rage in the car to his left. The crunch of metal on metal and the inaudible splinter of a pricey spray job inform Miro that the cars have met in damage. The next sounds are even less pleasing – the rage that had been so tightly contained has popped and has begun an intimidating (and vocal) approach towards the driver's door of Miro's car. Despite the commotion, the rain drives on, throwing sheets of water on the man's body as he glares ominously through Miro's now breath-fogged windows. Hastily fumbling in his pockets, Miro retrieves his beaten and bare wallet and removes his driver's licence. A quick fish in the breast pocket of his shirt provides him with a fountain pen and a small piece of paper.

Waving his personal details at the stranger, Miro ventures out into the rain.

Language and Ideas

Vocabulary

Imagery is created through alliteration and metaphor.

The writer uses strong verbs, adverbs and adjectives.

The word *fish* is used as a verb and not a noun.

Sentence structure

A variety of sentence lengths creates interest and shows control.

Short sentences create drama.

Ideas

The story has sophisticated ideas. The theme is clearly established: it is about conformity and loss of meaning in modern life.

Punctuation

Correct complex punctuation is used throughout the story.

Spelling

All words are correctly spelt.

Difficult and challenging words are frequently included.

Please note that a Standard level of sample writing has not been provided. Such a sample would not be as well written as this Intermediate sample. This sample has not been written under test conditions. However, it gives you a standard to aim for.

Writing Mini Test 3

The hunt

I woke up early. Dad and I were off hunting. We were spending three days together and missing work and school. It took me ages to get out of bed because it was so early. I had to get into my camo clothes and new big boots.

Dad was already awake and cleaning his gun. It got me scared because I hadn't seen a gun before. It made me scared of using one and killing something. I felt sick.

We had a quick breakfast and then checked that we had all of our stuff for the hunting trip. Dad got a new car for us to go in and it made me get excited again. I thought the trip would be fun.

We drove for three hours and then made it to the bush. The land was mostly flat but there were some trees and we knew that was where the wild boars would be. We would chase them in the car and then camp somewhere in the bush.

That *was* the plan, anyway.

It was Dad's first time hunting and he had watched a YouTube video to learn how to hunt. Not a good idea. I was beginning to get worried. It didn't matter thought because at least I got time off school.

We began our hunt when it was really hot. We drove into the bush and tried to find the boars. Dad was sure that the area was safe to drive in but he was wrong. The Jeep fell into an old river bed and it broke. We knew that the hunt was over.

Dad was great about it. It took two hours for us to be rescued but we got time to chat and Dad told me he was scared of hunting. I told him I had been too and this was a nice moment for us. The hunt might not have been good because we didn't kill things, but it was good because it brought Dad and I together again.

Structure

Audience

Attempts are made to engage the reader through the description of events and setting.

Character and setting

Simple verbs are included to capture the experience of the character.

First-person narrative is used.

Text structure

Events are recounted in chronological order.

Paragraphing

There are attempts to use new paragraphs to introduce a new thought or situation.

Cohesion

Ideas and paragraphs are occasionally linked with connectives.

Focus is on the son's perspective.

Language and Ideas

Vocabulary

Everyday words and some less common words are included.

Some simple adjectives and adverbs are used to enhance the recount.

Sentence structure

The text is written mostly with simple sentences. There is less variety in sentence lengths.

Ideas

There are links to the concept of the story—a hunt.

Punctuation

Simple punctuation is used throughout.

Spelling

Some words are spelt incorrectly.

Frequently used words and words with regular spelling pattern are included.

These writing samples have been analysed based on the marking criteria used by markers to assess the NAPLAN Writing Test.

The hunt

It was early in the morning. The birds and sun were still asleep and it was cold. Why was I awake so early? The hunt. Those two words had been in my head for over three weeks—ever since my dad had suggested we skip school and work for a few days and explore what it means to be 'a man'.

I got out of bed slowly and I got myself dressed in army greens. Dad had bought us special outfits designed to hide us in the bush. He said they were the kind professional hunters wore. The boots were hard to get on and they were really heavy.

I found Dad downstairs in the kitchen. He sat with a gun on his lap. I'd never seen a gun before. I was starting to get worried and feel sick. I don't think I can shoot a gun or kill an animal.

Breakfast was over quickly. I didn't feel like eating much, so I just had a small bowl of cornflakes. After breakfast we checked our supplies and gear and then got into the Jeep that Dad had hired for our trip. It was a pretty nice car and the new car smell got me excited about spending time with Dad.

After three hours of boring driving we reached what we could confidently call 'The Bush.' The land was flat and red. In the bush we hoped to find some wild boars. The plan was that we would spend our days chasing pigs in the Jeep and then camp when we found an open clearing.

That *was* the plan, anyway.

See, Dad had never been hunting before. He'd never even seen a wild boar in the flesh. But he had watched a YouTube video called 'Hunting Game in the Australian Bush'. I didn't really trust the video but he said it was really popular. I just felt happy to be getting time off school, so I didn't complain.

After lunch we began our hunt. Dad steared the Jeep into the trees and we headed south. The tutorial had said that the ground in these parts was reliable but it was wrong! As we were driving we ran into a deep old river bed. The car crunched to a stop and we knew it had ended our hunting trip.

Dad was great about it. While we waited to be rescued Dad told me how scared he was of guns and of killing. I told him I felt the same way. It was great to be honest with each other.

I guess, reflecting now on that failed hunt, that it was fate that we would end up spending our time together in the way we did. It made me realise that my dad is a gentle giant.

Structure

Audience

Some descriptive language is included in an attempt to engage the reader's imagination.

The introduction attempts to help orient the reader.

Character and setting

Verbs are used to capture the experience of the character.

First-person narrative is used to reveal the character's thoughts.

Text structure

Events are recounted in chronological order.

The reader discovers the importance of an event at the conclusion of the story.

Paragraphing

A new paragraph is used to introduce a new thought or situation.

Cohesion

Ideas and paragraphs are linked throughout by simple connectives.

There is continuity of ideas throughout the story.

Language and Ideas

Vocabulary

More frequently used words and some difficult vocabulary are included.

Adjectives and adverbs are used to enhance the recount.

Sentence structure

There is some variety in sentence lengths to create interest.

Ideas

There is a direct link to the concept of the story—a hunt.

The concept is made clear throughout.

Punctuation

Most of the punctuation is correct.

Some complex punctuation is used.

Spelling

Most words are correctly spelt but this one is incorrect.

Some difficult words are included.

Please note that this sample has not been written under test conditions. However, it gives you a standard to aim for.

Structure

Audience

Poetic devices/figurative language enhances the story.

Descriptive language engages the reader's attention.

There is awareness of audience expectations.

The introduction helps to orient the reader.

Character and setting

Strong verbs capture the experience of the character.

First-person narrative is used to reveal the character's thoughts and attitudes.

Text structure

Events are recounted in chronological order.

The reader discovers the importance of an event at the conclusion of the story.

Paragraphing

A new paragraph is used to introduce a new thought or situation.

Cohesion

Ideas and paragraphs are linked throughout by connectives.

There is continuity of ideas throughout the story—the focus is on the son's perspective.

The hunt

It was 4.36 am. The birds and sun were still asleep and a thick frost crusted up my bedroom window. So why was I awake at such a ludicrous hour? The hunt. Those two words had been rumbling around in my head for over three weeks—ever since my dad had suggested we skip school and work for a few days and explore what it means to be 'a man'.

Moving slowly out of my far too cosy bed, I got myself dressed in army greens. Dad had bought us special outfits designed to camouflage us in the bush. He said they were the kind professional hunters wore. The boots were hard to get on—there were at least a thousand lace holes—and once on the weight of them made me feel as though I were wearing lead weights on my feet.

I found Dad downstairs in the kitchen. He was caressing what looked like a shotgun. I'd never seen a real gun before. The hunt had seemed like a good idea when Dad suggested it, but the sight of the gun made me feel slightly nauseous. Was I really going to hold one of those things? Was I going to kill a living creature?

Breakfast was over swiftly. Dad had eaten much earlier so I rushed through a small bowl of half-stale cornflakes. Food had become as unappealing as the thought of the hunt. Having double-checked our supplies and gear, we clambered up into the back of the Jeep that Dad had hired especially for our trip. It was a pretty impressive vehicle and the smell of the new interior got me excited once more about the prospect of spending time with Dad in the wilderness.

After three hours of relatively mundane driving—made worse by Dad's embarrassing choice of music—we reached what we could confidently call 'The Bush'. The land was flat and red. There were clumps of densely clustered trees and it was in one of these that we hoped to find our game—wild boars. The plan was that we would spend our days crashing through the scrub chasing pigs in the Jeep and then camp when we found a relatively open clearing.

That *was* the plan, anyway.

See, Dad had never been hunting before. He'd never even seen a wild boar in the flesh. But he had watched a YouTube tutorial titled 'Hunting Game in the Australian Bush'. He told me it had received over 30,000 hits. It must have been good, right? In my mind I'd had my doubts, but why should I care? I was getting three days off school and I was spending it with Dad.

At the height of the day, when the kangaroos were all sleeping in the shade and presumably the boars were doing the same, we began our hunt. Dad skilfully steered the shiny Jeep into the undergrowth and we headed south. The tutorial had said that the ground in these parts was reliable—dry, not many holes or rough patches and certainly no large rocks to tackle. All I can say is never trust the Internet or 30,000 strangers.

Rounding a bend in the disused track we fell prey to a dry creek bed. The Jeep dropped down over a metre at speed. The crunching sound in the front end of the car and plastic puff of the air bags inflating informed us that the hunt was over.

Dad was great about it. We spent two hours waiting for a tow from the nearest town and in that time Dad confessed that he was petrified of guns. He hadn't even loaded his and was relying on his viewing of another tutorial to work out exactly how to do it. Since we were being open, I told him that I had felt exactly the same. Such frankness between father and son was unusual for us. It was great.

I guess, reflecting now on that failed hunt, that it was serendipitous for it to be cut short as it had been. The experience really helped me to discover my father, the gentle giant.

Language and Ideas

Vocabulary

More difficult vocabulary is included.

Poetic devices are used:
- hyperbole (exaggeration used for effect) informs the reader of the many holes for the laces
- metaphor captures the weight of the boots.

Adjectives and adverbs are used to enhance the recount.

Sentence structure

Short and simple sentences are used when appropriate.

A variety of sentence lengths are used to avoid monotony and create interest.

Ideas

There is a direct link to the concept of the story—a hunt.

The concept is made clear throughout.

Punctuation

Correct punctuation is used.

Complex punctuation is used.

Spelling

All words are correctly spelt.

There is frequent inclusion of difficult and challenging words.

Please note that this sample has not been written under test conditions. During a test you might not have the time to produce such a polished piece of writing. However, this sample gives you a standard to aim for.

Television does more harm than good

Television is bad for you. It is bad for your brain. Three reasons you shouldn't watch television are that it is full of ads, it has violence in it and it can make you fat. This is why television does more harm than good.

Ads on TV make kids want to buy bad things. There are heaps of ads on telly for things like junk food and toys. Kids always want to buy this stuff and that's why it is bad to watch television all the time. We shouldn't let them watch it.

There are heaps of bad shows on telly that make you want to do bad things like swear and hurt people. Kids like to copy what they see others do and that's why shows like this are bad for them. This is why television is harmful for people.

Ads and bad shows is a good reason not to watch television but what about the fact that it makes you all big and fat? You have to sit down and watch telly and this means you're being lazy. This makes you unhelthy. Kids have lots of energy and they need to run around and play. TV makes them lazy. We don't want our world to be full of fat lazy people.

Television is a killer. It kills our minds and bodies and we need to stop watching it. It is bad because it makes us want bad things, do bad things and be lazy. We should turn it off and go outside to be fit.

Structure

Audience

A simplistic outlining of the position that television is harmful is given.

The writer attempts to outline reasons to support the argument.

Persuasive techniques

The writer tries to use a variety of persuasive techniques, including emotive words and high modal words.

Text structure

The correct structure of a persuasive text is used, including introduction and supporting paragraphs, and a conclusion is attempted. A conclusion and/or introduction may be missing.

Paragraphing

The writer attempts to use a new paragraph to introduce a new idea.

Cohesion

Connectives are used infrequently.

Supporting lines of argument lack detail.

Language and Ideas

Vocabulary

The writer attempts to use language appropriate to the purpose: to persuade.

The writer attempts to use simple verbs and adjectives.

Sentence structure

The writer uses mostly simple sentences and some compound sentences.

Ideas

Ideas are simple and reasons are basic in an attempt to support the argument.

Punctuation

Simple punctuation is used. Sometimes punctuation is missing or incorrect.

Spelling

Most words are frequently used words with regular spelling. Some words are spelt incorrectly.

These writing samples have been analysed based on the marking criteria used by markers to assess the NAPLAN Writing Test.

Writing Sample Test 1

Television does more harm than good

Tiny pieces of information flying through space and landing into your innocent child's eyes. This is television. So how damaging is television to the human brain? And why do young people spend so much time sitting in front of it? There are three reasons why watching television may be harmful. Television is not just shows. There are advertisements encouraging young people to buy unhealthy products. The actual shows themselves may be harmful as they feature violence and mature themes. Finally, watching television makes people inactive, which is bad for their health. It is for these reasons that it can be said that television does more harm than good.

Television advertisements make viewers buy products they don't need. Advertisements every 7–10 minutes are guaranteed during every program. Lollies, video games, fast food and toys are forced upon young people and they are not healthy. This is bad for young people who always want new things. Why do we expose them to these products so much?

Also there are so many programs on television that many of them are bad for people. It's hard for parents to stop their kids from watching shows that contain violence and adult themes. Children may try to copy what they see on television and this will make them be violent. It is easy to see that this is a bad thing for young people and shows that television can be harmful.

Ads and violence seem pretty bad, but what about the fact that television makes you lazy and unfit? Sitting in front of the television stops people being active. Young people need to be active because they have a lot of energy. If they don't use this energy it can turn into fat. People don't play sport as much any more because they would rather watch it on television. This is a bad thing because people are becoming lazy and fat. People need to turn off the television, go outside and be active.

Television is a killer. It is killing the minds and bodies of young people around the world. It makes them want lots of bad products, behave in the wrong way and be unfit. It is important that society learns to say no to television because it is harmful to our health.

Please note that this sample has not been written under test conditions. However, it gives you a standard to aim for.

Structure

Audience

The writer attempts to alert the reader to his or her position—that television is harmful.

Emotive phrases engage the emotions of the reader.

Persuasive techniques

The writer tries to use a variety of high modal words to reinforce his or her position.

Rhetorical questions encourage thought in the reader.

Text structure

The correct structure of a persuasive text is used, including introduction, supporting paragraphs and conclusion.

Paragraphing

A new paragraph is used to introduce a new idea. The paragraphs are a little too brief.

Cohesion

Basic connectives are used to show connections between ideas and enhance the argument.

Each paragraph features reasons to support the argument.

Language and Ideas

Vocabulary

Language choices are appropriate to the purpose: to persuade.

The writer attempts to use a combination of everyday and more complex vocabulary, including strong verbs and adjectives.

Sentence structure

The writer uses a variety of simple and compound sentences.

Ideas

The writer uses good ideas that are relevant to the argument and are explained in the body of the text to support the persuasive argument.

Punctuation

Correct punctuation is used throughout the argument.

Simple punctuation is used.

Spelling

All words are correctly spelt.

Some difficult and challenging words are included.

Writing Sample Test 1

Television does more harm than good

Tiny invisible particles of visual information hurtling through space and landing onto the retina of your innocent child's eyes. Hello and welcome to television. So just how damaging is television to the squishy grey matter that is the human brain? And why is it that young people spend so much time sitting like zombies in front of the glowing screen? There are three good reasons why parents should be wary when deciding how much television they allow their children to watch. Television may seem to be full of frivolous and harmless narratives, but embedded within are advertisements enticing young people to consume unhealthy products. Often the content of the shows themselves may be harmful, projecting images of violence and promiscuity. Finally, the act of watching television itself results in inactivity and thus physically unhealthy young people. It is for these three reasons that it can be concluded that television does more harm than good.

Television advertisements encourage viewers to buy products they do not need. Sitting and enjoying the hottest show on television? Advertisements every 7–10 minutes are guaranteed. Confectionery, video games, fast food and expensive toys are just a few of the unhealthy products that are targeted at young people. Young people are vulnerable to these negative influences. Why expose them to unhealthy food options? Why expose them to unnecessary and expensive products?

Furthermore, there are thousands of television programs to which children can be exposed. The sheer number means it is impossible for parents to effectively regulate what their children are watching. Programs today contain images of violence that can impact negatively on the behaviours of young people, who may decide to emulate the violence in their own worlds. Themes of shows may also be too mature and unsuitable for innocent young minds. Once again, this can be harmful as the young viewers may accept such behaviour as normal.

Enticing advertisements and unsuitable content seem reason enough to accept that television is harmful. But what about the physical effects of sitting passively in front of the television for prolonged periods of time? It is this consequence of television that is the most disturbing. Young people must be active. Their high energy levels require activity if they are to have healthy bodies and minds. More and more young people are choosing to watch sport on television instead of participating in the sports themselves. Obesity is almost an epidemic among young people in the Western world and television watching contributes to this problem. It is essential that the image box is turned off and its viewers are pushed outside to exercise. The only sure way to good health is to exercise often. It is impossible to watch television for hours on end and be physically fit.

Television is a killer. It is killing the minds and bodies of young people around the world. It encourages them to demand products they do not need, it teaches them to behave in unacceptable ways and it forces them to be sedentary, leading to being physically unhealthy. Parents owe it to their children to take control and turn off the box.

Structure

Audience

The writer immediately alerts the reader to the position taken—that television is harmful.

Emotive phrases engage the emotions of the reader.

Persuasive techniques

High modal words enforce the writer's position.

Rhetorical questions encourage thought in the reader.

Repetition emphasises the writer's point.

Text structure

The correct structure of a persuasive text is used, including introduction, supporting paragraphs and conclusion. This structure assists in the development of the writer's position.

Paragraphing

A new paragraph is used to introduce a new idea.

Cohesion

Connectives and referring words are used to show connections between ideas and enhance the argument.

All supporting lines of argument are articulated fully and supported by evidence and/or reasons.

Language and Ideas

Vocabulary

Language choices are appropriate to the purpose: to persuade.

The writer uses strong verbs and adjectives.

Sentence structure

All sentences are grammatically correct, well structured and meaningful.

Ideas

Well-selected and relevant ideas are elaborated in the body of the text to support the persuasive argument.

Punctuation

Correct complex punctuation is used throughout the argument.

Spelling

All words are correctly spelt.

Difficult and challenging words are frequently included.

Please note that this sample has not been written under test conditions. During a test you might not have the time to produce such a polished piece of writing. However, this sample gives you a standard to aim for.

Writing Sample Test 2

The cage

It is so hot in this cage. My throat is dry and I need a drink. I feel like I could die.

There are others who are hot as well and they are all hanging together trying to keep away from the sun. They look so dirty and gross like they need a bath. I guess I look just as dirty. We've been in this box for ages and ages. It's pretty horrible. I can't even remember when we were put in here.

The box is so dirty too and it's making my feet dirty. Everyone is just going to the toilet on the floor which is really gross. I don't even want to stand on the floor it is so dirty. It smells bad. There are flies and maggots and I've seen others in here eat them.

There isn't much room in here. I think there is a street outside because it sounds like a street. Sometimes we are poked with a stick and it hurts really badly. They don't hit us. Just stick us.

There is a latch at the front of the cage and it was opened the other day. When it opened I heard bad noises like crying and screaming. I think there are less of us in here now. I bet bad things are happening. Being stuck in a cage is bad. I wonder where they go to.

The box is really tuff. I can't break it because I have tried but my nails broke. The people who caught us must be really clever because they built a box we can't get out of.

It is night again and I am scared in this cage. I am crouching with my pups because they are just babies and they are scared. Being a dog trapped in a cage is bad. Maybe tomorrow the men will take one of my pups away. I will just have to wait.

Structure

Audience

The writing lacks sensory detail to engages the imagination of the reader.

Some adjectives and verbs are used to maintain audience interest.

Character and setting

The writer attempts to create believable characters but fails to use descriptive language.

Character and setting are simplistic.

Text structure

The first paragraph is the story's orientation.

The complication is less easily identified.

Paragraphing

Writer attempts to use a new paragraph to introduce a new thought or situation.

Cohesion

Connectives are used infrequently.

The perspective may change within the narrative.

Language and Ideas

Vocabulary

The writer attempts to use simple verbs and adjectives.

Sentence structure

Writer uses mostly simple sentences and compound sentences.

Ideas

The story has more simplistic ideas. No clear theme is established.

Punctuation

Simple punctuation is used. Sometimes punctuation is missing or incorrect.

Spelling

Most words are frequently used words with regular spelling. Some words are spelt incorrectly.

These writing samples have been analysed based on the marking criteria used by markers to assess the NAPLAN Writing Test.

Writing Sample Test 2

Intermediate level — Sample of Narrative Writing

Structure

Audience

Writer attempts to engage the audience through strong verbs and description of the tongue.

Character and setting

First person narrative develops the character.

Writer tries to create the setting through descriptive language.

Text structure

The first paragraph is the story's orientation.

The complication of the story is easily identified—they are stuck in a cage.

The resolution is a cliff-hanger.

Paragraphing

A new paragraph is used to introduce a new thought or situation.

Cohesion

Connectives are used to enhance the story.

There is continuity of ideas throughout the story—the focus is on the mother dog's perspective.

The cage

It is hot in here. My throat is so dry that I can barely swallow. My tongue hangs limply from my mouth. This heat is certain death.

Looking around me I see others suffering from the heat. They clump together in the corner trying to get some shade from the sun. Looking at them with their messy hair and worried eyes, I realise that I probably look just as bad. We have been in this cage—for what feels like half of my life. I'm sure it hasn't been but it has been days since we were forced into this death crate.

The floor I stand on is filthy and my feet are black. It is smelly because everyone must use the floor as their toilet and the heat makes the smell worse. Flies have decided to make the filth home and their maggot babies wriggle through the dirt. I have seen some in here eat them because they are starving.

If I look to the right I can see outside of the cage. It is probably a street because it sounds like one. Lately a long stick has been poked into the cage. It pokes into our stomachs and hurts us. It pokes and pokes. I guess we're lucky it doesn't hit.

Last night the cage was opened. I know it was. The little bronze latch near the front of the cage was opened and then I heard sounds that made me shake with fear. There was whimpering and cries of pain. Then there was more room in the box—I think they are taking some of us. I wonder where they are taking them to. I bet it isn't a nice place.

I begin to wonder who built this contraption that may become my final resting place. The wooden slats are poorly carved and appear to have been nailed together with great haste. Or maybe just without any care. I tried to get out today. I scratched as hard as I could. Nothing happened except my nails were broken and hurt. The cage is too strong.

The sun is setting and I keep my normal position. I huddle with my two pups. They are so little and are hungry and thirsty all of the time. I am worried for my babies and hope they are not taken by the man with the stick. Maybe tomorrow this old dog will find out what lies outside of the cage.

Language and Ideas

Vocabulary

The writer uses strong verbs, adverbs and adjectives.

Attempts are made to use a variety of everyday and more complex vocabulary.

Sentence structure

A variety of simple, compound and complex sentences are used.

Ideas

The story has good ideas. Focus is on the idea of the cage.

Punctuation

Correct punctuation is used throughout the story.

Simple punctuation used.

Spelling

All words are correctly spelt.

Some words with irregular spelling patterns are used.

Please note that this sample has not been written under test conditions. However, it gives you a standard to aim for.

Writing Sample Test 2

The cage

It is hot in here. Not lying on a beach hot; suffocatingly hot. My throat is so dry that I can barely swallow. My once pink tongue is now a pearly white and hangs limply from my mouth. This heat is certain death.

Looking around me I see others suffering from the oppressive heat. They clump together in the far corner in a vain attempt to get some shade from the angry sun. Looking at them with their matted hair and desperate eyes, I realise that my own appearance must resemble theirs. We have been in this box—this cage—for what feels like half of my life. I'm sure it hasn't been but the sun has risen and fallen at least ten times since we were wrangled into this wooden crate of death.

The floor on which my tired and blackened feet stand is filthy. No one is let out to relieve themselves; all bodily functions take place in the cage. This contributes to most of the filth. The smell is indescribable and made increasingly worse by the heat. What's worse is that flies have chosen this place as their home and maternity ward. The maggots wiggle on the floor and some of the captives have taken to eating them. Extreme hunger and a desire to live often prompt one to do the unthinkable.

Turning my head to the right, I can just barely see outside the cage to the world beyond. I think we are on a street. I can hear the sounds of bicycle bells, children resisting their parents and the occasional growl of a car engine. Sometimes a long thin stick is shoved aggressively into the cage; it works its way into the stomachs of us captives. Poking. Prodding. We're lucky because it can't hit. There's no room to raise the stick high enough to do any damage, so the wielder of the stick doesn't bother. The poking is bad enough.

Two sun-rises ago I'm sure that the cage was opened. Towards the front of the box is a small bronze latch allowing a small part of the wall to be forced ajar. The sounds of whimpering and crying out in pain accompanied this event. I suppose we're one or two fewer in here now. That can't be a bad thing—surely it means more room to move and less filth? Yet the place is still congested—maybe they only take little ones? I can't help imagining where the door goes to and to where they were taken. Chances are it's not a nice place. There's nothing nice about our situation.

I begin to wonder who built this contraption that may become my final resting place. The wooden slats are poorly carved and appear to have been nailed together with great haste. Or maybe just without any care. Despite the ugly appearance of the box it is still strong. I have scratched at a panel for a whole day and barely a mark was made. My only reward for my effort was broken, bleeding and sore nails. The wood is strong. Our captors got that right.

As the sun begins to fade from the sky again, leaving only fingers of weak light to pierce the cage, I resume my nightly position. I huddle with my two pups. They are only ten weeks old and suffering badly from lack of water and food. They keep me alive but every night I fear it may be my last with them. The man with the stick may be selecting the smallest of our lot. Maybe they are prized more than us old dogs? The questions are trapped in my head, just like we are trapped in this cage. Maybe tomorrow I'll get my answers?

Structure

Audience

Poetic devices/language features enhance the story.

Descriptive language engages the reader's attention.

The writer shows awareness of audience expectations.

Detailed description helps to orient the reader.

Character and setting

Strong verbs allow the reader to experience life in the cage.

No character is introduced as the focus is on the cage itself.

Text structure

The text is well structured so that new areas of the cage are revealed slowly to create interest and suspense.

Paragraphing

A new paragraph is used to introduce a new aspect of the cage.

Cohesion

Ideas and paragraphs are linked throughout by connectives.

There is continuity of ideas throughout the story—focus is on the cage itself.

Language and Ideas

Vocabulary

Difficult vocabulary is included.

Adjectives and adverbs are used to enhance the writing.

Sentence structure

Short and simple sentences create drama.

A variety of sentence types and lengths is used to avoid monotony and create interest.

Ideas

Direct links are made to the concept of the story: the cage.

The concept is made clear throughout.

Punctuation

Punctuation is used correctly.

Complex punctuation is used.

Spelling

All words are correctly spelt.

Difficult and challenging words are frequently included.

Please note that this sample has not been written under test conditions. During a test you might not have the time to produce such a polished piece of writing. However, this sample gives you a standard to aim for.

SPELLING WORDS FOR CONVENTIONS OF LANGUAGE TESTS

To the teacher or parent

First read and say the word slowly and clearly. Then read the sentence with the word in it. Then repeat the word again. Give the student time to write their answer. If the student is not sure, then ask them to guess. It is okay to skip a word if it is not known.

Spelling words for Mini Test 1

Word	Example
1 lightning	The cause of lightning has only just been identified.
2 fierce	The child was involved in a fierce competition.
3 weird	The fridge made a weird humming noise.
4 tangle	The cables were left in a messy tangle.
5 village	A town is larger than a village, but smaller than a city.
6 governor	The governor was concerned about the impact of the urban sprawl.
7 sign	Jasper couldn't believe what had happened. It was a sign!
8 faith	He knew that his faith would one day be repaid.
9 aching	Even though his ankle was swollen and aching, he had managed to score the winning goal.
10 systems	Moles create complex systems of tunnels underground.
11 fail	Fireworks never fail to amaze me.
12 squad	Swimmers of all ages can become a member of a swimming squad.
13 development	It doesn't matter what stage of your development you are at.
14 enthusiasm	Joining a squad allows you to share your enthusiasm for the water.
15 colour	Samantha was shocked by the colour of her mother's hair.

Spelling words for Mini Test 2

Word	Example
1 police	A thumbprint was all that was needed for the police to catch the thief.
2 average	The average 30-year-old woman in the United Kingdom owns twenty-one handbags.
3 braces	Having waited what seemed like a lifetime, Harry finally had his braces removed.
4 Furthermore	Furthermore, the cost of living in Sydney is relatively cheap compared to that in Tokyo.
5 difficult	It was a difficult undertaking, yet Sami knew someone had to be responsible for it.
6 government	The protesters feared a violent backlash from their government.
7 whispered	The wind whispered through the trees.
8 mosaics	Upon the grass tiny slivers of moonlight shone to create mosaics.
9 witnessed	However, this beauteous sight was witnessed by none.
10 blackmail	Following the politician's election, the gang chose to blackmail him.
11 points	Would you like to highlight the key points in the passage.
12 executed	In hindsight the experiment could have been better executed.
13 paperweight	Clutching the glass paperweight, Andy struggled to remain calm.
14 beginning	Beneath his agitated feet the redwood floorboards were beginning to scuff.
15 scarecrow	If only Jasper had left that scarecrow alone, none of this would have happened!

SPELLING WORDS FOR CONVENTIONS OF LANGUAGE TESTS

Spelling words for Mini Test 3

Word	Example
1 invitation	It was less than ten minutes since the invitation had arrived.
2 intelligent	She was an intelligent young woman and knew what the invitation meant.
3 demonstrate	She must demonstrate her fine manners and her willingness to marry Sir Albert.
4 anniversary	Mother and Father celebrated their 50th wedding anniversary.
5 agriculture	I study agriculture this year. Do you?
6 commentator	The sports commentator fell off his chair when the team scored.
7 fundamental	It is a fundamental requirement of learning to surf that you know how to swim.
8 operator	I could not hear the operator on the other end of the phone.
9 reputation	Elms have a reputation for being ornamental.
10 established	Elms originated in Asia but they have established themselves as far as North America.
11 consequence	As a consequence of the development of Dutch elm disease the number of elms being sold is falling.
12 permission	James did not grant me permission to enter the building.
13 persuade	Ayden attempted to persuade me that he was a rock star.
14 acceptable	When you are attending an interview for a job, it is important that you ensure that your appearance is acceptable.
15 colleagues	You must ensure that you are polite to all people you meet at the interview, as these people may be your colleagues in the future.

Spelling words for Mini Test 4

Word	Example
1 crucial	It is crucial that young children drink full cream milk.
2 cautious	Mothers should be cautious when giving their young children skim milk as it does not provide enough calcium.
3 cease	If young children cease to drink full cream milk their bones and teeth can become brittle.
4 conscious	Despite having fallen over 20 metres to the ground, the man was still conscious.
5 device	The flotation device was not buoyant enough to save all of the stranded men.
6 column	The teacher informed us that we needed to write up our spelling words in a column.
7 amateur	The World Masters Games is a competition for amateur athletes.
8 protein	Vegetarians must ensure that they include alternative protein sources in their meat-free diets.
9 seize	"Stop! Guards, seize that man!" shouted the angry Roman emperor.
10 satellite	From a distance the satellite looked like a tiny blinking star moving slowly across the sky.
11 fault	"It's not my fault the car is broken!" exclaimed Judy to her frustrated husband.
12 maroon	The main colours for the Manly Warringah Sea Eagles are white and maroon.
13 integrate	The prisoner found it difficult to integrate back into society.
14 headquarters	He frequently had to attend parole meetings at the police headquarters.
15 mechanism	The clock's mechanism had a fault in it.

SPELLING WORDS FOR CONVENTIONS OF LANGUAGE TESTS

Spelling words for Mini Test 5

Word	Example
1 victimise	'Don't victimise those who are different' was the motto of our school.
2 vulnerable	The great elm tree is vulnerable to a number of new diseases.
3 substantial	A substantial number of wizards had gathered for the first of four important tournaments.
4 tremendous	The impact of the December 2004 tsunami was tremendous.
5 stomach	I could not believe that Gemma had such a flat stomach even though she had eaten three cheeseburgers.
6 sufficient	When baking cookies it is essential that you have a sufficient amount of chocolate chips.
7 rough	Often little boys play rough with their friends in order to understand the boundaries of acceptable behaviour.
8 paranoia	On day seven the paranoia set in. People began looking at one another suspiciously.
9 shortage	Food shortage always brings out the worst in people. This group was no exception.
10 provision	The only provision that existed in abundance on the island was bananas.
11 obtain	Jeff was trying to obtain his green P-plates, but the test seemed too difficult.
12 negotiate	Police negotiate with criminals on a daily basis and therefore require excellent patience and communication skills.
13 accusation	"The accusation that I hit the woman is entirely false," the defendant stated to the court.
14 anxious	Rubbing his hands continuously, the young man revealed to the interviewer that he was anxious.
15 celebration	The celebration planned for Craig's birthday was even bigger than the one for Bianca's birthday.

Spelling words for Mini Test 6

Word	Example
1 except	Everyone except Calvin was admitted to the show; Calvin didn't have enough money.
2 surprised	Children are often surprised to learn that the moon is not made out of cheese.
3 deficit	After 12 hours of shopping with my mother's credit card, a budget deficit halted my further spending.
4 chaos	"Did you see the chaos in the supermarket when the chocolate went on sale?" asked Samantha.
5 assault	The footballer was arrested on suspicion of assault.
6 cough	The boy's cough revealed that he had contracted tuberculosis.
7 because	His lips were cracking because of constant exposure to wind.
8 thought	Jack's tired eyes were thought to be like those of a dead fish.
9 eager	The children's hands were open and eager for something.
10 guerilla	In the Vietnam War the American soldiers often fell victim to the guerilla warfare tactics of the Viet Cong.
11 disappearance	The young boy had been wearing a maroon jumper on the night of his disappearance.
12 loiter	The police are on the lookout for a group of youths who consistently loiter outside the shopping mall.
13 furniture	The grandest piece of furniture in my house is my antique grandfather clock.
14 debris	The cyclone left a trail of debris all along the coast.
15 corps	The army corps was deployed to Fiji in October.

SPELLING WORDS FOR CONVENTIONS OF LANGUAGE TESTS

Spelling words for Mini Test 7

Word	Example
1 consequence	Janet told me that as a consequence of my wearing a hat I would have bad hair.
2 permanent	“The seating arrangement is permanent!” yelled the frustrated teacher.
3 atmosphere	In the dead of night, Georgie sat hugging her legs in bed. The atmosphere was tense.
4 imaginary	The fear of an imaginary being had kept her awake for over two hours.
5 accommodation	“Mother’s idea of comfortable accommodation is certainly unconventional,” she thought to herself.
6 perspective	It is essential that we take an international perspective on the issue.
7 processor	In the processor, mix two-thirds of a cup of yoghurt with 250 mL of low-fat milk.
8 classification	The classification of the contents of the entire storage container was a tiresome job.
9 exclamation	“Where’s your exclamation mark?” enquired Ms Adams of little Jacob.
10 paragraphs	In English class Mr James explained that our narratives must be written in paragraphs.
11 vocabulary	He also told us that a wide vocabulary was essential to express our ideas creatively.
12 personification	Finally, Mr James said that really effective stories use poetic devices such as personification.
13 digestion	Crocodiles have been known to eat large stones to help their digestion.
14 condensation	The condensation had started to build up on the windows, prompting Harry to turn on the car’s engine.
15 vertebrate	The most advanced organism on Earth is the vertebrate

Spelling words for Mini Test 8

Word	Example
1 orchestral	Grand orchestral sounds rumbled from the belly of the school hall.
2 indecision	Charlie was told to leave the group; his indecision was affecting their chances of winning the competition.
3 syncopation	The syncopation of the drums during the song’s coda was unexpected.
4 theatrical	Jo is the more theatrical of the twins; Sam is happier reading a book alone.
5 generosity	I will never forget the generosity of my host mother, reflected Komei.
6 tournament	The length of the tournament is dependent on the quality of the players participating.
7 quadriceps	Leg extension exercises are designed to specifically target the quadriceps.
8 collage	The term collage refers to art that has been created using a variety of different forms.
9 aesthetic	The combination of magazine and newspaper clippings with paint and fabric often creates a piece with aesthetic qualities.
10 preference	Of course, some people have a preference for traditional art made simply from paint and canvas.
11 spectrum	A broad spectrum of musicians performed at the charity gig.
12 disassemble	The young labourers were forced to disassemble the scaffolding at the end of the workday.
13 encyclopedia	Many children no longer look to an encyclopedia when they want the answer to a question.
14 parochial	The attitudes of the group were particularly parochial, and as a result Ji felt frustrated and resentful.
15 presumably	It is presumably the job of all mothers to clean the rooms of their children.

SPELLING WORDS FOR CONVENTIONS OF LANGUAGE TESTS

Spelling words for Mini Test 9

Word	Example
1 pharaoh	The word *pharaoh* originates from the Greek word *per-aa* meaning 'great house'.
2 antique	The word was originally used to describe the antique and grand royal court of the Egyptian king.
3 physical	It was not until the late 18th dynasty that the word was used to describe the physical king himself.
4 comfortable	The students looked very comfortable lying around on the beanbags.
5 enough	"Have you got enough rope to hold the boat steady?" enquired Lee.
6 answer	The answer to a good life is a satisfying, enjoyable and fulfilling career.
7 dinosaurs	The largest of the known dinosaurs is *Tyrannosaurus rex*.
8 weather	Anji was disappointed that the weather bureau had got the forecast incorrect for the second day in a row.
9 rhyme	William Shakespeare is renowned for his impeccable use of rhyme in his sonnets.
10 rough	The boys were told to stop playing tag. They were being too rough.
11 skeleton	The science teacher had a skeleton hanging next to the whiteboard.
12 colleagues	Even his colleagues at work had begun to complain.
13 succinct	The presenter was succinct with his message; surprisingly, Harry managed to understand what was being said.
14 nutrients	Ashley is frequently concerned that his children may not be getting the correct nutrients from their unhealthy diet.
15 tableau	The finale of *Hamlet* was a tableau of the dead characters arranged artistically around the stage.

Spelling words for Mini Test 10

Word	Example
1 sincerely	The boy was sincerely sorry to have missed his grandfather's funeral.
2 unfortunately	I had to admit to the parents that, unfortunately, their daughter was missing.
3 approximately	The line for the tickets had approximately 500 people in it.
4 horizontally	Exhausted and emotionally drained, Jill spread herself horizontally on the couch.
5 governmentally	The families were delighted by the prospect of a governmentally funded day-care system.
6 beautifully	The women were dressed beautifully in the traditional Palestinian attire.
7 sequentially	Alana was impressed by the sequentially numbered labels that adorned all of the filing cabinets.
8 technologically	Tania confessed to being technologically illiterate.
9 consciously	Amanda consciously made the decision to cease eating meat.
10 deliberately	We deliberately drove the long way home in order to avoid the afternoon traffic.
11 controversially	Gough Whitlam was controversially dismissed by the governor-general in 1975.
12 fundamentally	My mother is fundamentally opposed to the teaching of intelligent design at school.
13 suspiciously	The man in the dark coat leered suspiciously into the window of a parked car.
14 persuasion	I was impressed by my younger brother's resistance to the persuasion of his silly friends.
15 outrageous	The costume worn by Lady Gaga at her most recent concert was outrageous.

SPELLING WORDS FOR CONVENTIONS OF LANGUAGE TESTS

Spelling words for Sample Test 1

Word	Example
26 queen	The majesty of the queen left me awestruck.
27 guard	Ducking and weaving, the boy evaded the security guard.
28 piling	The children entertained themselves by piling stones on top of each other.
29 safari	Africa is a wild, sparse land and perfect for a safari.
30 alpha	The first letter of the Greek alphabet is alpha.
31 country	The Guringai people were the traditional inhabitants of the Guringai country.
32 eternity	JD paid $300 to get an eternity sign tattooed onto his inner arm.
33 burglar	It is believed that at 7:29 pm the burglar entered the premises and committed the crime.
34 permission	Mr Anderson gave permission for the three students to visit the local shops.
35 officially	On 18 July 1859 the Great Hall at Sydney University was officially opened to the public.
36 dramatic	Every year it plays host to graduation ceremonies, musical and dramatic productions, public lectures and book launches.
37 easily	The hobbits, with their love of nature, community and festive cheers, could easily be inhabitants of early England.
38 canoes	They celebrated the giants of the sea, which they watched while in canoes out on the ocean.
39 wonderful	If you want a wonderful little fish, you can't go past the guppy.
40 thrive	Guppies are tough little fish that can thrive in all varieties of waters—even brackish water.

Spelling words for Sample Test 2

Word	Example
26 frequency	The frequency was so highly pitched that the dogs moaned relentlessly.
27 bandage	The scrappy bandage failed to cover the young girl's wounds.
28 massacre	Sandy stood above the ant mound and contemplated the massacre his shovel had left behind.
29 accelerator	Switching swiftly from the accelerator to the brake, Hannah pulled the car to a halt.
30 mediocre	The food at West Point Deli is only barely above mediocre.
31 particle	Each minute particle contributes to the greater structure.
32 literary	My English teacher is always blabbing about the literary worth of Shakespeare.
33 receiver	The boy's mother slammed down the phone receiver and lurched towards the front door.
34 dangerous	Many believe that swimming across Tallebudgeera Creek is dangerous because of the sharks.
35 relief	"What a relief that the rain has finally slowed!" cried Detective Morris.
36 predators	The Atlantic blue marlin are so large that some have believed them to be predators of humans.
37 advertisement	To place an advertisement in the local paper one must pay approximately $50.
38 respiration	Asbestos exposure can disrupt an individual's respiration.
39 surrounding	The trees and ferns surrounding the small lake hid the uncertain faces of the adults.
40 reservoir	Intensely heavy rain swiftly filled the local reservoir.